Economies of the W

EDITED BY

NITA WATTS

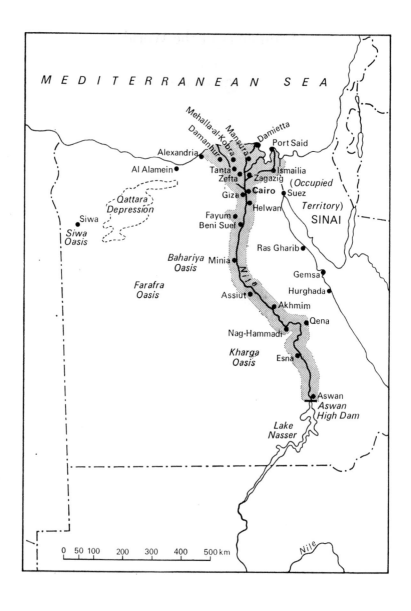

MEDITERRANEAN SEA

Mehalla-al-Kobra
Mansura
Damanhur
Damietta
Alexandria
Port Said
Al Alamein
Tanta
Ismailia
Zefta
Zagazig
(Occupied
Qattara
Giza
Cairo
Suez
Depression
Helwan
Territory)
Siwa
SINAI
Fayum
Beni Suef
Siwa
Oasis
Ras Gharib
Bahariya
Oasis
Minia
Gemsa
Farafra
Hurghada
Oasis
Assiut
Akhmim
Qena
Nag-Hammadi
Kharga
Oasis
Esna
Aswan
Aswan
High Dam
Lake
Nasser
Nile

0 50 100   200   300   400   500 km

Nile

The Egyptian Economy

1952–1972

BY

ROBERT MABRO

CLARENDON PRESS · OXFORD

1974

Oxford University Press, Ely House, London W.1

GLASGOW   NEW YORK   TORONTO   MELBOURNE   WELLINGTON
CAPE TOWN   IBADAN   NAIROBI   DAR ES SALAAM   LUSAKA   ADDIS ABABA
DELHI   BOMBAY   CALCUTTA   MADRAS   KARACHI   LAHORE   DACCA
KUALA LUMPUR   SINGAPORE   HONG KONG   TOKYO

CASEBOUND ISBN 0 19 877030 8
PAPERBACK ISBN 0 19 877031 6

© OXFORD UNIVERSITY PRESS 1974

PRINTED IN GREAT BRITAIN BY
RICHARD CLAY (THE CHAUCER PRESS) LTD,
BUNGAY, SUFFOLK

TO

MAURICE MARTIN

EDITORIAL PREFACE

Economies of the World is designed as a series for readers in universities, business, and government, and provides brief reviews of economic developments during the last 20–25 years in each of a number of countries. The countries selected for study are either of obvious importance in the world economy or interesting because of particular features of their economic structure or recent history, or because their experience throws light on more widespread problems of economic development.

Each volume contains a summary description of the pace and pattern of economic growth in the period covered; and it outlines the main economic problems confronting government in the country, the objectives of economic policy, and the chosen means of economic management. But each author then focuses attention on those aspects of the country's development which he considers most deserving of more detailed examination. The volumes do not attempt to provide comprehensive descriptions and analyses, but they give enough statistical data to support the author's conclusions and a bibliography to suggest further reading.

The series is intended for those interested in problems of economic growth and development outside the boundaries of the United Kingdom, and in the techniques of economic management available to governments. Some familiarity with the main arguments of economists concerned with such questions is assumed, but no more than can reasonably be expected of a second-year university student.

N.W.

CONTENTS

NOTES ON MEASUREMENTS
AND ABBREVIATIONS

EGYPTIAN UNITS OF MEASUREMENT

1 feddan = 1·038 acres = 4,200·8 square metres
1 kantar = 44·928 kg

CURRENCY

1 Egyptian Pound (£E) = 100 piasters
Exchange rate: September 1949–June 1962: £E1 = U.S.$ 2.872
             June 1962–March 1972: £E1 = U.S.$ 2.286
             March 1973–   : £E1 = U.S.$ 2.56
  between two years means fiscal year (1 July to 30 June)

ABBREVIATIONS

CAPMS	Central Agency for Public Mobilization and Statistics (Cairo)
IBRD	International Bank for Reconstruction and Development (Washington)
ILO	International Labour Organization (Geneva)
INP	Institute of National Planning (Cairo)
NPC	National Planning Committee (Egypt)
PCDNP	Permanent Council for the Development of National Production (Egypt)
UNCTAD	United Nations Conference for Trade and Development (New York and Geneva)

LIST OF TABLES

INTRODUCTION

'C'étaient de très grands vents sur toutes
faces de ce monde'
SAINT-JOHN PERSE

THE Egyptian economy has been one of my professional
interests during the past seven years. But my acquaintance
with Egypt is much older. I was born in Alexandria, brought
up and educated in this cosmopolitan town, a central part
of Egypt and yet alien. Egypt is the Nile Valley; the Mediterranean and its ports are the façade, an opening towards a
different world which may well represent what a certain
Egypt would have liked to be, not what Egypt actually is.
I began to discover the true Egypt when I went to university.
A year later, a group of students who soon became my best
friends introduced me to many aspects of Egyptian life in
Cairo and Upper Egypt—the populous quarters, the villages
and farms, not the archaeological sites. It all happened
around 1952, the year of the Revolution.

We believed for a short while that the young officers
would bring freedom and prosperity to the country. We
approved of the Land Reform and the nationalization of the
Suez Canal, rejoiced at the evacuation of the British troops
after seventy years of 'temporary' occupation and spent long
nights discussing the advantages and defects of the projected
High Dam. Most of us became involved in one capacity or
another in the industrialization of the country. We eventually
understood that small achievements are more valuable than
grand objectives; there are constraints.

My acquaintance with Egypt began to develop into
intimate knowledge when I started working on building
sites as an engineer. I was brought into daily contact with
skilled and unskilled workers in the towns and the countryside, with foremen, contractors, merchants, capitalists, lorry

drivers, policemen, and civil servants from the eternal pharaonic scribes to the Turkish under-secretaries of state. I learnt something about labour markets and wage differentials, monopoly profits, bribery and corruption, X-efficiency and cost-plus pricing, competition and oligopolistic collusion—as practised in the real world. Egypt's economic life became familiar long before economics. This experience influenced my understanding of the subject; things are usually the other way round. The long acquaintance with Egypt which some may view as an asset may well turn out to be a liability. The reader will judge.

In writing this book, I have attempted to conform to the intentions of the editor and publishers of the series. The brief was to produce a short and readable account of the structure, problems, and recent performance of the economy which would appeal to the keen undergraduate, the businessman, the specialist, and the general development economist. An almost impossible assignment! The restriction on length means that the book is not a comprehensive work of reference on the economy. It is an attempt at interpretation, a synthesis of the most salient elements of current knowledge and research which incorporates the results of original work. The portrait is in bold traits with finer shades in certain areas. Much is left outside the picture. I hope, however, that the features which best define Egypt's specific physiognomy are in sufficient relief.

The reader will be spared long footnotes and hefty statistical appendices but he is directed by complete references to the sources of all data and important statements. There is a wealth of statistical material on the Egyptian economy but little is usable without much processing and elaboration. Almost all data in the tables and the text are from primary sources. The results have been incorporated without much explanation of assumptions and methods. I have also drawn on the works of others—reputed scholars as well as humble students; they are always fully acknowledged. Although the Egyptian economy has been the subject of considerable research, much remains to be done. The student in search of a topic may well start by identifying gaps in this study. They are not all due to my shortcomings, nor to the restrictions imposed by the format of the book: some gaps simply reflect the state of the field.

The analysis concentrates on the period 1952–72. The choice of 1952 as a starting-point requires some comment. The political significance of that year is not in question (the *ancien régime* was overthrown and a new chapter of Egyptian history inaugurated); its economic significance is the subject of some debate. Some authors have argued that 1952 did not represent a break. The existing economic system, characterized by private ownership and capitalism, prevailed throughout the 1950s; the first comprehensive plan was introduced only in 1959/60 for the years 1960/1 to 1964/5; the nationalization which affected British and French economic interests in 1956 were not extended to a significant portion of Egyptian businesses until 1960 and 1961; the socialist laws were promulgated in 1962. I would argue also that 1952 did not mark a turning-point in economic performance: no downturn because the Revolution was peaceful, no sudden acceleration either, because economic conditions did not immediately change, except for the land reform. Contemporary Egyptian writings on recent economic development tend to overlook this continuity. They often claim, or at least strongly suggest, that every upward trend started with the Revolution, *fons et origo* of all achievements. To concentrate on a period starting in 1952 may reinforce this conventional but ill-informed view.

There are three reasons for overruling these considerations. The first and least important is statistical convenience. Many statistical series begin in 1952 and a desire to minimize the cumbersome task of adjusting and splicing together heterogeneous data played some part in the decision; and two decades is a sufficient period to cover in a book of this length. The second reason carried more weight. Nasser led the revolution in 1952 and died in 1970. This introduction to the Egyptian economy could thus be read as an economic appraisal of Nasser's regime, a self-contained chapter of the country's history. Much has been written on Nasser's life and politics but no overall assessment of the economic changes brought about by his policies during eighteen years of autocratic rule has yet been published. The third reason, perhaps the most controversial, provides an important theme for this study. Many authors have contended that, in the beginning at least, the Free Officers did not have a coherent and clear economic philosophy. Hence, the argument that no significant changes took place until the late 1950s or early 1960s. But this thesis, correct in so far as the economic system is concerned, is unduly restrictive. In fact the military regime took important economic decisions in the first years of its existence. Their significance in shaping the pattern of economic development, both in the short and long term, seems to have escaped the notice of earlier analysts. They may be better appreciated today simply because we enjoy a better vantage-point and benefit from hindsight. These decisions were (a) the agrarian reform (1952); (b) the building of the High Dam, an old and much-discussed project conceived under the previous adminis-tration to which Nasser became committed in 1952; (c) the setting-up in 1952 of a National Production Council* which prepared and appraised most of the projects later incor-porated in the First Industrial Plan (1958–60) and the First Five-Year Comprehensive Plan (1960/1–1964/5); (d) the foundation in 1954 of a national company with the govern-ment as a major shareholder for the construction of a steel-mill at Helwan. The implementation of these decisions had far-reaching effects. The land reform and the comple-mentary measures which followed influenced the pattern of agricultural development during the period. The High Dam, a bulky and indivisible project, strained the resources of the economy during the years of construction; and its impact may still be felt for many decades to come. Further projects, entailing large capital expenditures, will be required to realize the potential benefits of the dam while others may

* Formally the Permanent Council for the Development of National Pro-duction (PCDNP).

become necessary to counteract some of its adverse side-effects. Finally, the Revolution committed itself very early in the day to rapid industrialization and a deepening of the industrial structure; and the period is dominated by attempts to carry through this programme. The steelmill symbolized the commitment and the National Production Council paved the way for planning and strong government intervention in industry.

Despite a strong element of continuity in economic performance and the persistence of the old economic system, the first years of the Revolution in fact constitute a turning-point. A new orientation was taken, involving a large measure of state intervention both in agriculture and in industry, and later steps—e.g. planning and nationalization —followed logically from this earlier commitment. The suggestion is not that these steps were inevitable but that we can discern, with hindsight, a consistent purpose throughout the period. More fundamentally, the early policies of the Revolution had a profound influence on the structure of the economy, and long-term repercussions.

The presentation of the book reflects to some extent this theme. Chapters 1–3 introduce the economy: the historical background, the demographic features, and natural resources. Chapters 4–7 analyse in detail the major policies and real-izations of the Revolution: the Land Reform, the High Dam, planning and nationalizations, and industrialization and social policies. The final chapters contain an analysis of growth and of structural and distributional changes. The conclusion attempts to assess the significance of these changes for Egypt and the wider implications of the case study for the economics of developing countries.

I wish to thank the Social Science Research Council for financing a research project on 'Industrialization and Industrial Policies in Egypt' on which I am currently engaged with my collaborator Samir Radwan. To a large extent, this book is a by-product of the more specialized project. Miss Nita Watts, the editor of the series, read with patient care the final draft. The argument, not to mention the style, owes much to her skills. I owe a great intellectual debt to Edith Penrose, Patrick O'Brien, Bent Hansen, E. F. Jackson, A. H. Hourani, and Roger Owen. Most of them will be surprised to find their names mentioned here because they were not directly involved with this book. They helped and stimulated my thinking over the years and the influence of their teaching, writings, and discussions has been considerable. Samir Radwan has been such a close collaborator in recent years that neither he nor I can any longer identify the origin of our ideas. We do not, however, agree on everything. Judy accepted, not without amiable teasing, my absent-mindedness and the long hours of solitary work at night and during the weekend. She helped me most with her deep respect for mutual independence and her strength.

CHAPTER 1

HISTORICAL BACKGROUND

'Et nous avons si peu de temps pour naître
à cet instant'
SAINT-JOHN PERSE

The export economy: 1820–1910

EGYPT had her 'agricultural revolution' during the nineteenth century. The introduction of long-staple cotton in
the 1820s marked the beginning of a long transformation
which led through various stages and, despite changes in
political circumstances, to the emergence of an export-
oriented economy.[1] Agriculture, which hitherto had been
mainly, though not exclusively, devoted to the satisfaction of
subsistence needs, became integrated through the export of
a valuable primary commodity into the international
economy. The process started under Mohammed Ali (1805–
48), despite the monopoly system and an attempt at import
substitution, and was accelerated under his successors in the
1850s. The Cotton Famine, a consequence of the American
Civil War (1861–4), provided new market opportunities and
Egypt was able to respond. The agricultural, transport, and
financial infrastructures of the export economy were
developed, and the links between Egypt and the world
economy—trade, movements of capital, and foreign immigration—all strengthened.

Irrigation works were an essential component of this
'revolution'. They were undertaken under Mohammed Ali,
the Khedives, and the British. The area of cultivation was
pushed to the frontiers of arable land, and perennial irrigation enabled the peasant, especially in Lower and Middle
Egypt, to crop his plot more than once a year. The expansion
thus took place both at the extensive and intensive land
margins. The cultivated area increased significantly during

the nineteenth century but a ceiling—some 5·4 million feddans—seems to have been reached around 1905. Further

TABLE 1.1

Egypt's exports 1838–1912
(annual averages)

Years	Volume of cotton exports (millions of kantars)	Value of Egyptian exports (£E millions)
1838–42	0·19	n.a.
1843–7	0·24	n.a.
1848–52	0·36	2·2
1853–7	0·50	2·8
1858–62	0·57	3·1
1863–7	1·69	10·9
1868–72	1·59	9·9
1873–7	2·49	13·5
1878–82	2·52	12·1
1883–7	2·78	11·7
1888–92	3·89	12·6
1893–7	5·20	12·9
1898–1902	5·89	16·1
1903–7	6·28	23·1
1908–12	6·72	28·1

Sources: E. R. J. Owen, *Cotton and the Egyptian Economy 1820–1914*, Oxford, 1969; and C. Issawi, 'Egypt since 1800: A Study in Lop-sided Development', *Journal of Economic History*, 21 (1), 1961.

increases would have required very considerable investments in land reclamation and big dams. They were not obtained until forty years later, after the Second World War. It proved cheaper, meanwhile, to expand the cropped area,* which steadily increased from some 7·0 million feddans in 1900 to 9·3 million in 1952 and nearly 10·5 million in 1967. But this process eventually entailed sharply rising costs.

In its first stage, which may have ended in 1910, the agricultural revolution consisted essentially of better provision and regulation of water supplies. Excess capacity in land was brought into fuller utilization through considerable accumulation of fixed capital in irrigation, but without much increase in farm-capital intensity or in the use of material

* Cropped area = cultivated area × average number of crops per year.

TABLE 1.2

Population, cultivated area, and cropped area in selected years

Year	Population (thousands)	Cultivated area (thousand feddans)	Cropped area (thousand feddans)
1821	2,500–3,000	2,032	
1835		3,500	
1840		3,856	
1852		4,160	
1862		4,053	
1871	5,250		
1877		4,742	4,762
1882	6,804	4,758	
1890		4,941	
1897	9,715	5,043	6,764
1902		5,335	7,429
1907	12,751	5,403	7,662
1912		5,285	7,681

Sources: A. E. Crouchley, *The Economic Development of Modern Egypt*, London, 1938; *Annuaire Statistique*, various issues; *Population Censuses*, various issues.

inputs other than water. The ratio of farm capital—both fixed and working—to cropped area rose by a mere 10 per cent between 1895 and 1914.[2] Capital formation increased the effective supply of land but did not affect cultivation techniques—ploughing, sowing, harvesting, threshing, or storage. And agricultural development did not involve significant changes in the input package. In other words, capital deepening in agriculture (the capital–output ratio doubled between 1895 and 1914) resulted in 'horizontal' expansion. A complementary process of capital deepening on the farm failed to take place. And perennial irrigation, though it relieved the peasant from certain burdens, added new ones to his lot. Parasitic diseases—bilharzia and ankylostomiasis—became endemic and widespread and debilitated the human stock.

Other, but to some extent related, socio-economic developments favoured the emergence in the second half of the nineteenth century of an agrarian system best defined as a system of private landownership. The rights on land became exclusive and alienable through sale or lease, and, in the

1890s, labour was completely freed from its ties to the land. This system was characterized by great inequalities—landlessness at one extreme and very large holdings at the other. Another feature was factor mobility. Factor markets which, save for capital, are more flexible and competitive in this type of agriculture than is generally assumed, allocated labour to land within the framework of the usual tenure systems: share-cropping, fixed-rent tenancy, and direct cultivation with recourse to family and wage labour. The links with trade favoured the development of a monetized, profit-motivated, price-responsive agriculture which in turn strengthened those links. After the British occupation (1882), the role of the State in agriculture was largely limited to the improvement of the fiscal framework, the building, maintenance, and administration of the irrigation system, the maintenance of law and order in the countryside, and the enactment of social legislation in favour of the fellah, such as the abolition of the corvée and the kourbash and the protection of smallholdings against expropriation for bad debt (the Law of Five Feddans);[3] but no extension service, no attempt to expand education in the villages, not even a separate Ministry of Agriculture until much later.

Investment outside agriculture (after Mohammed Ali's reign and his ill-fated attempt to create under the aegis of the State a modern, diversified economy) followed the typical pattern that characterizes export economies. The favoured sectors are those which provide the necessary support for trade or supply services to the beneficiaries of the export boom. Thus the transport system was developed by both public and private enterprise. Railways, canals, and harbours facilitated the transfer of the crop from the interior to the main port and its shipment from there to world markets. Cotton ginning and pressing plants were erected, since elementary processing reduces the bulk and weight of cotton and hence transport costs. Foreign merchants and foreign capital established banks and commercial firms. They provided financial facilities and controlled the sophisticated organization of the cotton trade, including the futures market in Alexandria. Finally, urbanization absorbed considerable amounts of capital, especially in Cairo and Alexandria, where big landlords, merchants, bankers, brokers, and their agents chose to live. Foreign private enterprise found opportunities in public utilities, mortgage and land companies, and in construction. Egyptian and foreign residents seem to have invested significant sums in housing; there is evidence of considerable building activity in the late nineteenth and early twentieth centuries.[4]

Diversification of the productive structure through industrial development did not take place on a significant scale. After Mohammed Ali, investment in industry was limited to activities enjoying protection because of transport costs—sugar, beer, building materials, and the like. The State did not invest directly in industry except under the Khedive Ismail (1863–79). A policy of encouragement through tariffs or promotional measures could have opened up new opportunities; but Egypt, until 1930, was deprived of her fiscal autonomy by the Capitulations. The British rulers believed in free trade but apparently not in the infant industry argument.[5] They imposed an 8 per cent excise tax on domestic textile production, equal to the external tariff, when two British firms planned to erect mills at the turn of the present century. That one of them—the Filature Nationale—managed to survive, despite immense difficulties, until the 1930s suggests that much more could have been achieved with even a little protection. Classical economists and their modern disciples have told us the costs of industrializing in defiance of comparative advantages, and Egyptian economic history is rich in illustrations for their lessons. We know much less about the costs of free trade: the destruction of handicrafts and small manufacturing, the lost opportunities, talents that could have been used in industry, and the wasted time during which the inevitably long process of industrial training and 'learning by doing' could have taken place.

Investment in man increases the flexibility of the economy and its potential for development, but the State, especially under British rule, largely neglected education. In 1900 the Government spent £E 107,000, just over 1 per cent of its budget, on education; in 1913 the share had increased to 3·3 per cent. Egypt, however, was not entirely deprived of educational facilities. Cairo harboured for centuries the great theological university of Al Azhar which fed koranic schools throughout the country with teachers. Mohammed Ali introduced modern education for small élites and sent students to Europe, inaugurating a trend which has continued to the present day.[6] Missionary schools, mainly Catholic and French, were established in the second half of the nineteenth century to the benefit of the foreign community, local Christians, and very few Moslems. But all that affected a very small proportion of the population. In 1907 92 per cent of the population aged ten years and over was completely illiterate.[7]

The pattern of investment that obtained from the mid-nineteenth century to the beginning of the 1920s was suited to the contemporary needs of the export economy. It enabled the country to increase its agricultural production and its exports of cotton by providing the water, the land, the finances, and the infrastructure necessary for this expansion. But it also placed the economy on a path which it could not easily abandon should the circumstances that favoured export-led growth begin to change. The lack of a diversified productive structure and the low level of investment in human capital could seriously hinder the country if it decided to develop new resources and a new economic basis for sustained growth.

The export economy in difficulties 1910–1939

In fact, the circumstances that favoured the export economy began to change before the First World War. After the first decade of this century the economy failed to generate the minimal rate of growth necessary to maintain *per capita* income constant. According to Hansen and Marzouk, *per capita* real gross national income may have declined by some 20 per cent between the 1900s and 1945, about half the decline being attributed to the terms of trade and the remainder to a fall in *per capita* production. Although *per capita* income seems to have been continually decreasing during this period, *per capita* production recovered at a modest rate of 0·25 per cent per year between 1928 and 1939, but the gains were wiped out by the adverse movement of the terms of trade during the depressed 1930s.[8] Hansen and Marzouk also estimate that production per worker in agriculture had fallen by the end of the Second World War to two-thirds of its 1914 level.[9]

The new problems that faced the Egyptian economy during this period were manifold. Earlier development carried with it seeds of retardation and decline. Little room was left for increasing the cultivated area after the rapid expansion of the nineteenth century; and the cropped area which had expanded by some 60 per cent between 1877 and 1907 did not increase by much more than 10 per cent in the next thirty years. Multiple cropping and perennial irrigation damaged the soil; cotton yields, which had increased by 70 or 80 per cent (the data are not very good) in the last three decades of the nineteenth century, fell by more than 20 per cent in the first decade of the twentieth century. The problem was inadequate drainage, whose complementary role to irrigation was perhaps not fully understood. The rapid growth in total output delayed the realization that reduced soil fertility was a threat to future performance. The major regulators and barrages on the Nile—Aswan, Assiut, Esna, Zefta—were barely completed when a new transformation of agriculture was required. Fertilizers, drainage, and improved seeds were now needed to supplement or replace water as the 'leading input' of Egyptian agriculture. They were introduced after a lag and they had first to repair the damage and stabilize yields before they could contribute to increasing land productivity. Cotton yields did not recover the level of the 1890s until late in the 1930s.

Chemical fertilizers, hardly in use at the turn of the century, were applied in increasing amounts in the 1920s and 1930s. At the eve of the war, Egypt ranked tenth—after

Table 1.3

Some economic indicators 1917–1939

Year	Population (thousands) (1)	Cultivated area (thousand feddans) (2)	Cropped area (thousand feddans) (3)	Cotton yield (kantar/feddan) (4)	Use of fertilizers (kg/feddan of cropped area) (5)	Volume of cotton exports (thousand kantars) (6)	Value of Egyptian exports (£E thousands) (7)	Terms of trade Index (8)
1910–14 average		5,200	7,610	4·27	(9·0)	6,767	30,037	100
1917	12,751	5,269	7,677	3·75	4·8	4,074	41,519	71·1
1920		5,305	7,807	3·30		4,001	88,010	118·8
1921		5,354	8,060	3·37		4,792	42,473	56·8
1922		5,341	8,205	3·73	14·4	6,479	51,366	81·3
1923		5,387	8,104	3·81		7,473	59,832	89·1
1924		5,192	8,070	4·07		7,254	67,170	101·4
1925		5,420	8,213	4·14		6,424	60,466	125·1
1926		5,385	8,457	4·29		6,835	42,693	81·0
1927	14,218	5,544	8,661	4·01	26·0	7,383	49,164	92·0
1928		5,616	8,623	4·64	31·9	7,433	56,504	91·4
1929		5,549	8,634	4·63	38·0	7,625	52,430	86·9
1930		5,549	8,634	3·97		5,928	32,093	66·1
1931		5,485	8,547	3·78		7,397	28,074	54·2
1932		5,464	8,216	4·53	28·6	6,699	26,995	55·5
1933		5,384	8,283	4·75		7,854	28,848	54·0
1934		5,277	8,078	4·36	52·2	8,564	31,056	58·4
1935		5,229	8,054	5·11	81·0	8,577	35,693	63·0
1936		5,361	8,101	5·31	71·2	7,798	32,979	63·2
1937	15,933	5,281	8,358	5·37	79·0	8,900	39,753	50·4
1938		5,312	8,474	4·67	63·0	7,937	29,342	44·1
1939		5,338	8,522	5·35	56·9	9,103	34,081	40·2

Sources: (1) *Population Censuses;* (2) and (3) *Annuaire Statistique;* (4) D. Mead, *Growth and Structural Change in the Egyptian Economy,* Homewood, Ill., 1967; (5) S. Radwan, 'Capital Formation in Egyptian Industry and Agriculture', unpublished Ph.D. thesis, London, 1973; (6) D. Mead, op. cit.; (7) 1917–30, A. Crouchley, *The Economic Development of Modern Egypt,* London, 1938; 1931–9, D. Mead, op. cit.; (8) D. Mead, op. cit. (2) and (3) were compiled by S. Radwan.

seven western European countries, New Zealand, and Japan —in the use of fertilizers per acre of arable land.[10] The Government undertook a drainage project in the Delta; the length of drains increased from 6·3 million kilometres in 1917 to 9·2 million in 1937, or by some 40 per cent (to be compared with a 10 per cent increase in irrigation canals and a similar expansion of the cropped area).[11] Despite these efforts, plant production failed to increase by more than an average annual rate of 1 per cent between 1909–13 and 1935–9. As E. R. J. Owen puts it, 'the early increase in output was bought at the price of very much slower advances in later years' and 'much of the investment in the agricultural sector was necessary to repair damage already done to soil fertility'.[12]

The difficulties faced by the export economy were not due only to internal factors operating on the supply side. It was also vulnerable to external factors affecting demand. Two world wars and a Great Depression in less than thirty years, with short intervening booms in 1919 and the 1920s, gave rise to large price fluctuations which became much more significant than variations in output. The volume of cotton exports fell from a yearly average of 6,767,000 kantars (1910–14) to 5,624,000 kantars during the First World War (1914–18), but average annual earnings rose from £E 23·8 million to £E 37·2 million. During the 1930s, the average volume rose to 7,288,000 kantars (1930–4) and 8,463,000 kantars (1935–9), but average annual earnings were only £E 21·5 million and £E 25·2 million respectively. Egypt suffered a marked deterioration in her barter terms of trade during the inter-war period (neglecting occasional good years) and the income terms of trade were more unfavourable in the 1930s than at the beginning of the century (1903–7: 100; 1928–32: 93; 1933–7: 95) despite an increase of some 70 per cent in the quantum index of exports.[13]

Despite these circumstances, or perhaps as a result of attempts to mitigate some of their effects, certain structural changes occurred during this period. There was a spurt in capital formation in agriculture and a new spurt of industrialization. Changes were qualitative as well as quantitative. The water supply was increased and its regulation improved, thanks to the second heightening of the Aswan barrage (1933) and to a dam built by Egypt in the Sudan at Jebel-al-Awlia (1933-4). But as mentioned earlier, new items of capital formation and new inputs also made their appearance in agriculture. The ratio of farm capital to cropped area rose more rapidly than in the earlier period.

Though the scale of industrial investment was not considerable, the industrial structure began to change. A modern textile industry was established by the Group Misr in the 1930s: the local consumption of cotton increased from 78,000 kantars (1930-1) to 706,000 kantars (1939-40), output of yarn from 3,000 to 21,000 tons between 1928 and 1938, cotton fabrics from 8 million metres (1920) to 93 million (1938). There were advances in other branches of production: in Portland cement (output 24,000 tons in 1920, 375,000 tons in 1938) and in chemicals, paper, petroleum products, food, and other consumer goods.[14] The depression in agriculture and the new tariffs which Egypt was able to introduce after 1930 may have helped these modest developments. Industry ceased to be the exclusive domain of foreigners; and Egyptian capitalists and entrepreneurs were encouraged to invest in manufacturing and other modern enterprises. The developmental effort of the Government increased; the share of education in the budget, negligible in 1900, rose to 6·8 per cent in 1928-9 and 12·8 per cent in 1938-9, while Government expenditures on irrigation and public works absorbed a larger portion of the budget in the 1930s than in any previous decade, including the 1900s when many barrages were built.[15]

But these changes were still too small to affect significantly the character of the economy. The share of agriculture in total employment remained virtually constant at around 70 per cent during the first three decades of this century and its share in national income—some 50 per cent—remained high. The main public effort was in favour of agriculture, and the encouragement of industry, a new feature of policy, was extremely timid. The Government continued to adhere to a strict financial policy—balanced budgets or preferably small surpluses. And the greater concern for education was too recent to contribute to the economic development of the country during these years. But the significance of the 1930s becomes clearer if the structural changes of this decade are placed in a longer perspective: they announce and prepare the way for the more fundamental transformation of the economy in the next thirty years.

An interpretation of the economic development of the period 1858–1939

Two issues relevant to an interpretation of Egypt's economic development must now be raised. The first relates to population growth, the second to the utilization of export proceeds. Labour and foreign exchange are not the only factors that contribute to economic growth and development, but their role is important.

Population growth slowly but ineluctably transformed Egypt from a labour-short to a labour-surplus economy. Plans for importing labour were contemplated in the nineteenth century and mentions of labour shortages are found in economic reports written around 1900.[16] Soon afterwards the diagnosis began to change, and in the mid-1930s a new conventional wisdom was firmly established: Egypt is an overpopulated country.[17] Population had increased to nearly 16 million in 1937, a 25 per cent increment in twenty years. The rate of population growth in the late 1930s averaged 1·5 to 1·8 per cent per year and continued to rise to much higher levels after the Second World War. The man–land ratio (adult males in the agricultural labour force–cultivated area) rose from 0·36 men per feddan in 1917 to 0·59 in 1937.[18]

We do not intend to reopen at this stage the long controversy as to whether these increases drove the marginal product of labour in agriculture down to zero. Let us simply note that to state that Egypt is now a labour-surplus economy does not necessarily imply that disguised unemployment prevails in agriculture since internal migration transfers labour surpluses to the towns. A significant movement of population away from agriculture began in the 1930s, and thereafter the rate of growth of the agricultural labour force became considerably smaller than the rate of natural increase. The rapid expansion of the service sector in towns which began to characterize the Egyptian economy after the 1930s is both a sign and a consequence of overpopulation. This expansion often disguises serious problems of urban underemployment and poverty.

Another development also marked this period. While slowly incurring the liability that an increase in population pressure on land may represent, Egypt was settling liabilities of a different kind incurred earlier. A large foreign debt was contracted by the State under the Khedives Said (1854–63) and Ismail, at various dates after 1858.[19] In 1880, the Debt was assessed at £E 98·4 million, and it increased by £E 18 million in the next twenty years.[20] Payments abroad on account of the Public Debt (interest, redemption net of new borrowing, and annuities for certain loans) plus the tribute that Egypt was compelled to pay to the Ottoman Porte absorbed annually some £E 4·5–5·0 million in the years preceding the First World War. The burden is better appraised if we compare these amounts with export proceeds and government revenues (see Table 1.4).

After 1919, Egypt used surpluses accumulated during the war to repatriate the Debt. In 1914, foreign holdings of Egyptian Public Debt were estimated at £E 85·7 million; in 1934 they had fallen to £E 39·0 million. By redemption or repurchase Egypt paid her foreign creditors £E 46·7 million on account of the Public Debt.

The costs and benefits of the Debt to the country have never been assessed. Positive benefits might have accrued had the Khedives received the whole amounts for which Egypt became liable and invested them productively. They actually received less than 70 per cent of the contracted amounts. The practice of European bankers was to charge the Treasury for the loan as requested and to supply the smaller sums raised by public subscription; in addition, large commissions were paid to intermediaries, some loans were issued at heavy discount rates and others partly paid in depreciated treasury bonds.[21] It is difficult to determine the uses to which the amounts received were put. Since they were added to general government revenues they became fungible; they probably enabled the Government to increase

TABLE 1.4

Payments abroad on account of Public Debt and tribute, export proceeds and Government revenues 1884–1914
(annual averages)

Periods	Total payments abroad (£E thousands)	Export proceeds (£E thousands)	Government revenues (£E thousands)	Payments as % of export proceeds	Payments as % of revenues
1884–92	4,564	12,148	11,257	37·6	40·5
1893–7	5,043	12,936	10,878	39·0	46·4
1898–1902	4,379	16,055	12,462	27·3	35·0
1903–7	5,453	23,063	15,723	23·6	34·7
1908–14	4,245	28,227	16,668	15·0	25·4

Sources: Payments abroad: A. E. Crouchley, *The Investment of Foreign Capital in Egyptian Companies and Public Debt*, Cairo, 1936; Government revenues and export proceeds: A. E. Crouchley, *The Economic Development of Modern Egypt*, London, 1938.

its expenditure all round, on valuable projects and on items of questionable value and utility. This would, of course, also have been true of earmarked loans: they release some funds from other sources for other expenditures. We might make the extreme, and very unrealistic, assumption that all items of public current expenditures were constrained and that the amounts received from abroad were in fact devoted to investment—the purpose being to compute the rate of return on investment which would have enabled the country to break even in the most favourable circumstances. Allowing for the fact that some public investment undertaken in the 1860s and 1870s proved wasteful and that some was written off at an early stage, we may calculate that the more successful irrigation and infrastructural projects would have absolved the Debt if they had yielded over eighty years a minimum annual net return of 14–15 per cent. These rates would have to be higher if we allowed for fungibility.

It is doubtful whether many investment projects did perform so well. The inescapable conclusion is that the costs of the Debt, partly because of the Khedives' spending habits, partly because of the crooked financial practices of the time, were greater than its benefits. To evade repayment was out of the question: the initial pretext of the British occupation, after all, was to safeguard foreign lenders' interests.

Foreign capital did not finance only the Public Debt; private direct investment was also important. The inflows of foreign funds were significant in the 1890s, larger amounts were invested at the turn of the century, and a peak reached in 1907. A financial crash in that year shook business confidence, and foreign investment became more sluggish for several years; the recovery after 1911 was interrupted by the First World War.[22] Table 1.5 shows estimates of capital inflows and of interest and dividends paid abroad between 1884 and 1914. The net inflow on private account during this period is estimated at £E 34·8 million; but, despite this contribution, public and private net outflows were together as high as £E 111·3 million. A comparison of this sum with the costs of the Aswan barrage erected in 1898–1902 is suggestive: the costs of the barrage, the most significant item of public investment of the period, only amounted to £E 3·04 million![23]

After the First World War, foreign companies operating in Egypt chose to repatriate capital through repayment of debentures and purchase of shares held abroad. Crouchley estimates that the value of Egyptian securities held by non-residents fell from £E 71·2 to £E 45·2 million between 1914 and 1934.[24]

A picture begins to emerge. The growth of the export

economy coincided with a period of heavy indebtedness. In a first stage which ended around 1914, the inflows of foreign private investment were not sufficiently large to compensate for the servicing of the Public Debt. Thus, the benefits of export expansion were partly offset; 4 or 5 per cent of Egypt's national income was taken away and the Government was left with little revenue to spend on health, education, public administration, and the economy. After the war, when the export economy was on the eve of a period of difficulty, resources were still transferred abroad to service

TABLE 1.5

Capital flows and interest payments abroad 1884–1914
(annual averages; £E thousands)

Periods	Capital inflows: private investment	Dividends and interest: private	Net inflows: private account	Public Debt	Total net flows
1884–92	12	−277	−265	−4,564	−4,829
1893–7	1,065	−387	678	−5,043	−4,365
1898–1902	2,144	−994	1,150	−4,379	−3,229
1903–7	8,616	−3,465	5,151	−5,453	−302
1908–14	3,150	−2,938	215	−4,245	−4,030

Note: Minuses denote outflows. 'Public Debt' includes new loans.
Source: Computed from A. E. Crouchley, *The Investment of Foreign Capital in Egyptian Companies and Foreign Debt*, Cairo, 1936.

and redeem public and private debts. The large surpluses accumulated during and immediately after the First World War, which might have enabled the country to cushion the impact of the Depression and to prepare a lasting transformation of the economy, were eaten up by foreign indebtedness.

Throughout the period, while capital was flowing out of the country, Egypt's population and her need for complementary resources were growing. An increasing shortage of land called for larger investment to offset diminishing returns, but this was not forthcoming. By the 1930s the misery of the the fellah had become intolerable and underemployment a permanent feature of the economy. It became clear to many that new liabilities which for years to come might seriously threaten the economic development of the country had been incurred.

It is tempting to interpret Egypt's economic development as the inevitable transformation of an export-surplus economy into a labour-surplus economy. Myint's 'vent for surplus' seems relevant to the period ended around 1910 or 1914;[25] Lewis's 'unlimited supplies of labour' to the 1930s and the following decades.[26] This would imply a failure of primary exports to act as an engine of long-term economic growth and development. But the failure is not inevitable and the passage from Myint to Lewis not logically necessary. The imbalances in factor proportions which characterize the labour-surplus economy might not have appeared if the accumulation of capital (both human and material) had proceeded fast enough in the export-led phase and if natural resources had not been in such short supply. The failure or success of the 'export model of development' depends on the size of the exportable surplus, the circumstances in which it accrues, the country's ability to absorb its proceeds, the attitudes of the State and society, and the constraints imposed by the international community, among many other factors. But it is also true, as already suggested, that the export economy left to develop without interference in response to short-term profit opportunities may fail the country in the long run.

We have seen that foreign indebtedness incurred earlier for little benefit drained away considerable resources in the period of strongest export growth. In a sense this may be considered as a fortuitous circumstance. But it could also be construed as an aspect of a more general phenomenon: European interference in the Third World during the nineteenth century. In Egypt, there were no foreign enclaves in agriculture as in other export economies where colonization brought planters. But there were European bankers, merchants, courtiers, and unscrupulous adventurers and middlemen protected by the Powers. They helped the integration of

Egyptian agriculture into the world economy, which yielded certain benefits. Some conceived good investment projects which contributed to economic development. But they were also partly responsible for bad projects, the perpetuation of abnormal privileges, the circumstances and terms of the Debt, increased foreign intervention, and ultimately for the loss of independence.

We have also seen that the arable land frontier was reached at a rather early stage of development. Further expansion entailed increasing costs. Any observer taking the long view—some did—would have realized early in the twentieth century that economic diversification was essential. Mohammed Ali perceived this need and attempted to achieve it a century before; but the time was not ripe for success. But what about the Khedives, the British, and the semi-independent Government of the 1920s and 1930s? Some lacked the perception. Others lacked the means. The British and their successors took the long view in agriculture and ignored other sectors. Investment in man was badly neglected partly because of shortages of funds, partly because of a conscious colonial policy. Governments were, in any case, operating under severe financial constraints since their fiscal autonomy was constrained by the Capitulations which prevented them from taxing the rich foreign community and from imposing tariffs. Powerful vested interests became entrenched in land, trade, and finance, and hence in the political structure; and they made sure that Government policies would favour their sectional objectives.

The conditions necessary for the transformation of an export economy into a modern, industrial, and diversified economy did not exist. The export economy developed in an international context which discouraged its transformation. It reinforced powerful groups within the country which had good reasons to resist change. It perpetuated conditions of poverty, ill-health, and oppression in the villages, all inimical to long-run development. The natural conditions— the scarcity of land—which militated in favour of a transformation were themselves an obstacle: they constrained the growth of the economy at a time when productivity per man was low. And the historical circumstances were unfavourable: debt, pressures from abroad, colonial interests to satisfy, and for most of the time the frustrations that the loss of, and the struggle for, independence tend to entail.

CHAPTER 2

POPULATION

Introduction

THE Egyptian population displays the typical demographic features of the densely inhabited developing country. The rate of population growth is high. It rose from an average of 1·2 per cent per year before the Second World War to 2·5 per cent in the 1960s as a result of a sharp fall in death rates not compensated for by a similar decline in birth rates. Recent data suggest that this trend may be reversed in the 1970s, but the rate of population growth is unlikely to fall below 2 per cent per year. Both birth and death rates—especially infant mortality—appear to be high when Egypt is compared with industrialized countries. The age pyramid has a broad base, which partly explains low rates of participation in the labour force. Illiteracy and endemic diseases continue to plague substantial groups in the society, despite the considerable expansion of educational and health facilities and very praiseworthy progress achieved in these fields in recent decades.

Egypt is very densely populated. A large, though diminishing, proportion of the working population is occupied in agriculture, but population pressures on the land have stimulated internal migration, a socio-economic phenomenon of considerable significance.

Employment is one of the country's most worrying problems. Neither agriculture nor industry has been able to contribute to its solution; new entrants to the labour force thus tend to be absorbed into the ever-growing service sector. In Egypt, disguised unemployment is an urban rather than a rural phenomenon and its implications for the economic development of the country may be very different from those suggested by Lewis-type models in the theoretical literature,

It is estimated that in 1972 some 200,000 Egyptians, most of them skilled, were working abroad. Such migration is a recent but interesting phenomenon. Whether the costs entailed by the brain-drain are compensated for by the benefits arising from remittances and other savings is far from clear. The movement is not expected to make a substantial contribution to the employment problem save in the unlikely event of a successful political merger between Egypt and her underpopulated neighbours. We shall analyse the demographic background in this chapter and discuss issues relating to employment and migration in Chapter 9.

Population: level and rates of growth

The Egyptian population was estimated to be 34,076,000 on 1 July 1971. The Statistical Office publishes annually a mid-year estimate calculated on the basis of the latest population census and rates of growth inferred from birth and death registration. Egypt, however, has a long tradition of population counts. Table 2.1 reproduces data from population censuses taken at fairly regular intervals between 1897 and 1966. The quality and coverage of censuses have tended to improve over time, a consideration which may explain the

TABLE 2.1

Population in census years

Year	Population (thousands)	Average annual rate of growth (%)
1897	9,715	—
1907	11,287	1·51
1917	12,751	1·23
1927	14,218	1·09
1937	15,933	1·15
1947	19,022	1·79
1960	26,085	2·46
1966	30,076	2·40

Note: Rates of growth are calculated from the original figures and differ from those given in the source.
Source: CAPMS, *The Increases of Population in the United Arab Republic,* Cairo, September 1969, p. 26.

apparent fall in the rate of population growth between 1897 and 1927. The 1947 census is alleged to overstate the aggregate by 5 or 6 per cent because many respondents thought that the enumeration would be used for the issuing of ration cards. Too much has been made of this allegation, which is not well supported by indirect tests involving comparisons with earlier and later censuses, vital statistics, and more elaborate analyses of birth and death trends. The error may be limited to 2 or 3 per cent. The 1966 figures are from a sample census and hence not strictly comparable with other data in the table. These provisos suggest that the 1960 census is the best source of demographic statistics available at the moment.

Increases in the rates of population growth from an annual average of 1·79 per cent between 1937 and 1947 to 2·40 per cent between 1960 and 1966 seem to be uniquely due to a fall in death rates. Vital statistics do not reveal any trend—upward or downward—in crude birth rates between 1934 and 1966 (see Table 2.2). The year-to-year variations seem to be confined within a narrow range, with a lower limit of 37·6 per thousand in 1942 and an upper limit of 45·2 per thousand in 1952. In twenty-five out of the thirty-three years of this period, the crude birth rate has been consistently higher than 41·0 per thousand, but the picture begins to change after 1966. A slow decline in birth rates from a high level of 42·8 per thousand in 1963 has become more pronounced in later years; and the birth rate fell to 34·6 in 1971. This downward trend is worth noting but the period is too short to warrant strong inferences.

Crude death rates seem to have fallen very sharply after the Second World War—from 27·7 to less than 20·0 per thousand between 1945 and 1950. They have tended to fluctuate within the range 14–20 per thousand between 1950 and 1970. In general, average rates have tended to be lower in the 1960s than in the 1950s.*

* Vital statistics are often distrusted by students of the Egyptian economy because of incomplete coverage. A number of demographers have attempted to estimate vital trends by indirect methods from population censuses. One such

Fertility and mortality

The analysis of past trends of crude birth and death rates is of limited significance; it enables us to relate changes in the rate of population growth to these variables but does not provide an explanation of their movements. In any case, crude birth and death rates are unsatisfactory concepts. They conceal differences in behaviour between various socio-economic and demographic groups in society. Changes in aggregate rates could be due to shifts in the composition of the population, to changes in specific rates for constituent groups, or, more frequently, to a combination of both. Fertility and mortality are influenced by a wide range of variables; an analysis of specific rates may thus involve considerable disaggregation by age, sex, income, education, occupation, region, and duration and age of marriage, to mention a few significant factors. But a study of the determinants of mortality and fertility is essential to an understanding of demographic processes. The quality of population forecasts—an important ingredient of economic planning—and the ability to design effective population policies depend on such an understanding.

The evidence on differential patterns of fertility is scattered in a limited number of studies. They disclose, however, interesting and in some instances unusual features. Contrary to a common view about the impact of urbanization on

---

method is the 'reverse survival' technique which involves comparisons of at least two age distributions. Another, the 'quasi-stable population' method, has the definite advantage of requiring a single census. The procedure derives its rationale from the demographic properties of a closed population with stable birth and declining death rates: knowledge of the age distribution, the rate of population growth, and age-specific patterns of mortality permit the calculation of vital rates because these parameters are in unique combination. Estimates of vital trends by this method for Egypt have been generally consistent with data derived from registration statistics. T. Paul Schultz, for example, came to the conclusion that crude birth rates have been either constant at around 44·0 per thousand or slightly declining between 1947 and 1960.[1] Death rates were estimated to have declined from 28·0 to 17·0 per thousand in the same period. The inaccuracies of the major sources of Egyptian demographic data—recent population censuses and vital statistics—may not be as serious as is often suggested.

reproductive behaviour, differences in fertility between urban and rural areas seem insignificant. Data derived from the 1960 population census indicate that cumulative fertility rates were in fact slightly higher for Cairo and Alexandria

TABLE 2.2

Birth, death, and infant mortality rates
(per thousand)

Year	Crude birth rate	Crude death rate	Infant mortality	Year	Crude birth rate	Crude death rate	Infant mortality
1934	42·2	27·8	166	1953	42·6	19·5	146
1935	41·3	26·4	161	1954	42·6	17·8	138
1936	44·2	28·8	164	1955	40·3	17·5	136
1937	43·4	27·1	165	1956	40·7	15·3	124
1938	43·2	26·3	163	1957	38·0	17·7	130
1939	42·0	25·9	161	1958	41·1	16·5	112
1940	41·3	26·3	162	1959	42·8	16·3	109
1941	40·4	25·7	150	1960	43·1	16·9	109
1942	37·6	28·3	168	1961	43·9	15·8	108
1943	38·7	27·7	160	1962	41·3	17·9	134
1944	39·8	26·0	152	1963	42·8	15·5	119
1945	42·7	27·7	153	1964	42·0	15·7	117
1946	41·2	25·0	141	1965	41·4	14·1	113
1947	43·8	21·4	127	1966	41·0	15·9	127
1948	42·7	20·4	139	1967	39·2	14·2	116
1949	41·8	20·5	135	1968	38·2	16·1	131
1950	44·4	19·0	130	1969	37·0	14·5	119
1951	44·8	19·2	129	1970	35·1	15·1	n.a.
1952	45·2	17·7	127	1971	34·6	13·1	n.a.

Sources: Crude birth rates 1934–67: CAPMS, *The Increase of Population in the United Arab Republic,* 1969. Crude birth rates 1968–71: CAPMS, *Statistical Yearbook 1952–1971.* Crude death rates 1934–58: D. Mead, *Growth and Structural Change in the Egyptian Economy,* Homewood, Ill., 1967, p. 302. Crude death rates 1959–67: CAPMS, *Statistical Indicators 1952–1970.* Crude death rates 1968–71: CAPMS, *Statistical Yearbook 1952–1971.* Infant mortality 1934–1958: D. Mead, op. cit. Infant mortality 1959–69: CAPMS, *Statistical Indicators 1952–1970.*

(4·35 children born to a married woman) than for the rest of Egypt (4·14 children). Comparable rates from the 1947 census were 3·69 and 3·82 respectively. In 1947 and 1960, age-specific rates were higher in the two metropolitan centres

TABLE 2.3

Average number of children born to married women within specific age limits

Age	Cairo and Alexandria		Rest of country		All Egypt	
	1947	1960	1947	1960	1947	1960
Below 20	0·75	0·48	0·51	0·39	0·57	0·41
20–4	0·87	1·24	0·80	1·02	0·80	1·06
25–9	1·18	1·65	1·12	1·46	1·11	1·50
30–4	1·14	1·31	1·07	1·29	1·08	1·29
35–9	1·05	1·04	1·17	1·07	1·15	1·06
40–4	0·33	0·17	0·52	0·44	0·50	0·39
45–9	0·41	0·49	0·70	0·48	0·66	0·47
50 and over	0·07	0·30	0·05	0·09	0·02	0·02

Source: Bent Hansen and Girgis Marzouk, *Development and Economic Policy in the UAR (Egypt)*, Amsterdam, 1965.

than in the provinces for all brackets up to the age of thirty-five years. A disaggregation by educational attainment of married women in 1960 showed slightly lower fertility in urban areas for all groups save the illiterate. The number of children born to illiterate women is significantly higher in towns (4·81) than in villages (4·37). In all cases, however, fertility is inversely related to the mother's level of education, but there again the differences are more marked in urban than in rural areas.[2] El Badry, distinguishing fertility by occupational groups in the 1960 census, found the lowest rates among agricultural workers in predominantly rural districts.[3] A sample study by Rizk in 1957 covering 6,000 women from Cairo and Alexandria, the semi-urban centre of Mehalla-al-Kobra, and three villages tends to suggest an inverse relationship between the average size of completed families and social status. Differences in the educational level of husbands seem to result in significant fertility differentials. The same association was found with mother's education but, here again, in urban not rural areas.[4] Finally, Hansen and Marzouk have noted a marked decline in fertility between 1947 and 1960 for women in the lower age bracket (15–20 years).[5]

These results could not be entirely explained by either Malthusian-type theories or the transition theory of demographic behaviour. But the disaggregation suggests that both may be relevant. That the fertility of illiterate women, presumably poorer in rural areas than in towns, is higher in towns and that the fertility of agricultural workers is low may be construed as a Malthusian phenomenon. But this is just a presumption. For it is also possible that women are healthier in cities than in villages* or that rates of participation in the labour force of the illiterate women are lower in towns than in the countryside. A good test would require data on fertility rates by income groups and better information on health and female participation, which at present are not available. The theory of demographic transition which predicts a decline in fertility as urbanization and economic development proceed seems consistent with the other results surveyed. It receives further confirmation from an analysis of birth registration data from Cairo and Alexandria, which reveal a decline in fertility rates of 3 and 13 per cent respectively between 1952 and 1960.[6] This very significant difference between the two towns is worth noting. Alexandria has no rural hinterland; it draws relatively fewer migrants than Cairo, occupies a larger share of the population in modern-type activities (industry, export trade, the harbour), and has perhaps a better urban infrastructure. All that requires further investigation. Here again the presumption is that transition from a traditional agrarian society to a modern urbanized economy eventually results in lower fertility.

If this interpretation were correct we would expect the fertility of low-income groups (agricultural workers, rural migrants, and urban poor) to rise as their standards of living improve and the fertility of other groups to decline with increased education, urbanization, and economic development; as the two forces operate in opposite directions prediction of the aggregate effect is rather difficult. In the 1940s and 1950s their effects seem to have cancelled each other out; hence the relatively constant behaviour of birth

* The incidence of parasitic diseases, for example, is smaller in the towns.

rates and the unusual rural–urban differentials. But we noted earlier that crude birth rates have been consistently falling since 1963. The evidence on fertility discussed here may encourage us to think that this tendency is unlikely to be reversed. But it would be rash to expect an accelerated decline in birth rates in the medium term.

Modern schools of thought tend to analyse fertility in the framework of the theory of rational choice, and T. Paul Schultz attempted to study the determinants of fertility in Egypt in this way. His hypothesis is that reproductive behaviour is determined by 'a set of jointly determined choices that parents make over their lifetimes'.[7] The number of births that parents may want depends on such factors as their own levels of education and occupation, but also on the value placed on education, access to schools, length of compulsory schooling, children's and women's participation to the labour force, the availability and costs of contraception, and child mortality. Schultz does not mention, however, the support that parents require from their children in their old age—an important consideration which, in developing societies, may affect fertility rates of groups with varying access to social insurance schemes. There are benefits as well as costs in rearing children, and mortality tends to influence births because parents' objectives probably relate to surviving children.

To specify a satisfactory model of reproductive behaviour is an arduous task. Actual and desired births are imperfectly related; the time-lags may be long; decisions about number of children, their education, the timing of births and marriages, and wives' and children's employment are themselves interdependent; institutional and environmental elements play an important role in constraining options; foresight is far from perfect and children yield intangible costs and rewards. Parents' jointly determined choices depend on exogenous factors—the prevailing conditions of the economy and the availability of public goods—susceptible to significant changes over time. They would elicit complex adjustments and delayed responses.

Schultz attempted a multivariate analysis of fertility which involved single equations and simultaneous equation models in both structural and reduced forms. Regional data from the 1960 census were used. The analysis suffers, however, as the author himself recognized, from the weaknesses of Egyptian demographic statistics, and he wisely refrained from using the coefficients and statistical relationships of his models for projections or the formulation of precise policies. His results generally confirm the evidence surveyed earlier. Schultz also found that surviving fertility (measured from population censuses as ratios of children per thousand women of child-bearing age) is positively related to unpaid family work taken as a proxy for child labour; surviving fertility, however, is inversely associated with female participation in the non-agricultural labour force and also, rather surprisingly, with the level of agricultural activity in the region. Two provisos are in order here. First, unpaid family work is not a good indicator of child labour. In Egyptian agriculture children work both on and off the family farm and there is an important market for their employment as wage labourers during seasonal peaks. Second, agricultural activity and child employment are not independent variables in the Egyptian context, a consideration which may affect the results. The inverse relationship with agricultural activity (measured as the share of the labour force occupied in agriculture) seems, however, consistent with El Badry's findings on the low fertility of agricultural workers. But the results could not be fully interpreted without further evidence on the level and distribution of income in the various districts. Predominantly agricultural provinces may be poorer or include a larger share of landless labourers, in which case a Malthusian explanation would be plausible.

Other results are of interest. Marriage prevalence rates are directly associated with female education, but the indirect effect on marriages, through higher participation rates of educated women in the labour force, tends to reverse the direction of the relationship. Intermediate education seems, however, to imply lower fertility. In Lower Egypt, surviving fertility and marriage rates are lower and female participation higher than in Upper Egypt.

All things considered, Schultz cautiously predicted a substantial decline in fertility in the late 1960s: a conclusion borne out by recent data on birth rates. According to his estimates, the effects on fertility of a fall in the share of agriculture in the labour force should be more than compensated for by the reduction arising from the progress of female education, increased participation of women, and a decline in child employment. The downward trend in birth rates is expected to persist.

The question is whether the consequences of these changes on the rate of population growth are likely to be cancelled by further reductions in mortality. An analysis of age-specific rates indicates that, despite considerable progress, infant mortality is still relatively high. The rates fell from an estimated 400 deaths per thousand children under one year of age at the beginning of the century to an average of 165 in the 1930s and early 1940s. Steady and gradual progress brought the rates down to 110 at the end of the 1950s, but this tendency was not maintained and the performance of the next decade was rather disappointing. The dip to lower rates year by year from 1958 to 1961 proved to be ephemeral. Infant mortality stands now at around 120 per thousand as compared to 18 to 20 in the most advanced countries.

Once a significant drop in mortality rates is achieved through control of endemic diseases like malaria, further progress tends to depend on the improvement of nutrition, sanitation, and housing standards, the expansion of hospitals and medical services, and, in a country like Egypt, the eradication of bilharzia, a parasitic infection. Progress is bound to be slow because poverty, an unhealthy environment in overcrowded villages and towns, and debilitating diseases are the major causes of death. Infant mortality however, is, the exception. Substantial gains could still be achieved rapidly and at moderate cost if the government chose to direct medical and other resources in that direction.

Anti-tetanus injections, protein supplements to the baby's diet, and greater medical attention during pregnancy and birth are some of the relevant measures. A reduction in infant and child mortality rates could have a significant impact on the death rate in Egypt, given the age composition of the population, and could well lead to a higher rate of natural increase.

It may be argued, however, that a decline in infant mortality would affect parents' attitudes and increase their demand for birth control. The need to give birth to more children than desired in order to compensate for possible deaths would be reduced, and the desire for careful family planning eventually enhanced. As a result fertility and rates of population growth, after a lag, could decline. Progress on any front tends to become cumulative in the long run. The question is whether a poor society can shoulder the burden imposed while progress is being brought about.

The relevance of population growth to the problems of economic development explain the emphasis given in this section to demographic trends. Whether population is a contributing or a retarding factor in economic growth is a debatable question. Much depends on the stage of economic development reached, the supply of complementary factors of production, the employment policy, and a host of other variables. There is a broad consensus in the West in favour of population control, which has old intellectual roots in Malthus, the Puritan ethic, and the historical experience of certain countries. It is not value-free, but the thesis seems relevant to Egypt, though one may doubt its universal validity. The problems arising from population growth are one of the themes of this study and will often be investigated or referred to in the remainder of this book.

Other demographic features

Demographic theory predicts an increase in the share of the lower age bracket in a closed population with stable birth rates and declining death rates. Censuses show that the proportion of children (less than fifteen years old), which represented some 38–9 per cent of the total Egyptian population between 1917 and 1947, increased to almost 43 per cent in 1960. If fertility schedules remain constant the age distribution will stabilize itself in the long run. The population will be younger than before the decline in death rates, and the group of labour-force age (but not necessarily the labour force itself) will grow at the rate of natural increase. A decline in fertility, on the other hand, implies a lower proportion of children and a lower rate of growth of the labour force. The first effect is almost immediately felt, the second lags by some twenty years.

In Egypt, the burden imposed by children on society has been heavier since the 1950s than in previous periods. There were 8·3 children (less than fifteen years old) for every ten adults (aged fifteen to fifty-nine) in 1960 against seven children in 1947. Public expenditures on education and social services have tended to grow faster than national income. The costs borne by the present generation for feeding, rearing, and educating children have thus increased on two counts: a higher dependency ratio and more expenditures per head.

Dependency ratios tend to be higher in poor than in advanced countries although the latter generally have a larger proportion of old people in their population. But the lower number of children per adult more than compensates for this difference. 'Unto him that hath shall be given.' In this area as in many others, economic development exemplifies the Biblical dictum.

A high rate of population growth, not matched by a comparable increase in the habitable area or by significant emigration, implies rising population density. Density more than doubled in Egypt between 1927 (410 inhabitants per square kilometre) and 1966 (845 inhabitants). These averages conceal considerable regional variations largely due to the differential impact of internal migration. Cairo experienced a threefold increase (from 6,584 to 19,594 persons per square kilometre) during the same period. The rise was more moderate in certain agricultural provinces such as

Menoufia (41 per cent), Daqhalia (60 per cent), and Fayum (62 per cent).[8]

The economic implications of high and rising population density are complex. An increase in the man–land ratio in agriculture has a depressing influence on average incomes and also distributional effects. In Egypt it has been construed as prima facie evidence of growing underemployment and of marginal productivity of labour declining to zero. The reasoning, however, is fallacious partly because it confuses land, a multi-dimensional factor of production, with acreage, and partly because it neglects possibilities of substitution between land and other inputs and the effects on employment of crop reallocation. A high population density can permit economies in, say, the road infrastructure arising from a more intensive utilization of a smaller spatial network, and similar economies of scale in trade and distribution and the provision of a number of public services; market structures are to some extent favourably influenced by an intensive pattern of settlement especially in the tertiary sector. But there are diseconomies too, many relating to intangibles such as the quality of life. Low incomes prevent many Egyptian villages from expanding either horizontally (agricultural land is too expensive) or vertically (the mud hut is a one-storey building). Overcrowding is among the many factors that incite people to move, and rising density in rural Egypt thus adds to the migration push.

The rapidly growing, young, and densely settled Egyptian population suffers from social and physiological diseases. Illiteracy rates, not surprisingly, are much higher for females than males. Though extremely high at the beginning of the twentieth century, they have significantly declined after 1937. However, the absolute number of illiterates (aged ten years and over) has increased throughout the period from 7·3 millions in 1907 to 12·6 millions in 1960.[9] A considerable expansion of free primary education has taken place during the 1950s and 1960s. Between 1953/4 and 1965/6 the percentage of children of compulsory education age enrolled in schools increased from 46·0 per cent to

69·7 per cent.[10] Though female enrolment increased faster than male, the proportion of girls receiving primary education (55·7 per cent in 1965/6) remains lower than the proportion of boys (83·0 per cent).[11]

TABLE 2.4

Illiteracy rates (percentage of population, aged ten years and over, unable to read or write)

Year	Male	Female	Total
1907	87·0	98·6	92·7
1917	84·8	97·7	91·2
1927	76·1	95·6	85·9
1937	76·6	93·9	85·2
1947	66·1	88·2	77·2
1960	56·6	83·8	70·3

Source: D. Mead, *Growth and Structural Change in the Egyptian Economy*, Homewood, Ill., 1967.

The rural population in Egypt suffers from debilitating parasitic diseases—bilharzia and ankylostomiasis—which are among the main social diseconomies arising from perennial irrigation. Their impact so far has been more serious in Lower than in Upper Egypt where basin irrigation was practised before the construction of the High Dam. As a result of this project, these afflictions may now hit all rural areas. Amoebic diseases and eye infections, particularly trachoma, are widespread. As Mead pertinently put it, 'Egypt's main health problem is not one of major killer diseases, but rather of general poverty and weakness of the population making them susceptible to bronchitis, gastroenteritis and colitis, for example, three sicknesses which are relatively minor in developed countries, but which have accounted for 50 per cent of all deaths in Egypt in recent years.'[12]

CHAPTER 3
RESOURCES

'Ô monde entier des choses . . .'
SAINT-JOHN PERSE

THE natural endowments of a country, her geographical position, and climatic conditions influence the pattern of economic activity. They define an initial set of opportunities and constraints.

Geographical position

Egypt lies in the north-eastern corner of Africa, on the southern shore of the Mediterranean, at the cross-roads between North Africa and Western Asia, Europe, and the East. This privileged position and the absence of natural defences exposed her from time immemorial to foreign invaders—Hyksos, Persians, Greeks, Romans, Byzantines, Arabs, Ottomans. She attracted Bonaparte, and his short expedition (1798–1801) marked the beginning of her modern history and a new era of contacts with Europe. The most original feature of this expedition was the inclusion of a group of brilliant scientists in the French corps. Through their work, the monumental *Description*, Europe rediscovered Egypt and Egypt began to rediscover herself. Egypt also owes to her position the Suez Canal, a major international waterway opened to navigation in 1869. It created a new and significant European interest adding to other existing links: trade, investment, and immigrants. But until 1956, Egypt derived little direct economic benefit from the enterprise, and the canal proved to be a political liability. Whether it explains the British Occupation in 1882 is a moot historical point. It remains true, however, that seventy years later Britain was arguing against military evacuation because of the strategic importance of the waterway. In 1956, the nationalization of the canal brought war to Egypt, raised Nasser to the stature of a national and Arab hero, and inaugurated a new epoch in the country's relationship with the Great Powers.

While Egypt's political boundaries delineate an area of some 1 million square kilometres, physical constraints limit the habitable area to some 36,000 square kilometres—one-thirtieth of the total. The population is concentrated in the Nile Valley, the Delta, and a few scattered oases in the Western Desert. The Mediterranean coast, west of Alexandria, and the Red Sea littoral are sparsely populated. A few thousand semi-nomads live in Sinai, near the sea-shores and the edges of the Valley.

Deserts: Mineral resources

The contribution of the deserts—96 per cent of the total area—to the economy, though far from negligible, has not yet been very significant. The agricultural production of oases—dates, olives, vegetables—is small. Rain-fed cultivation of barley takes place along the Mediterranean coast, mainly for subsistence. The Government hoped to reclaim large tracts of land in the desert and irrigate them with underground or Nile waters from the High Dam but, as we shall see later (Chapter 5), suitable land proved to be relatively scarce and experiments with underground water in the New Valley costly and disappointing.

Another project, considered in the late 1940s, related to the production of hydro-electric energy. An immense natural depression—Qattara—in the Libyan desert, close to the Mediterranean, seemed to offer an interesting potential. The idea was to connect the Depression with the sea. The difference in levels would provide the water head necessary to activate the turbines and the natural reservoir would be used as an immense waste tank. It is doubtful whether any serious feasibility study was undertaken as the project has been made redundant by the High Dam.

Finally, the coastlines of the deserts on both the Mediterranean and the Red Sea have a real potential for a tourist industry. Egypt probably could profitably combine the attraction of her ancient monuments with that of her beaches. A determined promotion effort and the co-operation of foreign investment might help to realize this potential.

Mineral resources are either limited or yet unproven. However, the deserts supply the construction industry with gravel and fine sand suitable for concrete works; limestone is quarried near Alexandria, sandstone near Suez, alabaster near Assiut and Beni-Souef, granite and basalt near Aswan. Limestone, which is being increasingly used for fertilizer and cement, has become an important industrial raw material. Sinai supplied manganese, a minor export commodity, until the Israeli occupation in 1967—output in 1966 reached 186,000 tons. Phosphates, used as an input by the fertilizer industry for the production of superphosphates, are found near Kosseir in the Arabian desert, in the Dakhla oasis in the Libyan desert, and in Upper Egypt. Annual output has increased from some 400,000 tons in the 1940s to 650,000 in the 1960s.[1] Zinc, lead, chromium, tin, and gold exist in very small quantities, generally insufficient for economic exploitation. Natron, a natural sodium carbonate, is a traditional input in the production of caustic soda, one of the earliest modern industries in Egypt.

At present, the most important mineral resources are iron ore and petroleum. Before the erection of an iron and steel complex in the 1950s, Egypt used to extract and export very small quantities of iron oxides (3,000 tons per year).[2] Production of iron ore from mines located near Aswan— generally considered as being of relatively poor quality— reached 450,000 tons in 1970 and is entirely consumed by the domestic industry. Petroleum was discovered in Gemsa, sixty miles south of Suez, as early as 1908. Although one of the oldest in the Middle East, Egypt is not yet a very significant producer. Until 1956, the Anglo-Egyptian Oilfields Company, largely owned by Shell with a minority holding by the Egyptian Government, was practically the sole exploiter. Output of crude oil doubled during the Second World War, from 670,000 to 1,344,000 tons (1939 and 1945), and increased to 2,250,000 tons in 1952. The early fields at Hurghada and Ras Gharib on the Red Sea were later replaced by new discoveries in the same region and in Sinai. Although exploration was undertaken in the Libyan desert, the Fayum, and other areas, the former regions remained the major producers until the late 1960s. The loss of Sinai in 1967 was fortunately more than compensated for by the development of a large oilfield at Al Morgan and by discoveries in the Western Desert, especially at Abu Gharadig (1970) and Al Razzaq (1972). The output of crude oil increased by 150 per cent between 1966 (8 million tons) and 1971 (20 million tons). Large-scale exploration is being undertaken at present by the Egyptian General Petroleum Corporation in co-operation with foreign—mainly U.S. and Italian and, recently, Japanese—firms. Companies have been recently invited to bid for offshore concessions in the Mediterranean. Egypt's share of world production in 1971 was 0·8 per cent and the output of 20 million tons in that year may be compared with that of other Middle Eastern and North African countries: Iran, 227; Saudi Arabia, 223; Kuwait, 147; Libya, 133; Iraq, 83; Abu Dhabi, 45; Algeria, 36; Qatar, 20; Oman, 14.[3] Some oil experts expect Egypt to become a middle-rank producer in the late 1970s. Natural gas was discovered recently near Rosetta and at Abu Qir, and also Abu Gharadig where reserves are estimated at 63,000 million cubic metres—enough to meet Cairo and Alexandria's needs, say, for forty years. If these expectations are borne out, the deserts will play a significant role in the future development of Nilotic Egypt.

The Valley and the Delta: Agriculture

Despite the growing contribution of the desert, economic activity has been, and may remain for a long time, concentrated in the Nile Valley and the Delta. The Valley is a long narrow ribbon, in places only 2 km and seldom more than 25 km wide; the Delta is an inverted triangle with a base of 260 km and a height of 160 km. A lateral branch of the Nile, converted and extended as a main canal (the Bahr

Youssef) flows parallel to the River from Assiut to Fayum. The Fayum is a natural depression contiguous to the western edge of the Valley some 120 km south of Cairo. The Bahr contributed to the transformation of this small oasis into a rich agricultural province.

(a) *Settlement*. The pattern of human settlement has a number of interesting features. The 1966 Population Census recorded 1,664 villages in Upper Egypt and 2,369 in the Delta; 128 conglomerations—the capital, harbours, administrative seats of governorates, and districts—are classified as towns. The peasants live in villages built away from the banks of the Nile, near the edge of the desert or on small mounds (*kom*) made of the debris of ancient ruins. The rural habitat is not dispersed, with isolated houses on the fields, but concentrated in small, densely populated settlements— the *markaz*, the village, the *'ezba*, or the *nag'*.* This pattern has old historical origins and is largely explained by conditions prevailing in the past: the flooding of the land and frequent raids from nomads and bandits. The mounds on which villages were built afforded protection against high waters, and turned them into little islands during three months of the year. Concentration gave a sense of security and provided better means of defence against raids. The village today is a closely-knit community with complex social ties. When Father Ayrout asked children to add the missing features of a hut sketched on a blackboard, he was told to draw windows, stairs, doors, and then, to his great surprise, the neighbours (*giran*).[4] Without them the hut would not be fit for human habitation. These social factors and the price of agricultural land militate against a change in the mode of settlement. The habitat remains concentrated on land least suited for cultivation and the village, despite population pressures, is often unable to expand.

The larger rural settlements are market towns which have acquired administrative functions and, in privileged places,

* The *markaz* is the capital of a rural district, the *'ezba* the peasant settlement on an estate, the *nag'* a bedouin settlement.

some industrial plants. Very few are now renowned for a local handicraft, notable exceptions being Damietta with its carpentry, and Naggada, Akhmim, and Assiut with their silk and wool handloom weaving. Market towns, almost equidistant from each other (30 to 40 km) form a long string along the Valley and a tight network in the Delta. Some, though very populous (see Table 9.2), retain the features of big villages.

Egypt's main urban centres are: Cairo (4,220,000 in 1966, 4,964,000 with Giza and Choubra-al-Kheima), Alexandria (1,801,000), Port Said (283,000), and Suez (264,000). Cairo, a thousand-year-old Islamic foundation close to the ancient sites of Memphis, Babylon, and Fostat, has a privileged location at the juncture of the Valley and the Delta. The provinces of Middle Egypt, in the south, and the fertile Menoufia and Qaliubiya, in the north, provide it with a rich agricultural hinterland. It accounts for a large share of Egypt's modern economic activity, as a large commercial and industrial centre and the seat of the Government and most public administrations. Alexandria is Egypt's main harbour and owes her resurrection to the development of foreign trade in the nineteenth century. She had until the 1950s a relatively large foreign community and an active cotton futures market, and is second to Cairo in population, commerce, and industry. Her location, a few kilometres west of the Delta, sets her away from Nilotic Egypt, on which her trade depends, and accentuates her Mediterranean character. Port Said and Suez owe their importance to the Canal, transit trade, and a vast industrial complex (fertilizers and petro-chemicals). They were badly damaged, with Ismailia, after the 1967 war and partly evacuated. They are more isolated from the Delta than Alexandria and do not serve an important agricultural hinterland.

(b) *Soils.* This densely populated Egypt, with her five thousand villages and constellations of large towns, owes her existence to the Nile. Herodotus's old and often-quoted dictum has survived centuries of historical and economic changes. The Nile literally created with its alluvial deposits the soils which enabled an old agrarian society to settle and survive throughout seventy or eighty long centuries. These soils are Egypt's main natural resource. They may be described as calcareous alluvium deposited at the rate of one metre per thousand years, rich in unweathered minerals because of the volcanic rocks of the Ethiopian highlands which form the silt. Thus they contain organic matter but not in sufficient quantities for the high nitrogen requirements of plants; potassium, however, is in relatively good supply. They have a high clay content which makes them burdensome to cultivate, but with fertilizers, proper drainage, and correct doses of water they become among the most productive in the world. They owe to their common origin a great degree of homogeneity, the only difference being in the proportion of fine clay to coarser material which tends to increase from south to north and from the banks of the River to the edge of the Valley.[5] The most usual soils are silty clay loams and silty clays and because of this homogeneity crop allocation is not significantly constrained by the nature of the soils. Their origin explains the flat landscape of the Valley and the Delta and the sharp discontinuity between agricultural land and desert: no slow gradation between the Valley and the sands, no marginal cultivations, moors, pastures, or woodland.

(c) *Climate.* The climate, though less uniform than the soil, is not extremely varied. There are only two main seasons: summer and winter. The autumn and spring, short and undifferentiated, have little influence on plant growing patterns. Average temperatures in Alexandria, Cairo, and Assiut (Upper Egypt) for 1971 are shown in Table 3.1. The temperature hardly ever approaches freezing-point and plants are not subject to damage from frost; the relatively warm winter climate permits cultivation throughout the year. The growing period of most crops is relatively short, hence the wide scope for multicropping wherever water is available. Vegetables grow in all seasons and fruit is gathered several months earlier than in Europe, hence opportunities for exports which Egypt has so far failed to seize. Where the sea ceases to exert its moderating influence and the desert dominates, temperatures fall sharply at night. Differences of 15 °C. from day to night are not uncommon in Upper Egypt, and plants benefit from the resulting abundant dew. Climatic differences affect crop patterns. The higher temperature in Upper Egypt favours sugar-cane, onions, and lentils, while the humid Delta has the ideal climate for long-staple cotton. Rainfall is scanty and irregular in the Northern Delta, negligible elsewhere. Alexandria received 118 mm of

TABLE 3.1

Average temperatures in 1971
(degrees centigrade)

| | Winter | | Summer | |
	Max.	Min.	Max.	Min.
Alexandria	19·4	9·4	29·6	21·7
Cairo	20·6	9·6	33·9	21·0
Assiut	21·9	7·7	36·3	21·4

Source: CAPMS, *Statistical Yearbook, 1952–71.*

rain in 1971, Damanhur, 60 km further south, 79, and Cairo, only 8 mm; Upper Egypt from Assiut to Aswan is usually completely dry. Egypt owes both her water and her land to the Nile.

(*d*) *Water and irrigation.* The almost exclusive dependence on a unique source of water supplies had significant implications for agriculture. Some political scientists would even argue that it influenced the nature of both State and society. The strong, centralized state is a feature of Wittfogel's 'hydraulic society' explained by the infrastructure which requires control and regulation of a unique source of water supplies.[6] Whether Egyptian history can be meaningfully interpreted with this model is a question left to specialists. What interests us here is that the development of agriculture has been made possible by large public investment in irrigation undertaken in the nineteenth and the present centuries.

The basin system which irrigated land by natural flooding has been gradually replaced by perennial irrigation. Water is distributed to the fields through a network of free-flowing, deep canals, and storage of floodwater in barrage reservoirs enables a redistribution from high to low season. The perennial system introduces flexibility since it regulates both the timing of irrigation and the quantities of water supplied to the land. It has enabled Egypt to take advantage of her warm climate and the fertility of her soils to expand multi-cropping.

(e) *Factors of production.* The imbalance in factor proportions—scarcity of land and relative abundance of labour—has influenced agricultural technology in Egypt. Cultivation is both land- and labour-intensive, but the term 'intensity' does not have the same economic meaning when applied to these two factors. The difference arises from the role of capital. Capital invested in fixed irrigation structures adds to the effective supply of land by enabling multicropping; working capital in the form of fertilizers and other inputs adds to land productivity and increases yields. The intensive use of land is a fuller utilization of its capacity made possible by *complementary* investments. A fixed acreage, therefore, is not as binding a constraint as it may at first appear since land can be augmented in at least three ways: the length of the slack season may be reduced, the fertility of soils improved, and the crop pattern modified in favour of plants with short growing periods.

In Egypt land seems scarcer than capital but capital, in turn, is scarcer than labour. Hence the use of manpower rather than machines in most farm operations—from water-lifting to sowing, harrowing, harvesting, and threshing the crop. Labour intensity is the result of factor *substitution.* The abundance of labour and the nature of irrigation works (drains and canals) have also allowed considerable substitution of manpower for capital goods in the construction of fixed capital. Egypt's canals were often dug with bare hands. The classical model in which capital is initially produced by labour alone is more realistic than is usually assumed. Because of the complementarity of capital in irrigation and land, we could almost say that at times land was created with bare hands!

Animals, a form of capital which relieves and supplements labour in certain tasks on the farm, are land-consuming: in the absence of natural pastures acreage has to be devoted to fodder. In Egypt, however, the relationship is more complex because clover restores the fertility of land. In a sense, clover adds to land because it reduces the length of the fallow period and is a substitute for fertilizers.

(f) *Crops.* 'Given water, it is possible to grow almost any-thing on the fertile soils of Egypt.' This is perhaps true of field crops and most vegetables but high temperatures and low altitudes restrict the range of fruit trees to citrus, vines, figs, and a number of semi-tropical varieties (dates, mangoes, pomegranates, guyavas, custard-apples, and the like).

Crops are classified according to time of growing into three categories. (i) Winter crops (*shetwi*), which occupy the land between November and May, were previously associated with the basin system of irrigation. They comprise cereals such as wheat and barley, beans, fenugreek, onions, lentils, chickpeas, and clover. (ii) The autumn or Nile crops (*nili*), mainly maize, initially grown on unflooded lands. Water-lifting instruments were used during the flood season to irrigate these crops. They preceded winter crops by two months. (iii) The summer crops (*seifi*) are among the most valuable; they include cotton, rice, maize, millet, sugar-cane, groundnuts, and sesame; they grow during the driest season and are in a sense the reward of perennial irrigation. Vegetables belong to all three categories and many varieties grow practically in all seasons. Fruit trees have an annual cycle; some, however, have high water requirements in summer and could be treated from the point of view of irrigation as *seifi* crops.

Crop rotations are practised in Egyptian agriculture, two systems—the biennial and the triennial—being favoured. The former uses the land more intensively than the latter but has adverse effects on soil fertility. Examples of crop rotations are given below.

BIENNIAL ROTATION

1st year	November to February	Clover snatch crop or fallow
	March to October	Cotton
2nd year	November to April	Wheat or barley
	April to June	Beans and clover
	July to November	Maize

TRIENNIAL ROTATION

1st year	November to March	Clover snatch crop
	April to October	Cotton
2nd year	November to June	Clover (permanent) or beans
	July to November	Maize
3rd year	November to May	Wheat or barley
	June to November	Maize or fallow

An alternative to maize in the latter example is rice. Under this system the field is divided in two or three plots and the rotation is applied to each plot starting from year one on the first, year two on the second, and so on.

Crop seasons and rotations are not absolutely rigid, but they constrain to some extent land allocation responses to price changes. Rotations are partly a consequence of multi-cropping, but they are also necessary to counteract the damaging effects of cotton on the fertility of the soil (hence the fairly rigid sequence clover–cotton). The major constraint, however, is the availability of water which restricts reallocation of acreage between summer crops, especially the switching to rice. Although cotton, and sometimes rice, are more profitable than cereals, cotton acreage seems to be subject to an upper limit of some 2 million feddans, but an increase in water supplies is inevitably followed by an increase in the rice acreage. In general, Egyptian agriculture tends to respond swiftly to new situations. After the High Dam, *nili* maize was replaced by the higher-yield summer maize; to

TABLE 3.2
Area under main crops 1950–1971
(thousand feddans)

Period	Cotton	Wheat	Clover	Maize	Millet	Barley	Rice	Beans	Lentils	Onions	Sugar-cane
Average 1950–4	1,765	1,571	2,271	1,746	438	122	519	328	74	37	96
Average 1955–9	1,791	1,501	2,458	1,851	467	136	654	313	80	50	111
Average 1960–4	1,751	1,387	2,542	1,727	469	128	799	365	77	56	122
Average 1965–9	1,694	1,282	2,649	1,516	511	137	1,035	351	66	54	145
1970	1,627	1,304	2,748	1,504	501	83	1,143	330	47	46	186
1971	1,525	1,349	2,770	1,522	494	n.a.	1,137	289	65	n.a.	193

Note: Areas do not include interplanted onions.
Sources: Annuaire Statistique; CAPMS, *Statistical Indicators* and *Statistical Yearbook,* various issues.

satisfy a growing urban demand for fruit and vegetables landlords with access to capital or credit switched from field crops to fruit trees, and peasants have increased their production of vegetables wherever locational advantages or marketing and transport facilities have enabled them to respond.

The importance of long-staple cotton for agricultural incomes and exports has often created the impression that Egypt has a single-crop agriculture, but this has never been true. Throughout the nineteenth and the present centuries the larger proportion of the acreage has been consistently devoted to food crops and clover. Data on area of major field crops are given in Table 3.2; the rapid increase in the area devoted to vegetables and fruit is shown in Table 3.3.

TABLE 3.3

Area planted with vegetables and fruit trees
(thousand feddans)

Year	Vegetables	Fruit trees
1952	261	94
1960	513	131
1965	629	187
1970	717	244

Sources: CAPMS, *Statistical Indicators* and *Statistical Yearbook*, various issues.

(g) *Livestock*. Despite the absence of natural grazing land, livestock is an important agricultural resource; but livestock competes with field crops because of the dependence on clover for animal feed. The allocation problem in this respect is more complex in Egypt than in other Middle Eastern countries, like Iran, where differences in the quality of land tend to determine specific uses. Cattle are used for a dual purpose—draught operations and the production of milk and meat—and, as a result, are inefficient producers of dairy products. Moreover, the Egyptian *gamoussa* transforms fodder into protein less efficiently than the Friesian cow or the goat.[8] This use of cattle—together with donkeys and camels—for draught power reflects the poverty of Egyptian peasants and the imbalance in factor endowments. Mechanization, by displacing animals from field-work, would increase the productivity of livestock in its other use; but it would also displace labour and might, in the short term at least, aggravate the employment problem.[9]

TABLE 3.4

Livestock

(in thousands)

Year	Buffaloes	Other bovines	Sheep	Goats	Camels	Pigs
1952	1,212	1,356	1,254	703	165	27
1960	1,524	1,588	1,578	833	189	17
1966	1,646	1,630	1,947	791	176	10
1971	2,141	2,142	2,033	1,287	129	12

Sources: As in Table 3.3.

Man-made resources: the infrastructure

The much-maligned Khedives deserve credit for one achievement: they endowed their country, during the second half of the nineteenth century, with important components of a modern infrastructure. Egypt was one of the first countries in the world to build a railway (1851); and with 4,000 kilometres of track it had for a long time a high ratio of track per unit of inhabited area. It distinguished itself among developing nations with the early foundation of a Government Post Office (1865) and the introduction of a telegraph (the first line was opened in 1854). The design of Alexandria's harbour was extremely ambitious as it enclosed within the outer breakwater a larger area than any other Mediterranean port. Egypt remained, however, relatively poor in good roads, and public utilities were largely restricted to Cairo, Alexandria, the Canal Zone, and a few provincial towns. These early developments, partly explained by Ismail's concern with modernization, were both a prerequisite for, and a response to, the growth of the export economy.

At the beginning of the Revolution, in 1952, Egypt had 4,269 kilometres of railway track serving 699 stations and the railway rolling-stock included 881 engines and combined units, 1,459 passenger coaches, and 17,487 wagons for merchandise.[10] A comparison with 1970/1 indicates no increase in the length of track, while the number of stations was raised to 754; the number of locomotives and units increased by 14 per cent to 1,053, but this small rate of growth conceals considerable renewal involving a switch from steam to diesel engines for goods trains and the acquisition of diesel-combined units for the transport of passengers (their number rose from 60 in 1951/2 to 471 in 1970/1). Although this latter feature means that the increase in the stock of coaches from 1,459 in 1952 to 1,794 in 1970/1 understates to some extent the increase in capacity for passenger transport, the growth of output from 3,060 million passenger kilometres to 6,772 million (an increase of 120 per cent) during the period seems to have outstripped that of capacity; similarly the transport of goods more than doubled from 1,511 million ton kilometres to 3,287 million and does not seem to have been matched by a corresponding expansion of the rolling-stock (only 13 per cent in the number of wagons), although allowances should be made for changes in the quality of equipment. Veiled statements in official reports on railway transport reinforce the impression that the rate of utilization, and hence the depreciation, of the stock must have increased during these years, raising the requirements for gross investment.

In 1952 the Post Office distributed its services through 786 main bureaux and 565 village routes operated by the picturesque *tawaf* (usually riding a donkey); there were 128,000 telephones in the country and the telegraphic equipment included 2,580 Morse transmitters and only 48 teleprinters. Considerable expansion and modernization have taken place since: the number of main offices almost doubled to 1,514 in 1969/70, that of village routes more than trebled to 1,767 in the same year, and a large number of sub-post offices and licensed private bureaux were founded throughout the country—they numbered 1,390 and 2,492 respectively in 1969/70. There were 404,000 telephones in that year, more than three times as many as in 1952, and as the Morse equipment was being discarded the number of teleprinters rapidly increased from the mere 48 of 1952 to 498 in 1969/70. Data on the output of postal services are presented in Table 3.5. Here, facilities seem to have expanded

TABLE 3.5

Postal services 1952–1971

	1951/2	1960/1	1970/1
Inland ordinary mail (million)	87	121	153
Government ordinary (million)	17	19	16
Government registered (million)	22	23	24
Parcels (thousands)	768	879	383
Foreign incoming (million)	30	46	27
Foreign outgoing (million)	19	34	28

Note: Foreign includes letters and second-class mail (printed material).
Source: CAPMS, *Statistical Indicators*, various issues.

faster than output, and the decline in the number of official and foreign letters* in the 1960s, most of which occurred after the Arab–Israeli war of 1967, is worth noting.

Data on road transport are not very satisfactory. According to Issawi, by 1936 there were only 400 kilometres of paved roads and 7,000 of dirt roads.[11] Considerable investments in road construction were made in the 1940s, partly for strategic reasons during the Second World War, partly in response to the growth of car ownership. In 1951/2 the length of highways in the Valley and Delta was estimated at 14,395 kilometres (less than 200 kilometres of paved roads, the remainder being dirt tracks) and 2,619 kilometres in the desert (mostly paved). The length of paved roads in the

* The stagnation in the number of official letters between 1951/2 and 1970/1 is extremely surprising in view of the growth of government activity. We are unable to explain this feature of the statistics.

whole country rose to 13,889 kilometres in 1970/1 while that of unpaved track seems to have declined to less than 12,000 kilometres.

Having depicted Egypt's main demographic features, presented an inventory of the infrastructure and the main natural resources, and having briefly surveyed earlier economic developments, we may now turn to an analysis of the major economic policies implemented after 1952. The nature of Egypt's problems at mid-century can be easily surmised from the conclusions of these first chapters. The challenge, which governments began to perceive clearly in the 1930s and 1940s, was that of economic development, a process of structural transformation which would enable the country to sustain a high rate of economic growth, would reduce its vulnerability to outside shocks, provide meaningful employment to a growing labour force, and remedy the many ills—illiteracy, disease, and poverty—that enslaved a large proportion of the population. But natural endowments, human resources, and, above all, history restrict both the options and the means. The decisions of the past and the nature of the society and its institutions weigh on the future. Revolutions, as we shall see later, may instil vigour and determination in government policies, sweep away certain institutions, and promote new objectives. But they also inherit the country—its economy and society—as it stood at the time of the upheaval. They may bring in changes but cannot achieve a complete breakaway from the past.

CHAPTER 4

LAND REFORM

'Nous n'avons point tenure de fief ni terre
de bien-fonds. Nous n'avons point connu le
legs, ni ne saurions léguer. Qui sut jamais
notre âge et sut notre nom d'homme?'

SAINT-JOHN PERSE

THE revolutionary regime enacted a land reform law in September 1952, six weeks after the *coup d'état*. The decision should be construed first as a political act. The immediate purpose was to diminish the power of big landowners, the most representative and influential group of the *ancien régime*, and to remove a dangerous source of opposition to the young junta; hence the swift action, the priority given to this law over alternative measures for social and economic reform, and the determination shown in execution. The political implications did not escape the civilian Prime Minister, Ali Maher, a man of the past who objected to the project and was asked to resign. The first consequence was that the officers came into the open; General Mohammed Nageeb formed the new cabinet and the suggestion that the army would eventually return to the barracks, repeatedly made and sometimes believed, became less credible.

Political motivations, however dominant, do not rob land reforms of their social and economic significance. In Egypt the attempt to transform the agrarian system, even if it was criticized for lack of radicalism, was genuine, not a *trompe-l'œil* reform (as in some Latin American countries or the later stages of the Iranian programme) designed to attract U.S. aid or to boost the image of the ruler abroad but never effectively implemented. It aimed at correcting the maldistribution of landownership, seen as a serious aspect of the more fundamental problem of growing poverty and Malthusian overpopulation in the countryside, and it was conceived as an element of a 'development' package including industrialization and land reclamation. The three elements were interrelated. The agrarian reform was supposed to divert private capital from the land market to industry; land reclamation was to increase the area available for redistribution and hence the number of beneficiaries; land reform, reclamation, and industrialization were all expected to contribute in different ways to employment, the growth of income, and greater equality. The broad purposes were clear—to provide a solution to Egypt's economic problems, aggravated by a population explosion in a restricted area; the Government had the will and some of the necessary means.

The appraisal of a land reform can be undertaken at three different levels. It may involve, first, a discussion of the laws themselves and their objectives and stipulations in relation to the problem they purport to solve; second, an examination of the ways in which they are carried out; third, an analysis of their social and economic effects in both the short and the long term. A methodological question concerning the definition of a land reform arises here. The loose and confused concept of the U.N. reports of the 1950s, which includes under the term the whole range of agricultural policies, is very defective; but despite certain analytical advantages, the narrow definition which restricts the term to a redistribution of property could also be misleading. The successful fulfilment of the objectives of an agrarian reform usually involves a wider set of complementary measures. There is no real land reform without changes in the distribution of landownership; on the other hand, a policy confined to redistribution may defeat its own purposes and actually worsen the lot of those who were supposed to benefit. We shall find it more meaningful here to consider as an integral part of the land reform the supplementary provisions for new institutions and tenurial arrangements.

The agrarian question and the land reform laws

As already suggested, the agrarian question in Egypt before 1952 was essentially a problem of inequality and growing poverty.

Inequality had old historical roots and in modern times stemmed from the ways in which land was acquired and large holdings constituted in the nineteenth century. Under Mohammed Ali, a large part of Egypt's agricultural land, previously under the control of tax-farmers (*multazims*) or held to the benefit of families and institutions in the form of mortmains (*rizaq ahbasiya* or *waqf*) was confiscated around 1814 by the State. Some land—the exact amount is unknown —which had been granted (*rizaq*) to tax-farmers and not converted into mortmain remained in private hands with certain restrictions on the full rights of ownership. A part of confiscated land was registered in the name of villages in a cadastral survey; the rest was kept by the ruler or the State. The villages were responsible for the payment of taxes directly to the State. The fellahs had usufruct rights in their lifetime and no right in law to transmit the land to their heirs, although the practice seems to have been widespread. A change in policy in the later years of Mohammed Ali's reign announces the beginning of new private property rights. After 1829 he began to grant uncultivated land (*ib'adiyat*) to clients and high officials and also to members of his family (*jiflik*). One purpose was to encourage reclamation and investment, and to that extent the measure may seem enlightened. The evolution towards full ownership proceeded step by step. In 1838, *ib'adiyat* became heritable, and in 1842 alienable; more interestingly, fellahs were allowed by the 1846 law to pledge or transfer the village land they had in usufruct. The most significant legal development was Said's Land Law of 1858, which gave full ownership rights to the holders of *ib'diyat* and, with some restrictions (no rights of free bequest or endowment of *waqf* or rights to compensation if the land was requisitioned by the State), to fellahs who had cultivated a plot and paid taxes for five consecutive years. In

1891 and 1893, all remaining restrictions were lifted: all owners enjoyed the complete privileges of *mulk*.*

The origins of a dual development of land ownership—large estates and small peasant holdings—are now clear. But several other factors, besides the granting of sizeable tracts of land as *ib'adiyat* and *jiflik* by Mohammed Ali and his successors, contributed to the formation of large estates. One was a return to a tax-farming system in 1840 (under the new name of *'uhda*). Although partly abolished in 1850, re-activated later, and finally discarded in 1866, it led to the appropriation of large areas by a few families. There is some evidence that these estates were formed by dispossessing indebted fellahs who had accumulated tax arrears, and in some cases perhaps by eviction. Another factor was the practice of granting land abandoned by fellahs to big land-owners, or to civil servants in lieu of pensions, as the flight from the land—to escape the corvée, military conscription, or tax payments—already significant under Mohammed Ali, grew in importance during Said's reign. Later, with the monetization of agriculture and the development of the cotton trade, fellahs began to incur debts against the security of their land. Much fellah land was foreclosed for failure to repay loans. The problems of fellah indebtedness and dispossession began to arise in the 1860s and became very acute in the 1880s. Village notables played a part in the formation of large estates through a natural process of social and economic differentiation within the rural community. Bedouin sheikhs acquired large tracts of land through grants from the Government as part of a policy for settling nomads and through purchases by rich sheikhs towards the end of the century. Finally, foreigners came to own large estates through purchase, sequestrations resulting from their money-lending operations, and through the creation of land and mortgage companies. In 1901 they held 11 per cent of the cultivated area, and foreign estates represented some 23 per cent of all large properties.[1]

* In Arabic, full property rights; it is interesting to note that the word also means kingship.

By the end of the nineteenth century—and the picture did not change very much until 1952—the large landowners were the State itself, the Royal Family, descendants of high officials and village notables of earlier days, tribal sheikhs, and an urban class including foreigners and shareholders of land companies. Specific institutional practices were initially responsible for the formation of large estates; later, estates were constituted or added to through purchases in the land market. Small property, as we have seen, had its origin in the registration of village land under Mohammed Ali.

The initial inequality in the distribution of land, the emergence of a rich class of merchants and moneylenders in the second half of the nineteenth century, and foreign immigration all contributed to growing inequality. The role of Muslim inheritance laws is also interesting in this context. They tended to lead to excessive fragmentation of property, but the rich were more successful than the fellah in avoiding some of these effects. They could endow their property as private mortmain (*waqf ahli*), an option not always available to the fellah. The latter, when left with a small plot, usually leased or sold the land. Thus, inheritance laws may have contributed to increased inequality.

Table 4.1 illustrates some noteworthy features of the changing distribution of landownership in the decades preceding the land reform. Remarkably, the average size of medium properties and their share in the total cultivated area remained virtually constant between 1910 and 1952. The number of small owners more than trebled in fifty years, but although their share of the total cultivated area increased from some 20 per cent to 35 per cent, the average size of their properties fell by 45 per cent. A finer breakdown shows that most of the increase in small properties took place in the bracket 'less than one feddan'. Between 1910 and 1952 the number of owners in this bracket increased from 783,000 to 2,018,000 (to be compared with an increase from 464,000 to 624,000 in the bracket 'one to less than five feddans') and the average size of the property declined from 0·47 to 0·38 feddans. Although inheritance laws affected all groups in the same manner, medium and large properties seem to have escaped fragmentation.

However, the figures conceal considerable changes in individual or family ownership. A continuous displacement

TABLE 4.1

Landownership 1894–1952

Year	Small holdings (less than 5 feddans)			Medium-sized holdings (5 to less than 50 feddans)			Large holdings (50 feddans and more)		
	Area (000 feddans)	Owners (000s)	Ratio	Area (000 feddans)	Owners (000s)	Ratio	Area (000 feddans)	Owners (000s)	Ratio
1894	935			1,778			2,006		
1900	1,113	761	1·46	1,757	141	12·5	2,244	11·9	188·6
1910	1,370	1,247	1·10	1,636	132	12·4	2,459	12·4	198·0
1920	1,549	1,714	0·90	1,725	140	12·3	2,261	13·5	167·4
1930	1,715	2,053	0·84	1,755	144	12·2	2,307	12·8	180·2
1941	1,910	2,348	0·81	1,775	148	12·0	2,158	12·0	179·8
1952	2,122	2,642	0·80	1,817	148	12·3	2,042	11·8	173·0
	Percentages								
1894	19·8			37·7			42·5		
1900	21·8	83·3		34·3	15·4		43·9	1·3	
1910	25·1	89·6		29·9	9·5		45·0	0·9	
1920	28·0	91·8		31·2	7·5		40·8	0·7	
1930	29·7	92·9		30·4	6·5		39·9	0·6	
1941	32·7	93·6		30·4	5·9		36·9	0·5	
1952	35·5	94·3		30·4	5·3		34·1	0·4	

Sources: Annuaire Statistique 1914, 1921, 1934–5, 1944–5, and Statistical Handbook.

must have taken place over the years: large properties being subdivided into medium-sized holdings and the latter into small plots. But this fragmentation of the larger holdings was apparently compensated for by acquisition of land and the emergence of new proprietors. Large landlords, as a group, seem to have lost on one count only: their share of the cultivated area fell from a peak of 45 per cent in 1910 to 34 per cent in 1952. Despite this change, the distribution of land-ownership, extremely skewed from the beginning, became even more unequal.

In 1952, before the land reform, 2,000 owners held 19·7 per cent of the total area, some 1,177,000 feddans. At the other end of the spectrum more than 2 million persons owned between themselves 778,000 feddans or 13 per cent of the total area. These owners were virtually landless; some

lived in the towns or worked in the villages having leased
their plots to neighbours or relatives; others rented land to
supplement their holdings.[2] Finally, landless peasants
formed a sizeable group estimated at 1·3 million families (see
Chapter 10).

From an economic standpoint, the agrarian system in
1952 could be described as capitalist. We have seen that
private property was a well-established institution; cash
crops had been cultivated everywhere for more than a
century; the transport network linked the fields to the
market-place; finance and trade linked Egyptian agriculture
to the rest of the world. All the empirical evidence—on the
movements of rents and wages over time, changes in input,
use and crop reallocation—is consistent with the hypothesis
of profit-maximizing behaviour.[3] The complexity of tenancy
contracts, which often had provision for price fluctuations
or explicitly referred to Alexandria spot and future prices,
is itself an interesting indication of commercial awareness.[4]
Legend has made too much of the absentee landlord. Large
estates were generally well managed, either directly or
through the intermediary of agents and an elaborate
administrative set-up known as the *daira*.* The careless landlord is of course liable to be cheated by his managers; but the
agents in such cases had an additional incentive to maximize
the profits of the farm in order to increase their own take.

The factor markets, through lease of land and hiring of
wage labour, tended to reduce the dualism arising from the
distribution of ownership. The economic function of tenancy
is to break up large properties and to consolidate very small
parcels into holdings of operational size. In Egypt the
number of holdings (defined as units of farm operation) is
smaller than the number of properties. Thus in 1950 the
Agricultural Census enumerated 1,003,000 farming units
and 2,707,000 properties. Recourse to tenancy was widespread among both large landlords and small absentee
owners who could not draw a living from their minute plots.

* *daira* referred both to the estate and to the set-up responsible for its administration.

In 1950, 31 per cent of the owned area was leased either for fixed rents in cash or kind or under a system of profit participation. The sources, unfortunately, do not include share-cropping because the agreements were seasonal and limited to the duration of one crop; but another 30 per cent of the area may have been leased in this way in every season.

Tenancy contracts therefore took a variety of forms, but these differences (as Cheung has convincingly shown for agrarian systems very similar to the Egyptian)[5] are largely immaterial to the efficiency of resource allocation; preference for one type of contract over another depends on attitudes towards risks, the nature of the crop, and the transaction costs involved. Agricultural labour in Egypt was relatively mobile; direct cultivation and the existence of a pool of landless peasants favoured this mobility and the operation of a market for wage labour. Although large estates had a permanent workforce partly employed as share-croppers or for wages, recourse to temporary workers was prevalent because of strong seasonal variations in the demand for labour, and some small tillers also hired labourers during the seasonal peak while others, with too little land at their disposal, supplied their services outside their farms.

Because of these features, and the competitive nature of both land and labour markets, the pre-reform agrarian system may seem efficient in the allocation of resources. But there are qualifications. First, monopsonistic elements must have been present in certain areas. Second, the capital markets were much more imperfect than other factor markets and this has implications both for the distribution of income and for agricultural development, since working capital is required for the new inputs that contribute to the growth of productivity. Third, the system, however efficient, was extremely inequitable; the unequal distribution of wealth and, more fundamentally, the labour/land imbalance meant that wages were low and rents relatively high. That they were both set to a large extent by competitive forces in perfect markets is no consolation. Moreover, instability of incomes—a consequence of seasonality, price and yield fluctuations, and unreliability of labour and tenancy contracts—was an additional burden to the poor.

From a social standpoint, the pre-reform agrarian system could be described, in a certain sense of the terms, as feudal and dualistic. The late Doreen Warriner, sceptical about the meaning of feudalism, accepted the definition given by an Egyptian economist: a feudal estate 'means that the land-owner keeps a private army to defend his house and his person and that armed men stand guard over the crops'.[6] There were strong elements of social subjection on large estates and illegal abuses. An increase in the incidence of rural crimes and collective violence in the late 1940s suggests both that oppression existed and that it was resented as intolerable. Saab noted that peasants in Daqhalya occupied the Averoff estate twice in the space of three years and that the agitation continued after the sale of the holding by its foreign owners.[7] The cautious and scholarly Baer mentioned three rebellions in 1951 on estates, one belonging to the Crown Prince and another to the legendary Badrawi 'Ashur, as unprecedented events in modern Egyptian history.[8]

The reform of such a system should ideally aim to correct the maldistribution of ownership, remove the imperfections of the capital market, and increase and stabilize the income of the poorer peasants. But it should also avoid a disruption of production and undue interference with the allocative mechanism of the land and labour markets.

The Land Reform Law of 1952 fixed a 200 feddan ceiling on personal ownership. Owners could, however, transfer 100 feddans to their children, subject to a maximum of 50 feddans per child. They were allowed to retain, within the ceiling, the part of the estate of their choice and to sell land to their tenants in small plots (maximum 5 feddans). Private mortmain (*waqf ahli*) was abolished. All land above the ceiling was to be requisitioned within five years, the only exception being for fallow and desert land under reclamation. Landlords were entitled to compensation equivalent to seventy times the basic land tax, to be paid in the form of non-negotiable bonds with 3 per cent annual interest and redeemable in thirty years. The requisitioned land was to be distributed in small lots—2 to 5 feddans—depending on quality and the beneficiaries' needs. The order of priority was tenants and permanent workers of the estate, farmers with large families, and the poorest members of the village. The beneficiaries had to pay to the Agrarian Reform Authority in equal instalments over thirty years the compensation plus 15 per cent in charges as well as the annual interest of 3 per cent. They were not allowed to sell or sublet the land and subdivision through inheritance was not permitted. Beneficiaries were required by law to join a co-operative society which assumed, under the direction of an official, some of the functions of the displaced landlord—provision of inputs and credit, marketing of the crop, and maintenance of fixed equipment, mainly irrigation pumps.

The 1952 Law fixed rents at seven times the land tax and the tenant's share in the crop at 50 per cent (with equal participation in costs); and the minimum duration of tenancy agreements was fixed at three years. Minimum daily wages of £E0·18 for men and £E0·10 for women and children were also stipulated.

Subsequent laws extended the scope of land requisition, reduced the concessions made to landlords, alleviated the financial burden on beneficiaries, and changed to some extent the priority for distribution.

An amendment to the 1952 law limited the family holdings to 300 feddans.* A new law in 1958 extended the reform to charity mortmain. The Second Agrarian Reform Law of 1961 lowered the ceiling on individual ownership to 100 feddans. In 1962, all mortmain held by charities became subject to requisition. More land was later acquired by the sequestration decrees of 1962 and 1964 which confiscated the properties of certain landowners—a political action which followed the Syrian secession—and by a law of 1963 which expropriated foreign proprietors. In August 1969 the

* Including children and wives.

ceiling for individual holdings was lowered again to 50 feddans.

The concession enabling landlords to sell land in excess of the ceiling was withdrawn in October 1953 and in the same year it was decided to confiscate the estates belonging to the Royal Family without compensation. In 1958 the interest on compensation was reduced to 1·5 per cent and redemption extended to forty years. Although the terms of compensation under the 1961 law were generous (4 per cent interest and fifteen years' redemption) the privilege was shortlived. In 1964 all interest payments were discontinued, the bonds became irredeemable and completely worthless. Concessions to beneficiaries paralleled the tougher treatment of ex-landowners. In 1958 interest on their debts was reduced to 1·5 per cent, the supplementary charge to 10 per cent and the repayment period extended to forty years. The 1961 law fixed the beneficiaries' liability at half the compensation price; in 1964 this was reduced to one-quarter, the debt became interest-free, and the supplementary charges were removed. In the 1960s the agrarian reform was used to compensate families of officers or soldiers who fought in the Yemen war. Graduates from agricultural technical schools or faculties also became eligible for agrarian reform land.[9]

The land reform laws reflect an awareness of the main aspects of the agrarian problem—distribution of land-ownership, disparity of incomes and unsatisfactory tenancy arrangements—and of the requirements of a successful reform—institutions to replace landlords, payments by beneficiaries to ensure a certain level of performance. The legislation evolved over time, reinforcing and improving the initial measures of 1952. There was no change in the nature of the reform, in the direction of collectivization of agriculture and abolition of property rights; but there were changes in the extent and conditions of land redistribution. The legal framework is not, however, the whole story and a complete assessment of the land reform measures requires discussion of their implementation and effects.

Implementation of the Land Reform

Doreen Warriner often suggested that many a well-conceived land reform has failed because of delayed or defective implementation.[10] In Egypt, unlike Iraq, no delays arose from dissension among the ruling groups. The administrative tasks were facilitated by the existence of trained officials, a long experience with agriculture and irrigation, and the well-established legal framework of ownership with registration, cadastre, and title deeds. The Agrarian Reform Authority was from the beginning placed under dynamic and competent leadership. Thus the prerequisites of successful implementation were largely satisfied. Marei[11] and Saab[12] related some difficulties encountered at the beginning (mostly because of judicial intricacies in cases of joint ownership, absence of farm buildings and machinery on the expropriated areas, and disputes over the urban/agricultural character of the land), but they all seem insignificant.

We may note immediately, however, that the wage stipulations were never enforced. Statistics show a fall in rents after 1952, but it is not clear whether this phenomenon reflects the fall in cotton prices after the Korean boom or the application of the law. Most observers recognize that the laws on tenancy and rents were not universally respected, save perhaps in certain periods when the authorities threatened sanctions (1959–60) or installed a much-feared committee against feudalism (1966). Evasion was, and remains, possible through a variety of means. It is probably practised on a large scale by medium-sized landowners living in the villages and enjoying good relations with local officials.

The Agrarian Reform Authority concentrated its efforts on the requisition and distribution of land and the organization of co-operatives. Table 4.2 summarizes the statistics on land redistribution. It shows how much land was distributed each year and the total amounts distributed from the beginning of the reform to the end of any given year, and these cumulative figures can be compared with estimates of the total area requisitioned under the various laws. A cursory look at the table suggests that distribution has lagged behind expropriation and that the Agrarian Reform Authority has held throughout the period a considerable amount of land. This was inevitable at the beginning. Later, new laws brought in more land and replenished the balance

TABLE 4.2

Land redistribution 1953–1971
(thousand feddans)

Year	Total area requisitioned from 1952 to end of year	Distribution of Land Reform lands annual	cumulative
1953	211	16	16
1954	294	65	81
1955	374	67	148
1956	434	36	184
1957	n.a.	42	226
1958	544	43	269
1959	n.a.	6	275
1960	n.a.	23	298
1961	n.a.	28	326
1962	n.a.	106	432
1963	n.a.	90	522
1964	n.a.	122	644
1965	n.a.	26	670
1966	875	26	696
1967	n.a.	58	754
1968	n.a.	20	774
1969	n.a.	23	797
1970	n.a.	20	817
1971	n.a.	5	822

Sources: Total area requisitioned: calculated from S. Marei, *The Agrarian Reform and the Population Problem in Egypt* (in Arabic), Cairo, n.d., and other sources. Distribution: CAPMS, *Statistical Yearbook, 1952-71.*

before distribution had time to catch up. The Agrarian Reform Authority administers land directly pending distribution. It has substituted for the *daira* of the old landlord its own bureaucratic machinery, leases plots and collects rents, and in some places engages in direct cultivation. Public organizations have an inherent tendency to perpetuate themselves and some delays in distribution may well be due to a reluctance of the Authority to relinquish its functions. Yet 822,000 feddans had been distributed by 1971 and another 184,000 feddans from the public domains and Nile wastelands were distributed between 1960 and 1967.* By 1970 beneficiaries from the land reform proper amounted to 342,000 families, who had been given by that year 817,000 feddans, or an average of 2·39 feddans per family. The parcels received seldom reached the 5 feddan maximum allowed by the law, and there is some evidence that distributions tended to be more generous in the first stages of the reform than in later years.

Supervised co-operatives were created from the outset. Their role was to fulfil two important functions previously assumed by the landlord, the organization of production and the marketing of the crop. Membership of co-operatives is compulsory for beneficiaries and tenants on Agrarian Reform estates and involves a subscription to the capital of the institution. They are managed by a board under the direction of an official appointed by the Authority, the *mushrif*, who is often an agronomist; he has a staff of some twelve to fifteen people and wields considerable powers. A pyramidal structure was also created with local co-operatives grouped by district; these associations, in turn, were placed under a General Co-operative Society. The Ministry of Agrarian Reform in Cairo exerted the final control.

Until 1958 or 1959 very few farmers outside Agrarian Reform estates belonged to these co-operatives, but in 1957 the Government initiated a programme for extending the institution to other areas. In 1962 they became the sole suppliers of agricultural credit and later of fertilizers, seeds, and chemical inputs. At the same time, farmers were compelled to market their cotton and onions through the co-operatives, a regulation extended later to other field crops.

Before the land reform, in 1952, there were in Egypt 1,727 voluntary agricultural co-operatives with a membership of 500,000 and a capital of £ E661,000. The number of

* Additional to the areas shown in the table.

Agrarian Reform co-operatives was relatively small in the 1950s (187 in 1955, 303 in 1958) but other voluntary associations continued to be formed. Significant growth took place, however, in the late 1950s and early 1960s, the total number of government co-operatives increasing from 2,630 in 1958 to 4,406 in 1961. Expansion slowed down after 1965 (1965: 4,839 co-operatives with 2·4 million members; 1970: 5,013 co-operatives with 3·1 million members).[13] But during this period the increase in their capital was considerable, a reflection of the growth of their marketing, credit, and supply activities.

The social and economic effects of the land reform

Land reforms are usually expected to achieve several, sometimes conflicting, objectives. The relationships between the changes they bring about and economic development are complex. The Egyptian reform attempted first to tackle the maldistribution of wealth and hence to improve the standards of living and the social conditions of certain rural groups. It rested on a firm belief in the virtues of private ownership, which provides a framework for economic incentives, a measure of freedom, and some guarantee against social subjection. Land reforms, however, may defeat their own objectives if they create significant disruption during implementation, with subsequent falls in output, income, and employment. These are admittedly short-term effects. But land reforms could also involve social costs in the long term, if changes in the agrarian structure and the distribution of income had permanent adverse effects on savings, the allocation of resources, or other economic variables.

To avoid some of these possible adverse effects, the Egyptian reformers had recourse to complementary measures such as supervised co-operatives. Their role was to minimize short-term disruption by fulfilling functions previously assumed by landlords, and they were also expected to contribute to long-term development by providing credit and technical assistance to the farmer. But they necessarily involve restrictions on his freedom. An official bureaucratic organization has substituted itself for the private *daira* (in some cases, the old personnel were employed by the co-operative) leaving the impression that nothing has changed but the name. Moreover, the monopoly in marketing and supplies has turned out to be a double-edged instrument which, if misused, can adversely affect the pattern of economic incentives. Some of these defects, of course, are not inevitable, but the general point that a land reform may well be unable to achieve simultaneously desirable but con-flicting objectives remains true and is worth recalling in any assessment. There are trade-offs.

(a) *Redistribution of land ownership.* We have seen that between 1952 and 1970, 342,000 families received land from the Authority. But the land reform in fact reached a larger number of families because the first law authorized, for a short period, sales of surplus land in small plots. Some 145,000 feddans changed hands in this way,[14] and further sales were later induced by expectations of reductions in the permitted maximum size of holdings. Finally, the land reform rules applied also to the distribution of publicly owned land which in the past tended to be sold to big landlords.

There is no doubt that the disappearance of large estates reduced the degree of inequality. The Central Bank com-puted Gini coefficients* which show a sharp decline in their values—from 0·611 in 1952, before the land reform, to 0·492 after the first law, 0·432 in 1961, and 0·383 in 1965—and hence a significant movement towards greater equality.[15] But these figures should be treated with caution; the data on landownership after 1952 are not sufficiently disaggregated and there is an error in the 1965 figures which all sources uncritically reproduce. Aggregation of all smallholdings in the 'less than five feddans' bracket, which includes some 95 per cent of all owners, is the most serious defect. The distribution of landownership within this very large bracket

* Gini coefficients measure the degree of inequality between zero (perfect equality) and one (absolute inequality).

might have become more unequal. The Gini coefficients may thus exaggerate the improvement; it remains nevertheless true that the change towards greater equality was considerable.

A comparison of the structure of ownership in 1952 with that in 1965 (the latest year for which data are available) reveals interesting features. First, the average size of small properties increased from 0·8 to 1·2 feddans. The land reform is partly responsible for this change. Assuming that no other factor was at play during these fifteen years, one may calculate that the average size of holding would have risen to 1·05 feddans only. Since the net effect of inheritance (not taken into account in the calculation) is to lower the average size of holdings in this bracket, we are led to think that sales by big and very small owners, together with distribution of government land, made a significant contribution to the increase. Second, the number of medium-sized properties remained almost constant between 1952 and 1965, but their total area increased slightly (1952: 148,000 owners, 1,818,000 feddans; 1965: 148,000 and 1,956,000 respectively). We have seen that this feature of the structure of landownership goes back to 1920, and remained unaffected by the land reform. Not only did medium-sized landowners, many of whom live in the villages and represent the rural upper-income group, retain their share of the cultivated area, they may also have gained in social and political influence in areas previously dominated by big landlords. Third, the very large estates which covered 19·7 per cent of the area in 1952 have entirely disappeared. Fourth, the absolute areas previously occupied by the 50–200 feddans range did not significantly change, despite the reduction of the ceiling to 100 feddans; but their share in the total dropped from 14·5 to 12·6 per cent. The dual structure of the agrarian system, with relatively large capitalist farms at one end of the spectrum and small family farms at the other, has survived the reform; but the relative sizes of the landholdings of the two groups have drastically changed.

The Egyptian reform did not aim to satisfy the land hunger

of all tenants and landless workers. If the whole cultivated area had been expropriated and redistributed to the 2·8 million rural families in 1952, each would have received a plot of 2 feddans. Such a scheme would have been politically and administratively impossible and economically undesirable. It would have involved expropriation of very small and relatively poor rural and urban landowners and reduced the whole rural population to a standard of living barely above subsistence; and population growth would soon have

TABLE 4.3

Structure of landownership 1952–1965

	Owners (ooos)	1952 Area (ooo feddans)	Ratio (feddans per owner)	Owners (ooos)	1965 Area (ooo feddans)	Ratio (feddans per owner)
Less than 5 feddans	2,642	2,122	0·8	3,033	3,693	1·2
5 and less than 10	79	526	6·6	78	614	7·9
10 ,, ,, ,, 20	47	638	13·6	41*	527	12·8
20 ,, ,, ,, 50	22	654	29·7	29	815	28·1
50 ,, ,, ,, 100	6	430	71·7	6	392	65·3
100 ,, ,, ,, 200	3	437	145·7	4	421	100·0 (max)
200 and over	2	1,177	588·5	—	—	—
Total	2,801	5,984		3,191	6,462	

Note: * Adjusted figure.
Sources: CAPMS, *Statistical Yearbook*, various issues.

posed insuperable problems. A Soviet-type solution with collective organization and total expropriation was not contemplated.

The Egyptian land reform sought limited improvements in the distribution of wealth, and benefited the upper section of the low-income group. This outcome was inevitable, given the scarcity of land and the principles of the reform. Distribution of land to former tenants and permanent workers is justified on efficiency grounds, but benefits could have been extended to larger numbers if the ceiling on ownership had been lowered to 25 feddans in the second stage of the reform, in 1961. Complementary measures, in the form of food or cash subsidies to landless workers and regulation of work conditions for the *tarahil* (migrant labour employed in gangs for dredging drains and canals), could have improved the living standards of the very poor and further corrected the distributional bias of the reform. But such measures were never enacted and the minimum wage policy was never enforced.

It is often argued that landownership creates new economic incentives. The security gained by the tenant when he becomes a landlord encourages him to invest in land, improve cultivation practices, and adopt longer crop rotations; he is in a better position to take the long view. But the significance of these effects can be exaggerated. In Egypt, the distributed land was previously owned by landlords who did not lack these incentives. Tenancy contracts enabled them to determine cultivation methods, and—whether absentee or not— they were in a position to ensure compliance with the contract and to supervise the operations. In other agrarian systems the situation may be different, but in Egypt, the significance of land redistribution lies elsewhere—it reduced inequalities in the distribution of wealth and improved the social and economic conditions of 400,000 families.

(b) *The co-operatives and their effects.* The most interesting aspect of the supervised co-operatives established by the land reform relates to the organization of production. Each co-operative manages a land reform area as a single unit. Farmers retain both ownership and the responsibility for cultivating their own plot, but they are required to follow a number of practices: crop consolidation, triennial rotation, and co-operation in certain activities such as fumigation of crops and pest control. As Eshag and Kamal put it, 'the basic strategy . . . has been to combine the advantage of large-scale management with that of providing the incentive of private gain to individual farmers'.[16] Crop consolidation saves land and may increase yields, especially when the contiguous crops have different irrigation requirements. The triennial rotation implies a less intensive use of the land than the biennial and hence a reduction in total output in the short run; but this fall is rapidly compensated for by higher yields. The damage to soil fertility under the biennial system is considerable because of the greater frequency of cotton crops, the short fallow period, and the less frequent planting of clover. Finally, the undertaking of certain agricultural operations by the co-operatives may involve economies of scale and ensure the quality of performance. In this area, however, co-operatives have not in fact been very successful. Pest control, crucial for cotton which is subject to sudden attack from the boll-worm, became their exclusive responsibility after the 1961 disaster when a good third of the harvest was destroyed. The Government was largely to blame for their failure to supply pesticides in time. To prevent future disasters it could either have attempted to remedy the inefficiency of its own bureaucracy or abolished its virtual monopoly of supplies. However the solution was sought elsewhere, by asking the co-operatives to undertake pest control operations directly and to charge members for the cost. This system has a number of drawbacks. The co-operative supervisor—always an official—is often unable to organize wage-labour as efficiently as the farmer. Labour costs are high and administrative charges are added to the bill. The costs of cotton cultivation—the most affected crop —are unnecessarily raised and allocative patterns consequently distorted. Bureaucratic inefficiencies result in inadequate supplies of pesticides, and some corrupt officials make artificial shortages in order to benefit from black-market operations. Dumont relates instances when the absence of officials during the weekend has resulted in serious damage: because the boll-worm was sufficiently ill-mannered to attack the plant on Thursday afternoon.[17]

Co-operatives can, in principle, influence agricultural productivity through the supply of credit, fertilizers, seeds, and technical advice. They provide a convenient network, akin to an agricultural extension service, which the government may use to promote 'new inputs' and diffuse new techniques; and agricultural development in Egypt has reached a stage where it crucially depends on better inputs and improved methods of cultivation.

Increases in the volume, and changes in the terms, of rural credit were among the most important complementary measures to the land reform. The Agricultural Credit Bank was authorized to borrow money from the Central Bank and later to issue bonds up to the value of £E 30 million to finance its operations.[18] The volume of agricultural credit increased rapidly after 1956 (see Table 4.4). The increase

TABLE 4.4

Agricultural credit 1952–1970
(£E millions)

Year	Total loans issued
1952	16
1954	18
1956	18
1958	25
1960	37
1962/3	54
1964/5	65
1966/7	86
1968/9	69
1969/70	81

Sources: CAPMS, *Statistical Indicators* and *Statistical Yearbook*, various issues.

in bank and co-operative loans after the land reform exaggerates, however, the actual expansion of rural credit. Before the reform, landlords used to supply their tenants with seeds and fertilizers and moneylenders extended loans to farmers (no figures exist for these transactions). Institutions have taken over from private lenders after 1952. But, whatever the increase in the total flow of credit, farmers must benefit from the new arrangements because credit is now available on better terms. In 1961 interest on co-operative loans was abolished, and by 1962 all rural credit was being channelled through co-operatives. Interest on loans was re-established, however, in 1967 after the Arab–Israeli war, and fixed at 4·5 per cent. Not surprisingly, the volume of credit issued decreased from £E 86 million in 1966/7 to

£E 79 million and £E 69 million in the two succeeding years.

Interest-free loans lead to an inefficient allocation of scarce resources and discourage savings. They are difficult to justify on distributional grounds when they are extended to medium and big landlords. There is some indirect evidence suggesting that these groups receive a disproportionate share of total credit. In any case fiscal instruments rather than the price of credit should be used to improve the distribution of income (e.g. a reduction in land taxes to the benefit of small landowners). The fiscal instrument is available, since land taxes are levied on Egyptian agriculture.

Detailed breakdowns of loans by purpose and kind are available for certain years. The disaggregated figures for 1965/6 presented in Table 4.5 reveal a typical pattern. Medium-term loans for development purposes constitute a very small proportion of the total. Cash loans to finance the hiring of wage-labour and the purchase of other services represent 30 to 40 per cent of short-term loans. The bias of credit system in favour of the larger landowners (capitalist farmers who operate with recourse to wage-labour) is apparent here.

The total value of inputs supplied by co-operatives has considerably increased during the 1960s. The Government has a monopoly of supply for fertilizers, certain selected seeds, and pesticides, and uses the co-operatives as a channel. It is difficult to ascertain the extent to which co-operatives have been responsible for an increased use of these inputs. A high annual rate of growth in the consumption of fertilizers has been a remarkable feature of Egyptian agriculture throughout this century. Easy and cheap or free credit must, however, have encouraged greater use by small landowners (tenants were often supplied by the landlord, and medium or big landowners had easier access to credit). Co-operatives may also have played a significant role in extending the use of improved seeds.

The Government is increasingly using the co-operatives for disguised fiscal purposes. They have, in fact, become an

TABLE 4.5

Distribution of agricultural loans by purpose and type 1965/6
($£$E millions)

	Loans in kind	Loans in cash	Totals
Short-term loans (14 months)			
Cultivation	47·235	24·092	71·327
of which:			
seeds		4·633	
fertilizers		34·742	
pesticides		7·860	
financing of farm operations (wage-labour and other services)		24·092	
Marketing	—	1·857	1·857
Livestock	—	1·708	1·708
Operation and maintenance of machinery	—	1·212	1·212
Dredging	—	0·367	0·367
Other	0·188	0·649	0·837
Total	47·423	30·885	78·308
Medium-term loans (3–5 years)			
Purchase of animals	—	—	—
Purchase of machinery (including pumps)	—	0·485	0·485
Livestock breeding	—	0·218	0·218
Land reclamation	—	0·034	0·034
Conversion to orchards	—	0·004	0·004
Other	0·450	0·129	0·579
Total	0·450	0·870	1·320
Grand total	47·873	31·755	79·628

Source: Ministry of Agriculture, *Agricultural Economy* (in Arabic), special issue, July 1968.

instrument for the appropriation of the agricultural surplus. The compulsory marketing of the main crops, which the Government purchases at relatively low prices, and the sales of inputs at high prices, constitute an effective means of taxation. A good example is the sale of fertilizers at $£$E25 a ton in the early 1960s when the import price was $£$E15–16; similarly in 1970 cotton was purchased from farmers at

£E14·5 per kantar and exported at £E20·5 per kantar. This is an unfortunate use of the co-operative system, especially since the Government price policy is inconsistent with the development objective. High prices reduce the consumption of fertilizers which the co-operatives are supposed to encourage. The relative prices of inputs and commodities are distorted, leading to inefficient allocation of resources. An interesting study by the Institute of National Planning (I.N.P.) attempted to measure the loss in agricultural

TABLE 4.6

Value of inputs supplied by the co-operatives 1960–1971
(£E thousands)

Agricultural years	Seeds	Fertilizers	Pesticides	Pest-control equipment	Bags
1960	542	2,149	960	116	14
1961	561	1,942	1,539	352	137
1962	523	1,166	3,129	480	500
1963	731	3,025	1,894	482	700
1964	856	7,531	1,647	1,065	1,000
1965	1,202	8,993	1,785	55	1,174
1966	1,191	9,153	2,442	961	n.a.
1967	3,348	9,845	2,203	12	n.a.
1968	4,771	11,679	1,623	n.a.	n.a.
1969	4,661	10,966	1,655	48	1,554
1970	3,806	8,989	1,757	46	n.a.
1971	3,038	9,048	2,072	n.a.	n.a.

Source: CAPMS, *Statistical Yearbook*, various issues.

income and the balance of payment effects arising from these distortions.[19] The authors estimated that if the farmer had purchased his fertilizers and sold his output at world prices net agricultural income would have increased by £E 44 million between 1960 and 1967 (the annual average of £E 6·3 million represents 1·2 per cent of the average contribution of agriculture to GDP during the period). As fertilizers and field crops are highly tradeable the potential increment represents a foreign exchange gain in the Little–Mirrlees sense.[20] The study confined itself to the direct effects arising from higher yields on a given acreage. Changes in the price-structure would lead, however, to changes in the crop pattern and the more efficient allocation might add to the benefits. True, the computed potential increment appears to be small, but the exercise limited to fertilizers is just one example. The prices of many other items also—land, credit, water, pesticides, seeds—do not reflect scarcity values in Egyptian agriculture, and the total effect of all these distortions may well represent a significant loss of income.

We have argued that co-operatives hindered and helped; it seems however that the dynamic benefits arising from credit, improved inputs, new techniques, and the organization of production are more significant than the losses resulting from price distortions. To say that more could have been done does not imply an absence of achievement.

The contribution of co-operatives to improvements in land productivity in any historical period is difficult to assess because it cannot be easily separated from the contribution of other factors. We have calculated, however, indices (base 1948-51) of yields of seven crops for the years 1952-71; considering the period as a whole it is apparent that improvements have been impressive. In general, yields did not rise in the years corresponding to the first stage of the land reform, that is, between 1952 and the late 1950s. Cotton, the most important crop, performed badly until 1957 when yields just regained the 1948-51 average level; the yields of wheat, after an early rise (1952-4), remained stagnant until 1959; the yields of maize, the main ingredient of the peasant diet, did not improve during the 1950s. Rice is the only major exception to this pattern: by 1957, a 40 per cent increase in yields had been achieved, but they tended to fall or stagnate after that year. It is interesting to note that increases in yields in the late 1950s and 1960s coincide with the expansion of co-operatives. Other factors have been at play: public investment in irrigation, and more significantly in drainage, raised land productivity; the development of new varieties of cotton seeds by the Ministry of Agriculture, an activity which it assumed in the 1920s and which is unrelated to the

TABLE 4.7

Indices of yields for seven crops 1952–1971
(base: average 1948–51 = 100)

Agricultural years	Cotton	Wheat	Maize	Millet	Barley	Rice	Sugar-cane
1952	102	101	101	107	107	88	125
1953	109	112	105	105	109	98	127
1954	100	125	105	105	122	115	117
1955	83	124	107	108	115	130	130
1956	89	128	103	109	126	139	129
1957	100	126	96	111	128	140	130
1958	107	129	103	114	122	124	133
1959	118	127	92	118	127	132	136
1960	116	133	106	118	132	131	143
1961	76	135	115	121	140	133	132
1962	124	142	125	129	142	154	137
1963	123	145	123	134	141	145	130
1964	141	149	132	133	149	133	130
1965	124	143	167	142	137	132	130
1966	110	145	171	148	129	125	139
1967	121	133	165	150	115	133	137
1968	134	137	167	151	128	135	139
1969	150	130	181	152	125	135	144
1970	141	150	180	156	124	143	133
1971	150	165	174	154	134	140	n.a.

Note: Average yields 1948–51 (kg per hectare): cotton 527, wheat 1,834, maize 2,086, millet 2,697, Barley 1,880, rice 3,788, sugar-cane 68,809.
Sources: Computed from CAPMS, *Statistical Abstracts* and *Statistical Indicators*, various issues.

land reform, explains some of the improvements; the increase in maize yields in the late 1960s was largely due to new seeds and to a reallocation from *nili* to *seifi* cultivation made possible by the High Dam.

Some direct evidence on the impact of crop and land consolidation schemes promoted by the co-operatives is mentioned by Saab, Eshag and Kamal, and other students of the Egyptian Land Reform. They refer to a pilot experiment conducted in Nawag in 1955 where crop-consolidation led to impressive increases in cotton yields (608 kg per feddan in 1955; 849 kg in 1957; 1,061 kg in 1958). Eshag and Kamal supplied additional evidence for two areas, Kafr al

Sheikh and Bani Souef, where yields seem to have risen as a result of better cultivation practices (the information is unfortunately limited to two years only).[21]

The stagnation of yields in the 1950s should be interpreted with caution. It would be easy to jump to the conclusion that the land reform in its initial years had adverse effects on land productivity. The agrarian reform should be seen, as stressed in the introduction to this chapter, as a set of complementary measures and its impact assessed over a long period of years. The co-operatives were an essential component of the package and it is doubtful whether they would have been established and extended independently of the land distribution measures. As regards yields, these initial measures were, on balance, probably neutral. It is often argued, on the strength of an observed (inverse) relationship between yields and size of holdings, that a land reform must lead to an increase in yields. But this view should be qualified. First, the relationship which holds for family farms does not always apply to the 'capitalist' sector which is affected by redistribution. Second, there is no presumption that increases in yields must follow if the beneficiaries of the land reform are the former tenants of large estates—in Egypt, although their status changed after the reform, the size of their holdings remained practically the same. Some economists take an opposite view and believe that redistribution is likely to result in a fall in yields because of disruptions in the organization of production. We have seen, however, that the Agrarian Reform Authority in Egypt promptly stepped in to replace the landlord and assumed functions related to production. As repeatedly stressed throughout this chapter, the significance of the Egyptian reform for agricultural development lies in its conception and implementation as a large package of related measures.

CHAPTER 5

THE HIGH DAM AND LAND RECLAMATION

'Si haut que soit le site, une autre mer au
loin s'élève, et qui nous suit . . . très haute
masse et levée d'âge à l'horizon des terres,
comme rempart de pierre au front d'Asie'
SAINT-JOHN PERSE

THE main aim of the Land Reform was to redistribute
existing agricultural land. One of the purposes of the High
Dam is to increase the supply of land. The decision to build a
High Dam at Aswan was taken in the early years of the
Revolution. The Free Officers were aware that the scarcity
of arable land was a major obstacle to agricultural expansion
and that Egypt's poor endowment in natural sources of
energy had a retarding effect on industrialization. They were
concerned with economic development—that they lacked an
economic ideology should not obscure this point—and their
decisions reflected the views which young Egyptian intellectuals and reformers had begun to express in the 1930s and
1940s. In their quest for ideas, they discovered, after their
coming to power, that the Ministry of Public Works had a
file of important long-term projects and the High Dam was
one of them. Interest in the project was immediate. The
German firm Hochtief was asked in March 1953 to prepare a
design which was completed in December 1954. Despite
numerous disadvantages—which contrary to later views
were well known at the time—the project appeared on
balance to have sufficient merits to deserve attention. It was
expected to serve both agriculture and industry by providing
water to one sector and cheap electricity to the other. It
could also fulfil a number of secondary purposes from flood
control to improved navigation on the Nile and the provision

of a huge artificial lake for the fishing industry. The very size of the project, and the fact that it had been conceived but not implemented by previous governments, made it politically attractive. The Revolution had to prove in a visible and spectacular way its concern for the material welfare of the people, as well as its ability to succeed where the displaced regime had so badly failed. Great expectations were aroused by the decision to build the High Dam and Nasser thought, not without good reason, that it would immortalize his name. But inevitably the Dam has not, as yet, fulfilled its promises. Like all major undertakings of this nature, it has involved, and will continue to involve, heavy costs incurred with a view to greater benefits. Unfortunately, the burden of the costs is felt almost immediately while the benefits are slow to mature. Their realization calls for large-scale complementary investment in land reclamation, irrigation works, and industry, all of which are being considerably delayed by foreign exchange shortages and the consequences of the Arab–Israeli war of 1967. The unfavourable judgements which many observers today tend to pass on the High Dam are based on a narrow analysis of its costs and benefits so far. These observers may be correct if their concern is with the immediate effects of the Dam on the Egyptian economy. They are grossly misleading when they pretend to assess the long-term significance of a project not yet fully born whose economic life is expected to extend over many generations. The High Dam should not be viewed as an isolated project but as part of a much larger package. A substantial part of future investments in agriculture, electricity, the infrastructure, and industry will necessarily involve significant linkages with the Dam.

The High Dam is also the culmination of a development started a hundred years ago. It represents the final stage of an irrigation system introduced in Egypt in the nineteenth century and developed in discrete steps over the decades. An analysis of this system is essential to the full understanding of the significance of the Dam.

The main functions of the irrigation system are to redistribute the Nile waters over space and time. The first function involves a network of main canals (*rayah*) which feed secondary canals and the small channels that reach every field in the Valley and the Delta. The intake of the main canals is located behind elevation barrages, or regulators, built across the Nile. Their function is to control the supply of water to the canals by raising or lowering the water level upstream. The elevation barrages are at Esna, Assiut, Nag-Hammadi, on the two branches of the Delta, north of Cairo, and at Zefta and Edfina. The feeding of the smaller canals operates on the same principle: every secondary network is a microcosm of the main system based on the Nile. Irrigation calls for drainage as a remedy to waterlogging. Drainage is a mirror image of the irrigation system: small ditches feed larger and deeper channels and the waste water is ultimately collected in the main drains. Pumping stations at the mouth of the drains are the counterpart of regulators at the intake of irrigation canals.

The second function of the irrigation system derives from the hydrology of the Nile. The river has a very marked seasonal flow. Two months in the year—August and September—account for some 40 to 50 per cent of the annual water supply. Water is available in amounts generally well in excess of demand at the time of the flood, but in the absence of storage would not suffice for the requirements of summer crops. The solution to this problem is provided by reservoir barrages which insure a redistribution of water from the high to the low season and enable multi-cropping on most of the land. Such a barrage was built at Aswan at the turn of the century. Its initial capacity of 1,000 million cubic metres was increased by successive heightening in 1912 and 1932 to 5,000 million cubic metres. With the Aswan barrage perennial cultivation became possible in the whole Delta and most of Upper Egypt north of Assiut. Because of multicropping, an increase in the supply of water during the low season is akin to an increase in the supply of land.

The irregularity of the Nile flow is not confined to seasonal variations. Though the flood is in a sense a regular phen-omenon—it never fails to take place every year during a given season—the annual flow is highly irregular. The highest discharge recorded at Aswan in the past hundred years was 137 milliard cubic metres (1879); the lowest, 45·5 milliard cubic metres (1913).[1] The mean and the standard deviation of annual discharge between 1870 and 1959 were computed by Hurst and his associates[2] as follows (milliard cubic metres):

Period	Mean	Standard deviation
1870–99	110·0	17·1
1900–59	84·5	13·5
1870–1959	92·6	19·9

High floods threaten the Nile embankments which serve as dykes; if they were breached the water would damage crops, houses, and irrigation works in Lower and Middle Egypt where perennial cultivation obtains. A more serious threat to agricultural production arises from long sequences of low years—the old Biblical nightmare of irrigation officials (the seven lean years).

A good irrigation system is thus expected to fulfil a third function: the redistribution of water over long periods. Ideally the provisions for annual storage should be supplemented by facilities for 'century storage'. The High Dam was one among a set of alternative projects designed to achieve this purpose.

The historical development of the irrigation system in Egypt followed to some extent a functional sequence. The first phase, in modern times, began under Mohammed Ali and was linked to the development of long-staple cotton (1820). No attempt was made to interfere with the seasonal pattern of the Nile flow but the spatial distribution of water was improved (old canals were dredged, new canals dug, and two elevation barrages later built near the apex of the Delta). Multicropping became possible in Lower Egypt but in most areas elsewhere the land was irrigated by flooding (the basin system) and hence cropped only once a year. The second stage is marked by the building of the Aswan barrage under the British. The irrigation system assumed then its second function. But since storage enables an extension of perennial irrigation at the expense of the basin method, the need for an improved spatial distribution necessarily arises. The construction and successive heightenings of the Aswan reservoir were followed by the building of new elevation barrages and the digging of thousands of kilometres of new canals. With the High Dam, some sixty years later, the irrigation system entered a third phase and acquired a new role. Once again an extension of the spatial network was required to meet the increase in cropped and cultivated area. But 'century storage' solves at the same time all the problems arising from seasonal variations in water supplies. The capacity created to even out annual fluctuations also provides a bigger and more efficient buffer against seasonal irregularities than do the smaller reservoirs built for annual storage. In fact the High Dam made the Aswan barrage redundant long before the end of its physical life (save for hydro-electricity). The functions of the irrigation system are not merely additive: they involve substitution and complementarities.

The High Dam and alternative projects

The provision of 'century storage' is a technological feature of the irrigation system conceived for Egypt in the nineteenth century first by French and later by British engineers. At the turn of this century, Sir William Willcocks, one of the architects of the Aswan barrage, predicted that in order to complete the system another big reservoir would be required after fifty years. Later, in 1920, in an official report of the Ministry of Public Works, entitled *Nile control*, Sir Murdoch Macdonald proposed an ambitious scheme for the regulation of the River from source to mouth. A number of projects implemented in the 1920s and 1930s, such as Jebel-al-Awlia in the Sudan, and Nag-Hammadi in Egypt, arose from this scheme. The concept of 'century storage' was coined by Hurst, a British engineer who served the Egyptian government for fifty years from Cromer's days to Nasser's.

Proposals under this head can be divided into two groups. One treated the development of the whole Nile basin as a single entity. It has great intellectual appeal but would have required an enforceable international agreement or political unity between Egypt, the Sudan, Uganda, and perhaps Ethiopia. The proposal involved a large reservoir in Lake Victoria with a dam at Owen Falls, secondary reservoirs at lakes Kioga, Albert and Tana, a dam at the fourth cataract and a diversion canal away from the Sudd region in the Sudan where much water is lost in swamps. The second group of proposals were less ambitious and concerned specifically with Egypt's problems. In 1943 Macdonald advocated a third heightening of the Aswan barrage. The scheme was relatively cheap and would have provided sufficient protection against the dangers of a high flood or a lean year. The Nile regime, however, does not preclude the possibility of longer sequences of high and low discharges, and a much larger capacity was required for an expansion of cultivated and cropped area 'to the limit'. Another scheme conceived in the 1880s therefore received new attention. The Wadi Ryan is a natural depression in the Western desert which could be used both for storage and for hydro-electric power. The designed capacity was initially small: 5 milliard cubic metres, half of which could be recovered by free flow, the rest by pumping. It was thought later that a capacity of 10·5 milliard cubic metres was feasible with larger pumping stations utilizing electricity from the new power station on the old Aswan barrage.[3] The capital costs of this project were relatively low but it involved substantial operating costs throughout its life-span. The Wadi Ryan had strong supporters in the Ministry of Public Works, including Michel Baladi who resigned when the High Dam was preferred and Abdel Aziz Ahmad who constantly advocated it during his long polemical stand against the Dam. Storage in one of the lakes—especially Tana—was also contemplated; but the political reluctance to have a major developmental investment outside the Egyptian territory weighed against the idea.

A Greek entrepreneur, Daninos, whose fertile ideas about the hydro-electrification of the Aswan barrage and other

schemes date back to 1912, proposed in 1948 an outline of
the project that later became the High Dam.[4] He announced
'the sensational discovery that we had made in the Aswan
region, of the existence of an immense natural basin capable
of retaining by the construction of a single barrage, the flood
waters of two consecutive years'. He estimated the capacity
at 186 milliard cubic metres (not very far off the mark) and
argued the merits of a project which would fall in Egyptian
territory, provide more electricity than any alternative,
complete flood control, and reap all the benefits associated
with long-term storage. His ideas were examined by the
Ministry and apparently shelved but four years later they
were brought to the attention of the Free Officers and fired
Nasser's imagination.

An interesting aspect of the history of the Dam is that
engineers influenced and politicians made the choice
between alternatives. Later both together had the major say
in all decisions relating to the project. Economists were not
significantly involved. The state of their art is not entirely to
blame: it is worth recalling that cost–benefit analysis—
though less sophisticated and fashionable in 1952 than today
—was first developed to assess the worth of water resources
projects. In Egypt, however, irrigation was historically an
engineer's preserve, and although economic considerations
weighed heavily in their arguments in favour of, or against,
given projects, their approach was relatively crude and
consisted mainly of comparisons between total undiscounted
costs and benefits. The World Bank (IBRD), which offered
in 1955 to finance the Dam, may have been more professional
in their assessment but it is doubtful whether they examined
and ranked alternatives. Politics played an important role
in the government's commitment to the High Dam. As
already mentioned, the initial interest in the project in 1952
involved political considerations. After 1956 they became
dominant as the commitment became an issue of national
independence. Dulles, followed by Eden, had bluntly withdrawn the U.S. promise of financial support because of an
arms deal between Egypt and the Eastern Bloc. The Suez

Canal was nationalized in retaliation and Nasser explicitly stated that the revenues were needed for the Dam, which thus clearly played a role in the events culminating in the Suez war and became, though still in blueprint, a significant force in Egypt's history. It would have been politically difficult thereafter to reject the Dam and it is fair to add that the Government had no good reasons at this stage to believe that the project was economically unsound. It had received the blessing of the IBRD and later received Soviet approval. Some Egyptian engineers continued to oppose it, but world experts had been called in and their judgement was favourable. And the crude economic calculations that were made proved the project so overwhelmingly profitable as perhaps to excuse the neglect of a more refined analysis.

Construction, design, and costs of the High Dam

The construction of the High Dam officially began in January 1960 with Soviet technical and financial assistance. In 1958 the Soviet Government offered to help Egypt to undertake the project—a gesture of considerable political importance. They initially agreed on a £E 35 million loan at 2½ per cent interest repayable in twelve years; two years later a new agreement for an additional £E 78 million was concluded. The Soviets also modified in some respects the initial design formulated by Hochtief in 1954. The main change was in the location of the power station, to be sited now on the east bank with the diversion channel. In the original blueprints special tunnels were provided for the power station on the west bank. Another innovation related to sandfilling by a sluicing method successfully applied in the Soviet Union in similar projects. Both changes implied significant cost reductions. A board of international consultants opposed these modifications but they were overruled.

The High Dam is a conventional rock-fill structure. The conception is simple: to throw an artificial mountain across the valley in order to create a large reservoir. The site chosen —four miles south of Aswan—is very suitable because the Nile banks rise steeply from the bed and form a deep, natural

valley. The Dam has no foundations but lies on a thick
stratum of compacted coarse sand. Its weight and the thrust
of the waterhead are distributed on a very broad base. The
slopes of this artificial ridge are very gentle upstream, almost
horizontal in certain areas. The structure consists of four
rock-fill elements, moulded together with vibrated sand and
covered by a concrete blanket. The central element—which
may be construed as the main dam—has an impervious clay
core continued underneath by a cement grout curtain
(length, 560 m; depth, 180 m). Two other elements are in
fact the upstream and downstream coffer-dams. They are
necessary in all major waterworks to create and protect a
dry site. The ingenuity of the design was to incorporate these
temporary structures into the Dam itself. The fourth rock-fill
element, upstream, provides a solid lining to the edge of the
Dam near the base. The measurements of the Dam are as
follows: width at crest, 40 m; width at base, 980 m; length
at crest, 3,600 m; maximum height above bed level, 111 m
(the river bed is 85 m above sea level, the crest of the Dam,
196 m).

Since the Dam seals the valley a diversion channel is
required. The Nile now flows through an open channel
1,150 m long; then through six tunnels (diameter, 15 m;
length, 340 m) which lead the water to the power station:
then again in another open channel, 485 m long, which takes
the river back to its original bed downstream.

The Dam creates an artificial lake upstream (Lake Nasser).
The backwater curve is some 500 km long and extends south
into the Sudan, the width of the lake varies from 2 to 3 km
and the reservoir area exceeds 5,000 square km. The capacity
of the reservoir is estimated at 157 milliard cubic metres,
with a waterhead of 97 m (182 m above sea level). The
allocation of this capacity is as follows: 30 milliard for silt
deposits accumulating over 300 years (dead storage), 90 milliard of live storage, and 39 milliard of excess capacity for
flood control. This capacity is expected to ensure a regular
annual supply of 84 milliard cubic metres of water. This
estimate is based on Hurst's work on century storage.[5] Hurst

was concerned with the capacity of a reservoir (S) which would guarantee an annual supply (B), at most equivalent to the mean discharge (M) of the river over a century. The problem is relatively easy if we assume that the river discharges follow a normal frequency distribution, but natural events do not strictly follow this distribution. They have a tendency to occur in irregular groups: sequences of high values followed by others of low values are not infrequent. Thus the reservoir required, other things being equal, is larger in the case of natural events than for chance events entirely independent of each other. Hurst calculated that the capacity necessary to supply the mean discharge (M) would be unrealistically large. But according to his formula $\log S/R = -0.08 - 1.05 \dfrac{M - B}{a}$ (where a is the standard deviation of discharges and R the reservoir required to supply annually M), a live capacity of 90–5 milliard cubic metres would provide a constant annual supply of 84 milliard.

This, however, is the gross supply, part of which would be lost by evaporation or seepage (probably 10 milliard); another part represents Sudan's share (old share 4 milliard plus new share 14·5 milliard). Egypt is thus left with 55·5 milliard cubic metres, a net gain of 7·5 milliard over her old share of 48 milliard. This may appear a relatively small benefit. Criticisms of the Dam based on these considerations, however, are ill founded. First, the 7·5 milliard represent the *minimum* attainable,* and disregard the capacity for dead storage, though a decreasing portion of this additional capacity could in fact be utilized for 300 years. Second, Egypt could 'borrow' water from the Sudan, which is not expected to use its full quota in the years to come. Third, and more important, the aims of the High Dam are to reduce the variability of water supplies as well as to raise the mean. Finally, the Dam enables Egypt to determine the time pattern of water utilization in any given year. The 55–60 milliard cubic metres are available as an annual stock which can

---

* Assuming evaporation and seepage losses to be correctly estimated (see below).

be optimally allocated between seasons. Egypt's summer crops, the most valuable, would benefit significantly from seasonal reallocation of water.

The High Dam comprises a power station with twelve Francis turbines and a total annual capacity of 10 million kWh. Two main lines transmit the electricity generated to Cairo under 500 kilovolts and subsidiary lines connect the power station to plants in Aswan.

The expenditures incurred on the High Dam were estimated by the Government in 1971 as follows (in £E millions):

Preliminary studies	7·5
Infrastructure on site	12·5
Dam and diversion canals	117·0
Power generation	120·0
Flood control at the building site	2·0
Indemnities to the Sudan	20·0
Compensation to displaced Nubians	10·0
Egypt's contribution to the removal of monuments	6·0
Interest on Soviet loan	25·0
	320·0

Expenditures on related projects have so far amounted to £E 240 million broken down as follows: conversion of 836,000 feddans to perennial irrigation, £E 75 million; pumping stations, £E 15 million; reclamation of 650,000 feddans, £E 150 million.[6] The complementary investments required to realize the benefits of the Dam and to counteract some of its adverse effects are far from being completed.

In 1954 the IBRD estimated the costs of the Dam proper (excluding related projects but including interest on loans) at £E 209 million. The interest charge on IBRD loans is higher than on the Soviet loan and repayment periods shorter. The Soviet loan would have been more favourable to Egypt even if the commodities exported in repayment were significantly underpriced, and there is little evidence that they are. Wage and price inflation, inaccuracies in the initial estimates, and delays and unforeseen problems in execution explain the discrepancy between the IBRD estimates and actual costs.

Problems posed by the High Dam

The problems posed by the High Dam could be studied under a number of headings: structure, hydrology, environment, social issues, and agriculture.

(a) *Structural problems.* Every big earth-fill dam has unique characteristics which make its design and construction a new and difficult engineering venture. The science on which designs are based—soil mechanics—is relatively recent. Experience gained in other dams is limited (they are few in numbers) and may not provide adequate answers to problems posed in different circumstances. Structural risks are thus involved but we believe that the safety coefficient allowed for is probably high. Much expertise was drawn upon, and engineers have tended to be overcautious in their advice.

(b) *Hydrology.* The hydrological problems posed by large reservoirs are evaporation and seepage losses, sedimentation, and erosion of the river bed downstream.

Evaporation losses reduce annual availabilities. Experiments undertaken on the site estimated annual evaporation losses at 7·5 milliard cubic metres, but the effects of winds on the surface of the lake, when filled, are difficult to estimate with certainty. Critics suggested that losses could amount to 12·5–15·0 milliard cubic metres, in which case Egypt would loose most of the expected additional supply. Harold Keller put the figure at 10·5 and Government officials at 8·0–8·5 milliard cubic metres.[7]

Seepage is serious for two reasons: it can endanger the stability of the structure as well as reducing water availabilities. It is generally accepted that the grout curtain and the cushions of vibrated sand provide adequate safety. In fact, Soviet designers were so confident about stability that they intended at one stage to dispense with the curtain.

Execution flaws in the impervious core or the curtain could of course be dangerous and there is no way of knowing at present if the Dam is immune from such defects. Estimates of water losses from seepage are uncertain. This is an area surrounded by bitter controversy. Dr. Abdel Aziz Ahmed, who took grave personal risks in criticizing the whole project in 1960, argued that annual losses may be as high as 9 milliard cubic metres.[8] If he were right, Egypt would end up with less water than before. His argument hinged on a disturbing feature of the Nile mean discharge, significantly lower in the fifty years following the building of the old Aswan barrage than during the preceding thirty years. The question is whether the change is due to considerable seepage or is entirely independent of the Aswan barrage. His argument appears to have been refuted by experiments undertaken at the old barrage, measurements made by Swedish consultants on the Nubian sandstone, and by the expert opinion of Hurst and Black.[9] In any event, silt suspended in the reservoir will tend to seal all cavities and the geology of the site is such as to prevent significant seepage. The weight of informed opinion put seepage at 0·6–1·0 milliard cubic metres.

Sedimentation should not affect the live storage capacity of the Dam in less than 300 to 500 years, but it poses problems downstream. First, the clear water that flows from the diversion channel no longer deposits the fertilizing silt on the basin-irrigated lands in Upper Egypt. Second, its velocity is higher than that of water laden with silt. The clear water will thus erode the riverbed, reduce the water level, and endanger the foundations of all major works on the Nile downstream. Third, the brick industry will be deprived of an important source of raw material supplies. The significance of the first effect has been exaggerated, since most of Egypt's agricultural land under perennial irrigation did not benefit from the fertilizing virtues of the silt, though annual deposits on the Nile banks and canal beds were used for reclamation and to improve the physical condition of exhausted soils. The solution to the second problem is in the construction of protective structures at the site of all main barrages.

(c) *The environment.* The environmental problems are complex. The provision of an immense natural lake is likely to affect the very dry climate in Upper Egypt and increase rainfall, which may be construed as a benefit. But the shift to perennial irrigation in Upper Egypt is likely to spread bilharzia to that region. Any assessment of the Dam should attempt to put a value on such social costs: reduction in labour productivity, increased medical expenditure, etc.; but the unhappiness of the sick, though a cost, is not amenable to economic calculations. The High Dam affects ecological conditions both in the lake upstream and in the Mediterranean 700 miles away. The nutrients suspended in the lake are favourable to animal life and create an interesting potential for a fishing industry. This may compensate for the damage in the eastern Mediterranean where fish are deprived of the nutrients formerly brought by the Nile. Finally, the balance between sea erosion and silt deposits near the river mouths has been adversely affected and here again new engineering structures may be required to protect the coast. The problem is being studied at present by the Egyptian Government in co-operation with the United Nations.

(d) *Social issues.* The social costs arising from bilharzia have already been mentioned. The Dam has also led to a significant movement of population from Nubia to new settlements in Upper Egypt; and in the Sudan, the town of Wadi Halfa will also be flooded and the population settled elsewhere. The costs of forced population movements are difficult to evaluate. It is doubtful whether the indemnity paid to displaced Nubians and the expenditures on resettlement are an adequate reflection of the social costs. The compensation does not seem to account for the whole value of the capital—fields, date trees, and villages—destroyed; there is no way of evaluating losses and gains in welfare arising from cultural and environmental changes. The new set of economic opportunities may be favourable to some individuals while others find themselves ill-equipped and unable to respond. Uprooted minorities react differently to their new situation: in some cases forced change stimulates economic progress and helps the realization of hidden human qualities; in others, the first generations may fail to adapt.

(*e*) *Agriculture*. The implications of the High Dam for three important aspects of Egyptian agriculture deserve a word of comment. The first relates to the use of fertilizers, which will be required to replace silt in the basin-irrigated area. Let us note, however, that not all the additional requirements should be attributed as an extra cost to the Dam; an increase in the use of fertilizers arising from the introduction of multicropping in Upper Egypt does not constitute a *net* cost. Second, Egypt's soils may be adversely affected by the silt-free water in two respects: (i) because of evaporation in Lake Nasser the salt content may increase; (ii) the soil will be deprived of certain mineral particles (to be distinguished from fertilizing organic matters) which silt-laden water deposited on irrigated land. Similar arguments apply to drainage. Drainage will be required in the basin area where the retreating flood used to flush the land. Elsewhere, some new provisions may be needed because of increased salinity. But, again, extension of drainage arising from the intro-duction of multicropping should not all be treated as a net cost. The third aspect relates to the pricing of water. In Egypt water is scarce, yet it is supplied free to the farmers. Quotas instead of prices are used to ration this precious resource. The water quotas differ as between crops, and although the Government exerts some control on rotations, farmers have a certain amount of freedom in crop-allocation. That this system leads to allocative inefficiency through the wasteful use of a scarce input does not require elaboration. The High Dam, of course, has increased availabilities; but water is still in limited supply and society has purchased the increment at high cost. The official argument which refers to 'more abundant supplies' to excuse the absence of pricing is fallacious because requirements have also in-creased. The real argument against pricing is that the benefits derived from a more efficient allocation may be lower than the costs of implementation. The administrative and capital expenditures involved, given the nature of the irrigation system in Egypt, are likely to be considerable and the critics of the present method of rationing have not yet seriously examined these problems.

Expected benefits from the High Dam

The official list of expected benefits from the Dam (a) an increase of 1·2 million feddans in the cultivated area; (b) an increase of 850,000 feddans in the cropped area, through conversion from basin to perennial irrigation in Upper Egypt; (c) an increase in net agricultural output arising from changes in crop patterns; (d) productivity gains due to flood protection; (e) the creation of an additional source of electric power; (f) miscellaneous benefits including improved navigation on the Nile and a fishery industry on Lake Nasser.

(a) *Cultivated area.* Attempts to expand the cultivated area have been a permanent feature of agricultural development throughout the nineteenth and twentieth centuries. Water, of course, was the main constraint; but some 400,000 feddans were nevertheless reclaimed between 1892 and 1952 by the Government, big landlords, and specialized companies. The second heightening of the Aswan barrage and the construction of Jebel-el-Awlia, in the Sudan, during the 1930s enabled cultivation of this newly reclaimed land. Most of the work was done in the Valley, especially in the swamps of the Northern Delta. The only exception was a successful attempt by a Greek entrepreneur—Gianaclis—in the Western Desert, close to the Behera province. Gianaclis was a remarkable and patient innovator. He reintroduced grapes to Egypt and created a wine industry. Progress was inevitably slow, but unlike most private entrepreneurs he was willing to invest continuously for fifteen or twenty years before reaping the reward.

Land reclamation was part of the Free Officers' programme. The decision to build the High Dam was soon followed in 1953 by a reclamation project in the Western Desert, the famous Tahrir province. Gianaclis was clearly the model, but the enterprise proved to be extremely expensive and rather unsuccessful. The publicity given to Tahrir—much glamour is attached to desert reclamation— has obscured the more significant effort undertaken in the Valley. The Government intended to reclaim 255,000 feddans between 1952 and 1959, of which 234,000 were in the Valley and only 21,000 outside; and 79,000 feddans were actually reclaimed during this period (74,500 in the Valley, with the help of U.S. aid agencies and 4,500 in the desert). The start of the construction of the High Dam in 1960 called for a more significant effort and in the next ten years 805,000 feddans were reclaimed. The annual amounts are shown in Table 5.1.

TABLE 5.1

Land reclamation 1960–1970
(thousand feddans)

Year	Area reclaimed	Year	Area reclaimed
1960/1	28·3	1965/6	116·4
1961/2	89·3	1966/7	52·7
1962/3	122·3	1967/8	34·0
1963/4	159·4	1968/9	45·1
1964/5	137·0	1969/70	21·0

Sources: CAPMS, *Statistical Indicators* and *Statistical Yearbook*, various issues.

Provisional figures for 1970/1 put reclamation at 21,000 feddans during that year. The main effort was undertaken between 1962 and 1966 but the area reclaimed after 1966 is alarmingly low. Land reclamation targets were never fulfilled. The First Five-Year Plan (1960/1–1964/5) aimed at 885,000 feddans (100,000 in Northern Tahrir, 300,000 in the Oases and Sinai, and the rest in the Valley); the target was revised downwards in 1962 to 723,000 (520,000 in the Valley, 203,000 in the desert) but only 536,000 feddans were actually reclaimed, representing 87 per cent of the target for the Valley and 41 per cent for the desert. In 1965/6 and 1966/7 the target was relatively modest—175,700 feddans for the two years—and was practically achieved.[10] The Government has clearly revised its expectations downward partly because of financial constraints and the rising cost of reclamation (estimated in 1960 at £E190 per feddan but rising to well over £E310 in 1969), and partly because of the difficulties encountered in desert areas, especially in the New Valley.

650,000 feddans out of the 805,000 reclaimed between 1960 and 1970 are related to the High Dam. The cultivation of the remainder depends either on different sources of water supplies or on small Nile surpluses available before the Dam. The expected increase of 1·2 million feddans is far from having been achieved; and if the present annual rate of 20,000–30,000 feddans were to be maintained in the 1970s completion would require two long decades.

The question arises whether Egypt still possesses 550,000 feddans of land suitable for reclamation. A disturbing report produced by the F.A.O. in 1966 suggests a negative reply.[11] A survey of 14·5 million feddans undertaken between 1960 and 1964 by a group of international experts found only 88,000 feddans of class I soil (high potential similar to the cultivated area in the Valley), 190,000 feddans of class II soil (good fine-textured soil, some heavy clays, some loamy sands with heavy subsoils and some coarse sandy loams), and 565,000 feddans of class III soil of very mediocre quality (in all some 845,000 feddans). It is not clear how much of this land was reclaimed during the 1960s (the survey may or may not have included land scheduled for work and areas with work in progress). It is likely however that some of the best soils have already been reclaimed in recent years. The most favourable hypothesis is that Egypt is left with some 500,000 feddans of class III soil but very little in the higher categories; the worst that only 200,000–300,000 feddans of very mediocre land are still available. Costs of reclamation may well prove to be as high as £E400 per feddan at 1970 prices and the expected returns so low as to make the investment unprofitable.

Increases in cultivated area cannot be easily inferred from statistics on land reclamation. In most cases, there is a lag of three to six years between reclamation and the first crop. At this stage the quality of the land is generally low and the full potential is not attained in less than four to six years. Though 900,000 feddans have been reclaimed since 1952, the increase in cultivated area has not yet exceeded 360,000–400,000 feddans.

(b) *Cropped area.* The conversion of 850,000 feddans from basin to perennial irrigation is often mistakenly construed as implying an increase of 1·7 million feddans in cropped area. Three wrong assumptions are commonly made. First, that the conversion implies a shift from one to three crops which is incorrect because the triennial rotation favoured at present produces less than three crops a year. Second, that all the basin-irrigated area yielded only one annual crop. In fact the cultivation of only 625,000 feddans in Upper Egypt depended exclusively on flooding; an additional grain crop was produced on the remainder with pumped groundwater. Third, the assumption of a shift from one to three crops implies that all crops occupy land for a relatively short period of time. In fact, sugar-cane, grown on 135,000 feddans in the basin area in 1966, occupies land for ten months and hence leaves no room for a second crop. The conversion from basin to perennial irrigation of 850,000 feddans—almost completed by 1972—can in fact be expected to introduce multicropping to 490,000 feddans only.

(c) *Crop patterns.* The most important, but the least publicized, benefit arising from the High Dam relates to changes in crop allocation. Two factors are relevant here. One is the increase in water availabilities, the other is the improved seasonal regulation which permits larger allocation of water for summer crops. Significant benefits arise from a switch away from cotton to sugar-cane in Upper Egypt, a switch from wheat to rice in parts of the Delta, and from flood or *nili* maize to summer maize. Sugar-cane requires more water than cotton and is more suited to agricultural conditions in Upper Egypt where it yields a higher net income per feddan. Rice is an export crop, in which Egypt seemed to have a clear comparative advantage in the early 1960s, but world market conditions vary constantly and the problems of optimum allocation of land to rice, wheat, and cotton are extremely complex. The yields of summer maize are at least 20 per cent higher than of *nili* maize, and here the benefits of reallocation are clear.

In an article written in 1964, Wyn F. Owen expressed serious doubts about the ability of Egyptian agriculture to respond to the new situation by simple alterations of the crop pattern.[12] Fortunately he was wrong. In 1952 the areas of summer and *nili* maize were 27,000 and 1,677,000 feddans respectively; in 1971 they were 1,171,000 and 351,000 feddans respectively. The sugar-cane area increased from 92,000 to 193,000 feddans during the same period and rice from an average of 545,000 (1950-4) to 1,140,000 (1967-71). Without suggesting that these adjustments have achieved an optimal allocation, one may note that they reveal a very significant response.

There may be still room for further changes. One of the vexed questions is wheat, which the Government has consistently encouraged through subsidies and compulsory cultivation. However, substitution of clover, rice, or maize for wheat has often been advocated. Clover is complementary to cotton in Egyptian crop rotations and an input for livestock production. A considerable expansion in clover unrelated to a policy for livestock thus may well result in sharply diminishing marginal revenues. Reallocation between grain crops should be influenced by relative world prices because these crops are eminently tradeable and Government policy should aim to enhance the limited flexibility allowed by physical and technological constraints. The transmission of correct price signals is essential. Protectionist policies in favour of any grain crop to the detriment of others seem both economically irrational and difficult to justify on non-economic grounds.

In his 1964 article, Wyn Owen argued that the High Dam water would be entirely used up by crop reallocation together with an increase of 400,000 feddans in the cultivated area. The issue of the optimum allocation of the water increment between old and new land thus arises. The optimum position is attained when the net benefit of the marginal unit of water is equalized in all uses. On old land, the net benefit is the difference between the value added of the substitute crop and that of the original crop per unit of extra water used, *minus* interest and depreciation on complementary investment that may be required (mainly drainage). On new land, the benefit is the value added of the crop per unit of water *minus* the interest on land reclamation expenditures. It seems that nobody has attempted to do the calculations. It is possible that the benefits from 'horizontal' expansion were initially higher than those from crop-reallocation on old areas. But, as the costs of reclamation are increasing and the agricultural quality of soils scheduled for reclamation declining, the relative advantage may be narrowing until it eventually disappears. At that point—and the question is whether it has already been reached—land reclamation should cease and resources be diverted to the old areas.

(*d*) *Benefits from flood control.* These are relatively minor. Excess water from flooding reduces yields in the basin area. The conversion to perennial irrigation, allowing greater flexibility in the timing of certain agricultural operations (watering, planting) and by lengthening the crop growing season, may also result in higher yields. Finally, the High Dam regimen saves resources previously devoted to the protection of embankments and the repair of flood damage.

(*e*) *Electricity.* The hydro-electric power station at the High Dam has a potential of 10,000 million kWh, or double the potential of thermal stations existing at the time of its completion. Total consumption in 1970 was around 7,000 million kWh and excess capacity in electricity is now enormous as can be surmised from the following indices: consumption index (1952 = 100; 1969/70 = 660); capacity index (1952 = 100; 1969/70 = 1,135). Since operating costs of hydro-electric stations are very low, the marginal cost of electricity at source is today virtually zero.

(*f*) *Other benefits*. Improved navigation on the Nile is a minor benefit. The development of fisheries on Lake Nasser requires significant investments in cold storage and transport, and feasibility studies are here again required.

Conclusion

The High Dam is a big and lumpy investment project: a beautiful textbook example of 'indivisibilities'. Although its main purpose is to provide water and electricity, its effects may prove wide-ranging and involve multifarious costs and benefits. They are in the nature of externalities; and some are difficult to evaluate because of intangibles, indirect reper-cussions of a complex nature, or uncertainties and lack of knowledge.

The structural characteristics of the Dam ensure a very long physical life (in the absence of nuclear wars) which may extend well beyond its economic life. The gestation period is also long. Though completed in the shortest possible time, construction extended over seven to eight years. A period of similar length is then required to fill the immense reservoir: eight or perhaps ten consecutive annual floods. The High Dam is essentially an 'intermediate' project: its profitability is that of the industries which will be set up to utilize its electricity and the agricultural projects which will use its waters. Long time-lags will necessarily arise before full utilization. Related projects cannot be undertaken all at once because of their scale and the complementarities involved. Their own gestation period is sometimes very long: the reclamation of a plot of desert land, for example, may extend over ten years. The stream of future benefits depends to some extent on the time pattern of comple-mentary investment and is likely to increase over the years.

The High Dam thus implies a very low social rate of time preference since the initial period during which very substantial costs are incurred with small immediate benefits is relatively long (at least fifteen years).

To attempt a cost–benefit analysis of the Dam—a Promethean task—is not possible at this stage. Accurate information on the characteristics and the time pattern of all related projects would be required and uncertainty about this time pattern would mar the exercise even if a complete file of projects (with their feasibility studies) happened to exist. Projects should be carefully evaluated *ex ante*. *Ex post* exercises are purely academic, especially in the case of a project which, unlike a factory or a bridge, will not be reproduced in the future. In any case, the time for an *ex post* analysis has not arrived, because the complementary projects without which the High Dam is a sterile monument have not yet been completed.

Whether Egypt was right or wrong to build the Dam in 1960 is an unanswerable question. Those who argue that she was wrong should consider that countries do not choose freely the timing of large projects involving considerable foreign assistance. Egypt cashed in on the Cold War. The international circumstances of the 1950s were unique and the opportunity they represented for Egypt might not have recurred. Those who argue that she was right are engaging in premature or incomplete evaluation.

Finally, it is worth recalling that the significance of the Dam reaches beyond economics. It may have slow but important social repercussions if electricity is introduced in the villages, affecting patterns of living and attitudes in rural Egypt. Though much remains to be done, it has created a sense of achievement and national pride. It has also made Egypt dangerously vulnerable in war and may weigh in the formulation of foreign policy and play a role in future Middle Eastern conflict. These are among the costs and benefits which the economist cannot quantify; but they matter too.

The major task today is to make the best possible use of the High Dam. This requires a careful evaluation of the complementary projects which will realize its potential benefits. The agricultural issues relate to the allocation of water between old and new areas and the opportunity costs of further reclamation of desert land. The evaluation of industrial projects should treat electricity delivered at Aswan or in other locations which may be supplied by the existing transmission network as a free good. Other uses, which imply new investment in distribution, should take these capital costs into account. Other projects should be studied: for example, the introduction of electricity in villages for domestic and productive uses, fisheries and tourism on Lake Nasser.

The High Dam should indeed become a central element of a new long-term plan. It has significantly changed the features of the economy, adding to its resources, offering a new set of potential linkages with all the major sectors and imposing new constraints. To ignore these facts is both wasteful and dangerous. Benefits forgone by unnecessary delays in the utilization of existing capacity are for ever forgone. Delays in remedying the adverse effects of the Dam may, in certain cases at least, entail heavy damages and losses. But there is no evidence that the High Dam and its implications have become an integral part of official thinking on planning and development policies. It is unfortunate that the completion of the Dam has coincided with a period of financial and political difficulties. The Arab–Israeli conflict has diverted scarce funds away from investment into armaments and defence expenditures and economic development is not today the main priority; the Government has other worries and its energies are absorbed elsewhere. Even so much more could be done than seems in prospect at present to realize, within these constraints, some of the potential benefits of the Dam.

CHAPTER 6

INSTITUTIONAL CHANGES

Introduction

THE Free Officers' concern with economic development was not limited to the expansion of the cultivated area and the redistribution of landownership. Measures taken in the early years of the Revolution suggest that they had, from the very beginning, other objectives. The first relates to the diversification of the economic structure, mainly through industrialization. This involved at one stage greater encouragement to private industry, Government participation in new industrial ventures, and an increase in the rate of public investment in electricity, agriculture, and certain services. It rapidly evolved and led to the transformation of the economic system from free private enterprise with moderate Government intervention to a new situation in which the involvement of the State in the economy through planning and the operations of a large public sector became significant.[1]

The need for economic diversification was an old and important theme of the national movement which was closely related to another concept, that of egyptianization. Egyptian intellectuals and some politicians had always resented the dependence of the economy, arising from its narrow export specialization in cotton, on world conditions which escaped the country's control and its vulnerability to international economic crises and wars, which was so patently demonstrated between 1914 and 1945. They also resented the control exercised by the small but prosperous foreign community (146,000 in 1947) and by Egyptians of Levantine stock, more foreign than 'national' in their culture, habits, interests, and ways of life. These aims of the national movement—egyptianization and economic diversification—found a concrete but limited expression in the 1920s with the foundation of the Bank Misr. Talaat Harb and his companions created the first bank entirely owned and controlled by nationals. The purpose was to divert Egyptian capital from agriculture to other sectors in order to establish a wide range of new firms—in industry, trade, insurance, transport, and construction—which, like the Bank, were wholly financed and managed by Egyptians.

The foundation of the Bank Misr, however, was a private initiative, sometimes encouraged and helped and at other times attacked and hindered by the politicians of the day. Governments, until the Second World War, were generally timid in undertaking measures leading to a significant diversification of the economic structure. True, a commission was set up in 1917 to examine the state and prospects of industry and to formulate new recommendations, but little action followed the report.[2] Tariffs, established in 1930 and raised on several occasions afterwards, were primarily designed to yield revenues; nevertheless they helped the nascent textile industry and became after the war an important policy instrument. Two Five-Year Programmes for public expenditures on irrigation and social infrastructure were drawn up and approved by Parliament in 1935 and 1947; but, here again, implementation was incomplete and sluggish. Changes in the economic system involving nationalization and comprehensive planning were neither conceived nor probably conceivable at that time. The *ancien régime*, however, took steps towards egyptianization, especially during the late 1940s when it imposed ceilings on the proportion of foreign manual workers (limited to 10 per cent) and salaried employees (25 per cent) and on the proportion of capital held by non-Egyptians (49 per cent) in joint-stock companies. Arabic became the official language for book-keeping and all commercial documents. Finally, the egyptianization of the judicial system was completed in 1948 with the abolition of the Mixed Courts.

The Revolution seemed determined, from the start, to carry out the objective of economic diversification with much greater vigour than the old regime. It created, as early as 1952, a new institution (the Permanent Council for the Development of National Production) for the study of investment projects, which developed later into a Planning Commission. On egyptianization the officers tended to be more cautious during the first years of their rule, partly for economic reasons—they hoped to encourage foreign investment—but mainly for political reasons, in an effort to reassure the Powers about their intentions and to obtain support and recognition, especially since they were engaged in delicate negotiations with the British Government over the evacuation of military bases. Later, however, the national-ization of the Suez Canal (1956) led to a radical policy of egyptianization, extended within a few years to all the economic activities and institutions still in the hands of foreigners.

Another broad objective of the Revolution was social welfare. We have seen that this objective was reflected in the agrarian reform laws; but it was also pursued in other areas, mainly in education, health, and the provision of social services. There is a close link between the nationalizations, the so-called 'socialist laws' which granted new benefits to manual workers in construction and industry, and the 'employment drive' which committed Government adminis-trations and the public sector to recruiting large numbers of new employees. In the fields of education and labour legisla-tion we can discern elements of continuity between the Revolution and the previous regime. Public expenditure on education had been rapidly increasing since the 1930s and Taha Hussein, the blind writer who became Minister of Edu-cation just before the Revolution, had propagated the view that 'education, like water and air, should become a free good'. In 1946 the Government started on a programme of rural welfare consisting in the establishment of Combined Centres (they comprised a surgery, a school, an agricultural extension service, and a social welfare unit in the same building) in villages; but the scheme ran into difficulties, partly because of problems of recruitment. Labour legislation had its origin in the 1920s and had evolved considerably by the time of the Revolution.

Elements of continuity between the old and the new regime do not rob the Revolution of its significance. The Revolution did not invent many new ideas and objectives: it is easy to trace back the origins of certain notions and projects, as we did for the land reform and the High Dam, to earlier periods and to find antecedents to a number of recent policies; but the Revolution had, in certain instances, the will to pursue these policies, and in other cases the means and the help of favourable circumstances for implementing them. The difference between the old and the new Government—and these differences matter—lies in the type of action Nasser was prepared to undertake and in the speed and scale of action. In this chapter we shall discuss planning, national-ization, and the emergence of the public sector; in the next the related issues of industrialization and social policy.

Planning

(a) *The Permanent Council for National Production.* The Government created by decree No. 213 of 1952 a Permanent Council for National Production, an independent body attached to the Cabinet Office and presided over by the Prime Minister. Its role was to study development projects in agriculture, electricity, commerce, transport, and industry; to examine means for the encouragement of industry in order 'to develop manufacturing into the main sector of the economy', reorganize domestic markets, promote exports, and attract both foreign and local capital; to revise the fiscal and the tariff structure; and finally to propose legis-lation. The brief was not only broad but urgent, as the Council was given only one year to produce a three-year programme. The Council had authority to initiate the implementation of projects either directly or in collaboration with other Government agencies or in partnership with the private sector, and it was expected to follow up execution and performance and to submit annual reports.

The Council—which included ministers, engineers, economists, industrialists, and bankers as well as various other specialists—set up committees and seemed, judging from the wide range of projects studied and the ambitious inventory survey of the country's resources undertaken during the first year, to have operated swiftly and efficiently. An analysis of the development budgets of the Council for the fiscal years 1954/5 and 1955/6 reveals an interesting pattern with the infrastructure receiving the largest allocation. The very early concern of the Revolution with land reclamation is also apparent as well as an emphasis on electricity, seen as a prerequisite of industrialization. The share of industry, small in the first year, increased markedly in the second. The novelty of this programme in comparison with Government budgets under previous regimes lies precisely in the appearance of industry as an item of public expenditure and in the large

TABLE 6.1

Development budget of the Permanent Council 1954/5 and 1955/6

	1954/5 £E thousands	%	1955/6 £E thousands	%
Irrigation and drainage	9,780	23	6,905	13
Agriculture	4,167	10	2,718	5
Land reclamation	6,478	15	9,043	17
High Dam	—	—	2,850	5
Industry (incl. petroleum and mining)	3,017	7	8,213	15
Electricity	7,290	17	10,168	19
Transport	11,420	27	13,851	25
Storage (grain silos)	100	1	500	1
Total	42,252	100	54,248	100

Source: Computed from data in PCDNP, *Report* (in Arabic), 1955.

allocations to electricity and land reclamation. We cannot but disagree with O'Brien's statement that 'most of the investment proposed by the Council remained traditional public expenditure',[3] as irrigation, drainage, and transport, the items he had in mind, accounted for 50 per cent of the Budget in 1954/5 and 38 per cent in 1955/6.

The significance of the Council for industrialization lies also in the choice of projects which gave special emphasis to capital- and intermediate-goods industries. The Iron and Steel Mill and a factory for the production of railway wagons, both at Helwan, as well as a fertilizer plant as Aswan, were among the first projects recommended by the Council and were all largely financed by the State and other public institutions. The Council prepared plans for a paper-mill in which the Government became a major shareholder in 1957; it encouraged the foundation in 1953 of a private firm for the production of electric cables, established in partnership between French and Egyptian capital, and the important Nisr company for tyres and tubes which was given a Government contract to supply all the tyres needed by the public services. The Council thus initiated significant structural changes in manufacturing by promoting two entirely new industries, rubber and iron and steel. In areas related to manufacturing, electricity and petroleum received considerable attention. Works for a hydro-electric power station on the old Aswan barrage, started under the previous Government in 1947 but continually delayed, were resumed in 1953; and the construction of two thermal power stations (Cairo-North and Al-Tebbin) was given high priority. New incentives were provided by the Mining Law of 1953 for petroleum exploration which had slackened after the Second World War; and new concessions were granted, the most important to Coronoda Oil in the Western Desert (1954); the capacity of the Government refinery at Suez was increased; and the construction of two refineries—one at Alexandria and the other near Cairo, at Mostorod—started around 1954.

The origin of two institutional developments—planning and the public sector—which acquired significance in later years should be sought in the foundation and the early activities of the Council. It is interesting to note in this connection that the decision to establish this institution is alleged to have been inspired by Ahmed Fouad, a Marxist economist very close to Nasser. The links between the Council and the planning institutions that succeeded it have been perceived by students of the Egyptian economy and the years 1952–7 were aptly described by some as years of 'partial planning'. But the significance of Government participation in new industries—a departure from its traditional role which called for new institutions outside the ministerial framework and established the embryo of a new bureaucracy with its vested interests—did not receive much attention though it unmistakably marked the birth of the public sector.

(*b*) *Transition to comprehensive planning*. On planning the evolution was rapid. In March 1955 a National Planning Committee composed of Ministers—in reality a Cabinet sub-committee—was formed and entrusted with the task of 'drafting a national comprehensive plan for social and economic development'. The significance of this act was not so much in the committee it established but in the explicit mention, for the first time it seems, of a comprehensive plan. In January 1957 a new organization was created under the same generic name; it had a two-level structure with a Higher Committee under the chairmanship of the President responsible for the guidelines and the final approval of the plans and the planning committee proper (commonly referred to as NPC). This committee absorbed all previous committees and councils previously concerned with planning. The Council for National Production and its sister organization the Council for Public Services (established in 1953 with a similar brief to the PCDNP for education, health, and social services) were formally abolished as they had accumulated planning and executive functions (the management of the Government share in mixed companies) which would be more efficiently discharged by separate agencies. And indeed, on the day of the promulgation of the National Planning Act (13 January 1957), another decree established the Economic Organization, a public agency in charge of Government interests in the mixed sector.

It may seem at first, as abundantly stressed by all writers on the Egyptian economy, that in 1957 the Egyptian

Government 'meant business'. The NPC was to draft a detailed and comprehensive Five-Year Plan (initially scheduled for the calendar years 1960-4, later changed to fiscal years 1960/1-1964/5) as the first stage of a ten-year programme. The NPC was thus given ample time to prepare the planning document, a surprising feature, given that the revolutionary Government in 1952 demanded a preliminary design for the High Dam within three months and a development budget from the PCDNP in the first year of its existence.

'Partial planning' was to continue during the three-year interval between the abolition of PCDNP and the first comprehensive plan: in 1957, two quinquennial programmes, for industry* and for agriculture, drafted by the relevant ministries were adopted and became operational the next year. Paradoxically, the transition from the multi-sectoral development budget of the PCDNP to the comprehensive plan of the NPC was effected through unco-ordinated investment programmes prepared by agencies concerned more with their sectional interests than with the broader requirements of the economy. The forceful and ambitious Aziz Sedki, then Minister of Industry, may have been largely responsible for these developments as he was in search of a role both for himself and for his newly founded department. Although he may be credited with an industrialization spurt much harm was done. First, the Ministry of Industry appears to have been more interested in the number of projects it initiated than in their quality (the ambition was to open a new factory a day), and the First Industrial Plan is a confused and hasty document responsible for a number of disastrous ventures. Second, sectoral programmes tend to be inherently defective for the lack of a macro-economic framework to ensure that the main interdependencies between the projects and the rest of the economy are taken into account. Third, the distribution of planning functions to the ministries during this period had implications for the

* This investment programme was officially called the First Industrialization Plan.

First Five-Year Plan as the NPC became restricted in their choice of projects to lists and priorities dictated by the departments.

The First Five-Year Plan and after

Much has been written on the preparation and contents of the First Five-Year Plan as four major books in English on the Egyptian economy were researched and completed in the early 1960s when the plan, though not fully implemented, appeared to be of considerable significance; the interested reader is referred to these sources.[4] We shall concentrate here on a few salient points and on issues where we may differ from contemporary opinion.*

The preparatory work for drafting the plan was perhaps the most exciting and rewarding episode of the history of planning in Egypt. The NPC drew on the best talent available in the country and abroad. They gathered an enormous amount of statistical data on the development of the economy after the Second World War; attempted to construct input–output tables, consistent sets of national accounts, and commodity balances for 1954 and 1959; and experimented with a number of planning models. Students of the Egyptian economy owe to this work numerous and valuable sources of quantitative information, and the science of economic planning benefited from the theoretical advances made by Frisch, Tinbergen, Hansen, and others during their periods of association with Egyptian planning agencies. It is worth noting, for example, that Tinbergen's semi-input–output method which suggested for the first time the use of world prices as shadow prices—an idea expounded later by B. Hansen in his de Vries lecture[5] and reinvented by Little and Mirrlees in their Manual on project appraisal[6]—seems to have been developed during the preparation of the Egyptian plans. However, little use was made of all this preparatory work in the design of the plan.

A brief analysis of the contents of the plan is in order. The

* The discussion of actual performance during the Plan period forms an integral part of Chapter 8.

long-term objective was to double the national income in ten years, the more immediate aim being to raise the level of national income by 40 per cent during the first five years. Two aspects of this plan are of interest: the investment programme and the sets of national accounts which expound in figures the views of the planning authority on how the economy should develop.

The sectoral pattern of planned investment, presented at a fairly disaggregated level in Table 6.2, reveals something about priorities and areas of special emphasis. Contrary to common opinion, agriculture was not neglected in favour of industry as its share in total planned investment equals that of manufacturing. One is almost tempted to say that the planners interpreted literally the concept of sectoral balance, a recurrent theme in NPC memoranda and other documents. Certain features which the plan shares with earlier development budgets are easy to discern, for example the relatively large allocations for electricity, land reclamation, and transport and a concern with exploration and production of petroleum, which accounts for virtually all investments in mining. In manufacturing, the emphasis is on intermediate-goods industries ($3b$ and $3c$ in Table 6.2) which received some 53 per cent of the total allocation to manufacturing (57 per cent of planned net investment in that sector). Capital goods, however, were neglected, for most investments under heading $3d$, 'machinery and transport equipment', were scheduled for consumer durables and private cars. The urban bias is apparent in 'dwellings'; in fact very little provision was made for the old villages of the Valley and the Delta, since item $6b$ includes the resettlement scheme for Nubians displaced by the High Dam and housing on newly reclaimed land. In transport, railways as usual take the lion's share. The emphasis in services is on education but this item is relatively small (2·4 per cent of total planned investment). Few resources were allocated to health, including family planning, despite the significance of the population problem and endemic diseases as obstacles to economic development; tourism, which could have been promoted with considerable

TABLE 6.2

Total planned gross investments in the First Five-Year Plan
(1960/1–1964/5) by sectors
(at constant 1959/60 prices)

	£E millions		Percentage	
1. Agriculture	383·2		23·4	100·0
(a) Vertical expansion		50·8		13·3
(b) Land reclamation		173·4		45·2
(c) Irrigation and drainage		111·7		29·2
(d) High Dam (excl. electricity)		47·3		12·3
2. Mining (incl. crude petroleum and exploration)	52·4		3·3	
3. Manufacturing	383·8		23·4	100·0
(a) Food, textiles, clothing		79·8		20·8
(b) Wood, paper, rubber, chemicals, petroleum, non-metallic		154·9		40·4
(c) Basic metals and metal products		48·6		12·7
(d) Machinery and transport equipment		63·1		16·4
(e) Others (incl. replacement)		37·4		9·7
4. Electricity (incl. High Dam power station)	138·5		8·5	
5. Transport, communications, and storage	269·2		16·4	100·0
(a) Railways		100·0		37·2
(b) Road transport		55·3		20·5
(c) Rivers, maritime, air, pipelines		37·9		14·1
(d) Suez canal		35·0		13·0
(e) Telecommunications		31·2		11·6
(f) Storage		9·8		3·6
6. Dwellings	140·0		8·6	100·0
(a) Urban		113·0		80·7
(b) Rural		27·0		19·3
7. Public Utilities	47·6		2·9	
8. Services	101·7		6·2	100·0
(a) Education		39·2		38·5
(b) Health		9·0		8·8
(c) Scientific research		6·1		6·0
(d) Tourism		9·6		9·5
(e) Others		37·8		37·2
9. Changes in Stocks	120·0		7·3	
Total	1,636·4		100·0	

Note: Investment figures exclusive of land.
Source: General Frame of Five-Year Plan for Economic and Social Development July 1960–June 1965, Cairo, 1960.

benefit in the early 1960s, seems to have been neglected, and the allocation to scientific research, a noteworthy feature of the plan, was misdirected to nuclear physics and to the establishment of yet a new university, when it could have been more profitably employed for industrial research (adaptation of imported technology to Egyptian conditions and development of new products from local raw materials), agriculture (new seeds and techniques), or medical purposes.

Finally, Egyptian planners did not forget changes in stocks, a common omission in many plans, but the predicted increase ($£E$ 120 million) appears to be unduly large.* Whether the NPC believed that the planned expansion of industry and agriculture would lead to such a significant building up of stocks or whether they allowed for larger amounts than required as a safety factor against under-estimates in other investment items remains an open question.

The aggregate level of investment is high as it implies an average investment ratio of more than 20 per cent during the five years to be compared with an actual investment ratio of approximately 14 per cent in 1959-60. As the plan does not provide a breakdown between domestic and foreign savings little can be said about expected foreign borrowing and the problems of financing capital formation between 1960/1 and 1964/5. Discussion on this subject in the literature has tended to be misleading. Planners, however, indicated that the economy would generate a balance of payments surplus of $£E$ 40 million in the last year of the plan and hence that domestic savings would be growing faster than investment during the five-year period. The assumptions underlying this optimism remain very puzzling.

The sectoral developments envisaged by the planners suggest that they underestimated the difficulties of curbing the almost autonomous expansion of the service sector in an economy with a high rate of population growth. They

---

* The average annual increase of $£E$ 24 million represents 1·5 per cent of the gross national income in the middle year of the plan ($£E$ 1,570 million in 1962/3 at constant 1959/60 prices).

expected the share of agriculture in gross value added to fall from 31·2 per cent in 1959/60 to 28·5 per cent in 1964/5, that of industry (mining, manufacturing, and electricity) to rise from 21·2 per cent to 30·0 per cent, and that of the tertiary sector (including construction and transport) to fall from 47·6 per cent to 41·5 per cent during the same period. This pattern departs from earlier developments on two counts: it involves a fall in the share of services in national income despite its steady rise since the Second World War and a faster rate of industrial growth than hitherto achieved. In fact, industry was expected to contribute £E 267 million to a planned increase in gross national product (at factor cost) of £E 513 million, or more than 50 per cent, and agriculture was expected to grow faster than the tertiary sector (28 per cent and 22 per cent increases in the contribution to GNP respectively).

A comparison of planned increases in employment with gross value added reveals the assumptions about growth of labour productivity. Gross value added per worker was expected to increase between 1959/60 and 1964/5 by the following percentages: agriculture, 11 per cent; industry, 48; construction, 5; transport, 13; trade, 28; services, 10. Prima facie these figures seem reasonable for agriculture, unduly pessimistic for transport because of autonomous increases in the Suez Canal traffic, and far too generous for industry where despite (or perhaps, because of) the emphasis on capital-intensive sectors, a rate of growth of labour productivity averaging 8 per cent per annum seems almost inconceivable.

It is difficult to understand the low rate for construction, which implies little or no change in building techniques, in a plan which included the High Dam, heavy engineering works, and complex industrial structures. It seems that the NPC assumed a high degree of underemployment in trade, hence the relatively high rate (5 per cent per annum) in that sector. Since output in the services is generally equal to wages, the concept of labour productivity has little meaning in that sector. The NPC forecast simply says that they expected real wages in the services to grow at about 2 per cent per annum.

As already mentioned, planners made little use of the preparatory work and of the advice received. Though the low quality of the data (that of the input–output tables and other statistical constructs) and the complexity of planning models developed in abstract are much to blame, other short-comings either remain inexplicable or seem difficult to excuse. They have been attributed in fact to insufficient time as the NPC was compelled by the Higher Committee to revise its target rate of output growth from 3·5 per cent to 7·0 per cent per annum, but the obscure point in the story is the reasoning which led the NPC to adopt initially such a low objective. Judging from the performance of the economy after 1945, one wonders whether any plan or special effort were required for the economy to achieve a lower rate of growth than currently attained. Time was in fact plentiful, but was partly wasted as much work went into the preliminary draft, and partly misused as resources were diverted to the con-struction of non-operational models. It also seems that the methods and principles and criteria utilized in designing the plan were faulty in some respects.

The criticisms fall into three broad categories. The first relates to the absence of policy guidelines for the imple-mentation of the plan. The issue does not arise so much for investment, since the Government and public enterprises were expected to undertake most new projects, as for other variables: savings, output, employment, exports, and the balance of payments. The plan included forecasts for all these aggregates and assumed that economic agents from house-holds to private corporations and the public sector would automatically respond to the stimuli of investment expendi-tures in a way that would fulfil the predictions of the plan. O'Brien has emphasized this lack of co-ordination with the private sector in the planning process, and the absence of explicit macro-economic policies that would enable the Government to elicit the desired responses.[7] Hansen and Marzouk have criticized the plan not for failing to specify precise policies—better left, in the interest of flexibility, to the annual budgets—but for the absence of preliminary studies on the feasibility of targets and on the consistency of forecasts in relation to alternative sets of policy measures.[8] These criticisms reveal something of the true nature of the First Five-Year Plan, which is no more than a public investment programme, different from earlier development budgets and partial plans by its more systematic coverage of all sectors of the economy.

The second group of criticisms, directed to investment criteria and methods of project appraisal, relate therefore to the essential part of the plan—to what it actually offered rather than to what it claimed to be. As mentioned earlier, the NPC was constrained in its choice of projects by the procedure which entrusted ministries with selection and the establishment of priorities. The correct procedure should have involved closer co-operation between the NPC and other official, as well as private, agencies and the adoption by all parties concerned of uniform criteria. As things stood projects were selected, with varying degrees of competence and care, according to different and ill-specified methods. We suspect that engineers and technicians—as for the High Dam —played an important role in initiating and preparing the study of most projects, not only in the Ministries of Irrigation and Public Works but also in the Ministries of Agriculture and Industry. In making the case in favour of the project they wished to promote, they included some crude calculations of value added per unit of capital invested, potential foreign exchange savings, and, if substantial, employment effects.

Maximizing the crude value added/capital ratio was probably the criterion most commonly used. Hansen and Marzouk criticized this procedure on the grounds that it treats factors of production other than capital, especially labour, as a free resource. This raises the complex issue of the shadow wage of labour. Hansen and Marzouk argue that it should be equal to the market wage in agriculture, which tends to reflect the marginal productivity of labour in that sector.[9] But this suggestion should be qualified because (a) it ignores the implications of population growth on the marginal productivity of labour and wages in agriculture, and (b) it assumes that labour is a homogeneous factor of production fully employed in all sectors of the economy. As projects create employment throughout their lifetime, the relevant shadow price of labour should express relative scarcities in the future rather than in the present; and population growth may well imply a lower shadow price than today's market wage. In Egypt, many projects create employment for certain categories of workers who otherwise would be given unproductive jobs in the Government or would remain unemployed in the private service sector. Ironically, while shadow wage rates for unskilled workers may be positive, those of educated manpower—save managers, technicians, and specialists—are sometimes close to zero.* The Egyptian plan could not be legitimately criticized for an excessive employment bias in the choice of projects (employment, on the contrary, was not given sufficient weight, and the Government had to remedy this defect by expanding the civil service) but rather for failing to assess the relative scarcity of various categories of labour and of other non-capital resources.

The maximization of foreign exchange savings was another argument often advanced in support of 'good' projects for selection by the planning board. This amounts to a crude import substitution or self-sufficiency criterion, which may well defeat its purpose because it neglects comparative advantage and treats all domestic resources as non-tradables. Unfortunately, Tinbergen's excellent advice on the use of 'foreign', or more precisely border, prices in project evaluation was not heeded. And although the introduction to the plan stated 'it was also considered that the expansion of the various sectors should contribute to improving our position with the outside world, in order to be more of an exporting

---

* Allowances, of course, have to be made for the social costs of extra consumption if employment in the new project entails higher earnings than in the alternative job.

than of an importing country . . .' [*sic*][10] neither the investment programme nor other sectors of the plan seem to deal effectively with this objective. Exports are expected to take care of themselves, and to fill automatically the gap between production and domestic demand, as if prices, trade promotion, and market connections abroad were irrelevant to the issue.

The third category of criticisms concerns a number of forecasts which appeared, either *a priori* or with the benefit of hindsight, as highly unrealistic. One relates to the level of imports, expected to decrease from £E 229·2 million to £E 214·9 million (at constant 1959/60 prices) between 1959/60 and 1964/5; another questions the forecast for household savings, expected to increase from £E 26·3 million to £E 80 million, implying a rise in the average propensity to save from less than 2·5 per cent in 1959/60 to 5·7 per cent in 1964/5; a third notes a surprising feature of the forecast for value added in construction, expected to decrease (at constant prices) from £E 52 million to £E 51 million between the base year and the end of the plan despite the considerable investment programme. Errors of judgement, however, are inevitable in what was, after all, a first attempt. As Hansen and Marzouk put it, 'nobody expects a country's first plan to be a masterpiece'.[11]

All considered, Egypt's First Five-Year Plan, despite the macro-economic forecasts and the attempts at relating investment to a target rate of growth for the economy, is in the tradition of earlier development budgets and partial plans: a blueprint for public investment. Although a follow-up machinery was established, institutional arrangements for implementation were never made. In fact, the detailed annual plans were often completed six or nine months after the beginning of the year to which they referred and the Ministry of Planning had no means of influencing, advising on, or carrying out economic policy, which remained the exclusive prerogative of other departments.

With the First Five-Year Plan comprehensive planning died in Egypt. One sad feature of these developments is that

Egypt lost many of its ablest economists and planners in the 1960s; many, either disheartened or enticed by the prospects of high earnings, took up appointments with international organizations or in rich Arab oil-producing countries. The learning process was discontinued and the country was not able to benefit very much from the experience gained by the first team. The Second Five-Year Plan never materialized though it is known that a draft was prepared. A provisional three-year plan is supposed to have been in existence for 1965/6–1967/8, but we were unable to trace it. The Arab–Israeli war in 1967 must have inhibited for a while any new attempt. In 1972 a ten-year plan was announced but it would be unwise to try at this stage to analyse the meagre information available on its contents.

After 1964/5 annual public investment programmes con-tinued to be drawn up and new projects examined. The concern with public investment has been perhaps the most constant feature of the history of planning in Egypt. The sectoral pattern of investment in these programmes did not differ very much at first from that of the First Five-Year Plan. Excess capacity in industry did not deter planners from allocating relatively large sums to that sector. In the late 1960s, after the completion of the High Dam, the share of industry increased. We tend to agree with Hansen's view that a developing country may be better off devoting its scarce professional resources to building up a file of 'good' projects rather than attempting to plan comprehensively. Provided of course that both project appraisal and the management of the economy through fiscal, monetary, and trade policies are in able hands.

The public sector

(*a*) *Emergence and development.* A considerable trans-formation of Egypt's economic system took place between 1952 and 1964. When the Free Officers came to power public ownership of means of production was limited to the irri-gation and transport infrastructure (including the railways), a petroleum refinery at Suez, a few military factories, and the very small proportion of the cultivated area in the Public Domain. By 1963 public ownership had extended to all financial institutions, public utilities, and transport (except taxis), and to almost all industrial establishments of significant size, to large construction and haulage firms, department stores, and big hotels. The public sector also controls the export–import trade and the marketing of major agricultural crops. Urban estates (save in instances where property was confiscated or sequestrated),* most of retail and part of wholesale trade, and small businesses in all economic sectors are left, however, in private hands. The agrarian reform, as mentioned in an earlier chapter, did not abolish private ownership in agriculture, but reclaimed land in the desert remains Government property with tenurial arrangements—direct cultivation by the relevant Public Organization—akin to state farming.

The expansion of public ownership and control over important economic sectors proceeded in discrete steps during the decade following the military *coup d'état*. As already suggested, the origins of the new public sector should be sought in the early days of the Revolution, well before the nationalization of British and French interests in 1956. The first steps were taken in 1952 with the agrarian reform, the creation of the PCDNP, and the decision to give urgent priority to reclamation of desert land. The Land Reform Authority became immediately involved in the management of expropriated estates and hence in agricultural production and trade; we have seen that the agency, because of inevitable lags between expropriation and distribution of new titles, held throughout the 1950s and in the early 1960s considerable amounts of land. The role of the PCDNP has already been discussed. Finally, the Government became involved in investment and production activities of yet another kind with the foundation of the Permanent Agency

* Strictly speaking, sequestration is a temporary measure which should be distinguished from confiscation. Sequestration, in principle, does not alienate property rights, but in many instances it led in fact to dispossession. In other cases, owners eventually regained possession or received some financial compensation.

for Land Reclamation and the Public Organization for the Tahrir Province. These initial measures which gave birth to a new public sector were clearly related to the Free Officers' concern with economic and social development.

In July 1956 Nasser announced the nationalization of the Suez Canal. The immediate chain of causation which led to this event—an apparent retaliation to the withdrawal of the U.S. and U.K. offers to finance the High Dam—is well known. The link with the country's need for economic development was thus explicitly made. But another powerful force was at work, a desire for national economic independence which involved the egyptianization of major foreign assets. Our contention is that these objectives were those of the Revolution from the start. The events of 1956 simply provided an opportunity which Nasser seized with some audacity. It is difficult to believe that the initial programme of a revolutionary movement whose leaders derived much inspiration from their formative years in the 1930s, when the themes of egyptianization and national economic independence were developed and vigorously preached by the intelligentsia and new political groups, did not include the eventual nationalization of the Suez Canal.

The Suez Canal Authority represented a substantial addition to the public sector. The 1956 war led naturally to the sequestration of British and French assets in Egypt and those of certain Jewish residents. The Government thus became the owner of seven important commercial banks, specialized credit institutions such as the Crédit Foncier and the Land Bank, and five major insurance companies. These measures gave the State control over half the banking sector and over two-thirds of all insurance business transacted in Egypt. These sequestrations were followed immediately by egyptianization measures, for the Laws 22–4 of January 1957 required all foreign banks, insurance companies, and local branches of foreign commercial concerns to change their legal status to that of 'sociétés anonymes égyptiennes', with Egyptian majority shareholding and Egyptian management.

Later, in 1961, Belgian economic interests were sequestrated, a gesture of protest after Lunumba's assassination.

The Government share in industry and finance had sufficiently expanded between 1952 and 1956 to justify the setting-up of a new institution, the Economic Organization, in January 1957. Government holdings in mixed enterprises, before the sequestrations of 1956, amounted to the substantial sum of £E 17 million. The paid-up capital of companies controlled by the Economic Organization soon after its foundation was estimated at £E 59 million.[12] The Organization continued to expand rapidly through both nationalizations and creation of new companies as it succeeded the PCDNP in its role of Government investor.

From then on, three factors, mutually reinforcing each other, explain the rapid expansion of the public sector through successive waves of nationalization. First, egyptianization which the Government could pursue with great ease after 1956 as the failure of the foreign military intervention in Suez strengthened the regime internally and removed the external obstacles to the policy. Second, the development drive which called for the implementation of development programmes with a large and growing volume of public investment. This factor naturally increased Government involvement in the economy but it also posed problems of financing the plans and the issue of co-operation with the private sector. Nationalization can be construed as a relatively simple, though radical, solution to both problems. Third, the momentum of State involvement in the economy and that of the expanding public sector itself may have been very powerful in the Egyptian context. Nationalization of major firms in one area led to further nationalizations because of the Government reluctance—partly explained by the centralized and monolithic character of the Egyptian State, partly by Nasser's own inclinations—to share with others the control of a sector in which it had acquired an important stake. Moreover, the Egyptian public sector, already large in 1957, had a tendency—common to all giant organizations—to spread its activities and extend its control.

This tendency was enhanced by some of its early successes, notably those of the efficient and well-managed Suez Canal Authority. It was reinforced by internal pressures from civil servants always jealous of the private sector and now provided with a new scope for interesting jobs and quicker promotion, greater power for the ambitious and more wealth for the corrupt; also by external pressures to employ new graduates and other entrants to the labour force as well as retired officers and political clients of the regime for whom the Government could no longer provide a sufficient number of rewarding jobs.

Our argument is that these forces are more relevant to the understanding of nationalizations and the growth of the public sector than alternative explanations which focus on apparent changes in ideology or on *ad hoc* and impulsive reactions to external events in the Congo, for example, or in Syria. The socialist ideology was formulated at a later stage providing an *ex post* rationale for earlier moves and a convenient pretext for further action, and events like the Syrian secession explain the timing of certain decisions, the immediate causes rather than the fundamental tendencies. This emphasis on socio-economic forces is consistent with the view that nationalization is ultimately a political action related to Nasser's persistent drive for hegemony, since economic pressures and motivations operating in a specific historical context often underly political decisions of this nature.

Thus a rapid expansion of the Economic Organization, not only through public investment but through affiliation of a number of major firms belonging to the Misr Group and the Abboud empire, occurred between 1957 and 1960, long before any mention of socialism. The factors discussed above seem to have been at work. They led, in February 1960, to the nationalization of the Bank Misr, a purely Egyptian concern which often operated in close contact with the Government. As the public sector controlled after 1956 a large share of the country's banking activities, the inducement to absorb one of the last big banks, seen both as a powerful rival and a complementary institution, must have been great. More fundamentally, the regime was wary of independent centres of economic power, often suspected of disguised political opposition and capable of delaying or frustrating its development plans. Whether the threat was imaginary or real is another question. But this attitude was reflected as early as 1957 by a law forbidding any bank to hold more than 25 per cent of the shares of any joint-stock company, a law clearly directed against Misr and designed to prevent the emergence of similar groups. The regime also needed to control means of finance for its programmes and ensure full co-operation for their implementation; and its autocratic tendencies favoured absorption rather than the establishment of flexible modes of collaboration.

The logic that led to the compulsory affiliation of certain firms to the Economic Organization and the absorption in the public sector of the Bank Misr is behind the big waves of nationalization of June and July 1961. Major options— Government involvement in the modern sector of the economy, egyptianization of foreign assets, public control of important sources of profit and finance, removal of powerful private centres of economic decision—had already been made and there was no reason to stop half-way. The nationalizations of mid-1961 preceded the Syrian secession (28 September 1961) and could not be construed as a political reaction to an external event as in 1956 (Suez Canal) or later in October 1961. But economic difficulties at home— an apparent inability to meet the plan targets during its first year, a catastrophic failure of the cotton crop in 1961, and problems of employment creation—may have hastened the decision.

The laws of June 1961 created a state monopsony in cotton, egyptianized all companies dealing with the cotton trade, and gave the public sector a 50 per cent share in cotton-export firms. The Khedivial Mail Line, part of the Abboud empire, was nationalized as well as the four largest cotton ginning and pressing companies. Laws 117–19 of July 1961 decreed the nationalization of all banks and insurance companies still in private hands and of fifty large industrial, commercial, and transport firms, the nationalization of half the capital of eighty-three companies in manufacturing and construction, and, finally, State participation in 145 medium-size industrial firms through transfer to the public sector of all individual share-holdings in excess of a £E10,000 ceiling. Laws 122 and 123 transferred public utility concessions—Electricity in Alexandria and Tramways in Cairo—to the public sector.[13]

The Syrian secession from the United Arab Republic provided an opportunity for sequestrations of an explicitly punitive character (October–November 1961). The regime needed scapegoats, and as nobody in Egypt, save perhaps the Government itself, was responsible in any way for the disaster, it proved expedient to pursue the nationalization under a new pretext. The property of 167 wealthy Egyptian families, many of Levantine origin, was sequestrated on 22 October. In November the list was extended to some 600 persons. Though sequestration was later lifted in a few individual cases, the measure was tantamount to confiscation in most instances, and the public sector thus acquired yet another chunk of private wealth.

The nationalization policy did not extend to small firms and establishments whether in commerce, manufacturing, construction, or transport. The regime was interested in the large- and medium-size concerns of the modern sector as they are relatively easy to manage and provide sources of profit for the State and employment for officers and technocrats; small establishments have nothing of value to offer. The policy was not extended to agricultural land and urban real estate, for systematic expropriation would have created insuperable managerial problems and, more significantly perhaps, alienated the middle classes, the very social groups which the regime represented. The land reform and the nationalization of the modern sector affected mainly the rich bourgeoisie, a small group of Egyptians politically associated with the *ancien régime* and foreigners whose loyalty to the country was often suspect. A more radical land reform and large-scale expropriations of urban property would have led to the dispossession of officers, technocrats, civil servants, and rural landowners, all members, relations, or supporters of the regime itself. There were political obstacles to an expansion of public ownership outside modern concerns, but no great impediments to a full take-over of any remaining share in the modern sector. And indeed, a series of laws and decrees enacted between 1962 and 1964 completed the take-over: companies in mixed owner-ship after the acts of July 1961 became fully nationalized and firms missed out by earlier laws were transferred to the public sector. By the end of 1964, the Government owned most assets and means of production in the modern sector; the movement which began in 1952–3 with small public partici-pation in mining and manufacturing had transformed with-in twelve years, through a succession of steps, the whole character of the economic system.

Two minor but interesting developments after 1964 are worth mentioning. The first is the emergence of a 'new' private sector consisting mostly of small firms, repair work-shops, and commercial intermediaries often established in discreet partnership with public sector employees. The size and significance of this sector are not known but there is evidence of some linkages—either through sub-contracting or sometimes, as suggested by occasional reports in the Egyptian press, through black-market operations—between public companies and private firms or middle-men.

The second development relates to timid moves towards liberalization. After the Arab–Israeli war, the Government relaxed restrictions on private activity in the export trade and the response can be gauged from the increase in exports of 'private sector goods' such as leather products, handicrafts, fruit and vegetables after 1967. The value of footwear exports, for example, increased from £E189,000 in 1965/6 to £E844,000 in 1967/8 and £E4,108,000 in 1968/9; that of furniture exports, from £E85,000 to £E96,000 and £E766,000 in the same years; and similar increases are recorded for handbags, travel goods, and films.[14]

In 1972 a number of sequestrations were lifted, and very

recently suggestions that the Government may sell certain enterprises to the private sector have been made. There are no signs, however, of any significant reversal of earlier policies. The public sector not only retains the importance attained in 1964 but continues to grow through new investments.

We have chosen to emphasize in discussing the expansion of the public sector in Egypt the early origins and the continuity of both the movement itself and the underlying forces. Anouar Abdel-Malek, partly followed by O'Brien, focused on discontinuities, more precisely on the apparent changes of attitude towards the private sector and the industrial bourgeoisie in the late 1950s.[15] They tend to contrast the early years of the Revolution when the regime sought the co-operation of local and foreign capitalists and a later period when Nasser nationalized their assets and transformed the economic system. History has more than one facet and different aspects are perhaps complementary. We believe, however, that the demise of the private modern sector was brought about by forces which operated from the start and rapidly gathered momentum rather than by fundamental changes in Nasser's attitudes. The capitalist bourgeoisie, considering its composition, its political sympathies, and the economic power concentrated in its hands, did not stand great chances of survival under his regime. He moved against this bourgeoisie when the circumstances seemed favourable and when pressures partly built up by his own policies—egyptianization, State involvement in the economy, establishment of a public sector, planning and control—appeared to reduce the range of choices.

(b) *The public sector and the economy.* Any appraisal of Egypt's public sector and of its significance for economic development is necessarily partial and tentative given the present state of research; and it is doubtful whether political conditions in Egypt will permit any studies in depth on the subject for a long time. We shall limit ourselves in this section to a few preliminary remarks on the issue. It is necessary to

distinguish two sets of questions, one relating to firms established by the Government or with its help as a result of
various development programmes, the other to the nationalizations themselves. The first set involves two main questions:
whether the planning authorities chose projects which have
yielded a social rate of return higher than—or at least equal
to—that of alternative undertakings, and whether the public
management of these concerns was efficient. The second set
overlaps with the first on the issue of efficiency but comprises
a further question on the significance of nationalization for
economic growth.

We suggested earlier that the methods of project appraisal
adopted by the NPC and other agencies are deficient and
that no serious attempts were ever made to optimize the
sectoral allocation of scarce investible resources. This is a
common state of affairs in developing countries and elsewhere. The implication is not that all selected projects
would fail more satisfactory tests but that the risk of erroneous
decisions, especially for marginal projects, is high. There is
no doubt that resources were wasted in undertakings
motivated by military objectives, as in the aircraft industry
which absorbed some £E 80 million without any tangible
results. Non-economic objectives, however, do not provide
excuses for all planning errors. Insufficient attention to
sectoral linkages led to the establishment of dairy factories
under the First Industrial Plan without complementary
investment in milk production. The costs of the import-
substitution strategy with its emphasis on certain branches
of production, such as steel, passenger cars, and other
consumer durables, were not properly appraised because the
objectives of the strategy were too readily taken as absolute
imperatives. Finally, the tendency to avoid careful appraisal
of projects expected to make losses in the short-run on the
grounds that they may yield substantial external economies
in the long term is dangerous; the selection of these projects
requires perhaps more care and caution than others because

of uncertainties and the difficulties involved in valuing external effects.

The issues of management and efficient operation of public corporations arise for all firms whether directly established by the Government or nationalized. Empirical evidence on the performance of public organizations in Egypt is scanty. And a complete appraisal would also involve comparisons with privately managed firms which are difficult to make. We may draw, however, certain conclusions from a knowledge of the administrative and managerial structure of the public sector and from the principles which regulate its operations.

Let us note from the start that in theory at least, the type of ownership may be largely irrelevant to the issue of management. Management and ownership are generally divorced in large modern corporations and the control exerted by shareholders on firms in many advanced countries is not important. The main difference between a private and a public corporation is that the former distributes some profits to shareholders while the latter remits them to the State, but these differences need not matter if profits in the public sector remain an important indicator of success. In the absence of a stock market, the informed judgement of a ministry or a public commission could perhaps be relied upon to appraise success. Public concerns thus could be run on the same principles as private firms and public managers and employees given the necessary incentives for efficient performance, initiative, and innovation.

We may add that public firms should indeed be allowed much of the freedom that characterizes private enterprises and given similar incentives, as their contribution to the economic development of the country and their ability to allocate efficiently scarce resources partly depend on these factors. Firms cannot attempt to plan correctly production or investment if their access to markets is restricted. Freedom to prospect foreign markets and promote exports can result in significant economic gains as firms will sometimes be able to utilize excess capacity and draw on specific talents and the initiative of their personnel. Autonomy in pricing—save in the case of monopoly—is essential for an efficient allocation of resources; and some discretion on recruitment, wages, and incentive schemes is an important prerequisite for efficient performance. Finally, firms should be allowed to grow, diversify, and expand whenever profitable opportunities are perceived. This implies a degree of freedom—the use of part of their profits for expansion or access for investment loans to banks and other financial institutions—which may appear to conflict with the requirements of comprehensive planning; but the difficulty of reconciling the two objectives may not be insuperable. Restrictions on the freedom of firms in investment entail economic losses to the economy as the entrepreneurial talent of managers will be under-utilized and the inducement to innovate and explore new opportunities completely removed.[16]

In Egypt, public companies and organizations do not generally enjoy these types of freedom.* The rigid and pyramidal structure of the Egyptian bureaucracy tends to prevail in the public sector. Public companies in the same branch of activity are affiliated to a public organization which supervises and controls their operations. All important decisions must be referred to and approved by the organizations which are themselves attached to the relevant ministries. Public managers have, of course, a certain degree

* In a few cases, the Public Organization for the Tahrir Province, the Suez Canal Authority, and the High Dam, a large degree of autonomy was granted to the organization and its manager. But this was seen as an exceptional measure justified by the urgency or the importance attached to the objective pursued. The Free Officers expected considerable political kudos from the reclamation of the Tahrir Province; the efficient performance of the Suez Canal was essential to Egypt's international image, and the rapid completion of the High Dam was deemed necessary for both political and economic reasons. The Tahrir Organization seems to have abused its privileges, the Suez Canal Authority put them to good use, while the body in charge of the High Dam spared neither effort nor money to keep the construction schedule. There is no doubt that the regime was able to show flexibility and to depart from rigid or doctrinaire principles in certain circumstances: thus, the co-operation in building the High Dam with Osman Ahmed Osman, a large construction firm which escaped complete nationalization.

of autonomy in the day-to-day life of their firms. Though output targets are not generally imposed, foreign trade controls interfere with their production plans. Their freedom in matters of employment, pricing, and investment and their access to markets for their inputs and products are restricted. The labour laws prevent them from dismissing workers save in very exceptional circumstances; and in such cases applications for dismissals are subject to a long and troublesome procedure. Wages are determined according to rigid schedules and wage increases uniquely depend on length of service, not on ability or performance. Profit-sharing, introduced in 1961, provides a collective but limited incentive; the wage system, however, fails to create any inducement for the individual. The main industrial and agricultural products are marketed either by the organization to which the company belongs or by some other public board. Direct access to markets is possible for a few commodities and services, but most dealings between companies and the rest of the economy involve public organizations. Import orders are generally placed with public organizations dealing with foreign trade after approval of the foreign exchange allocation by the exchange control authorities. Most export orders are channelled in the same way. Here again there are exceptions and some public companies can import directly after securing a licence. Firms which export a significant portion of their output are allowed some initiative in promotion and dealings with foreign clients. But as a large proportion of Egypt's foreign trade is undertaken under bilateral agreements the scope for these activities is small. Exchanges of views take place between companies, the relevant organization, and the ministry on issues of prices and investment, but the decisions ultimately rest in the hands of higher authorities. Firms have in principle no claims on the use of their profits or their foreign exchange earnings but they no doubt refer to their successes or their prospects when they apply for import licences or press for special allocations in the annual investment plan. Rigid organizational structures do not completely preclude dialogue, exchanges of views and information, or initiative; and membership of the public sector does not entirely deprive the firm of its identity or its motivation for success. But the scope for initiative is considerably limited and the motivation for efficient performance reduced. More fundamentally, the system does not recognize the role of the firm as the main 'source of truly dynamic growth'.[17]

Among the many constraints on firms in the public sector, the price and foreign trade controls lead to very considerable Prices and foreign trade controls lead to considerable inefficiencies. The problem of pricing is extremely complex because of the multiplicity of objectives that the Government attempts to achieve with a single instrument. Price controls have a long history in Egypt and thus preceded the emergence of a large public sector, but they were confined to a limited number of commodities and to rents. The main purpose was to improve in some respects the distribution of income. Price policies have been used at various times mainly to influence the crop allocation between cotton and wheat. Price controls could be used for both distributional and allocative purposes in the case of monopolies since they may, on the one hand, reduce monopoly profits, and on the other close the gap between marginal costs and prices. The degree of concentration in Egyptian industry is high; it is thus possible that price controls imposed on certain industrial products in the 1950s yielded social benefits. In the 1960s the expansion of the public sector created a situation in which a very large array of prices is determined by the Government. The method generally used—costs plus a 'fair' profit margin—is inherently defective. It does not necessarily benefit the consumer as inefficiently produced commodities remain expensive; it does not differentiate between monopolies and other firms and it destroys an important indicator of performance by allowing the firm a margin of profit whatever the level of its costs.

Cost-plus pricing cannot be defended on distributional grounds. Marginal-cost pricing—difficult to apply in practice —is the relevant method if the Government is concerned with monopolistic behaviour. In other instances, taxes and subsidies are the relevant instrument. In fact, price and tax policies in Egypt—save for a few commodities such as bread and for rents—are not designed to improve the distribution of income. In agriculture, as we have seen in an earlier chapter, prices are used as a fiscal instrument. The heavy reliance on indirect taxes, which affect prices to the consumer, has a regressive impact on the distribution of income because of heavy imposition on commodities such as textiles, sugar, and tea, all important items in the family budgets of lower-income groups. Rates of indirect taxes have been frequently raised during the 1960s and the share of indirect taxation in the Gross Domestic Product at market prices has risen from 6·6 per cent in 1959/60 to 14·1 per cent in 1969/70. In addition, price surcharges were introduced in 1965/6 on a large array of commodities including fuel, fertilizers, and pharmaceuticals.

This pricing system contributes (with other factors, of course, such as foreign trade controls) to the misallocation of resources and leads to inefficiencies. It provides firms with little incentive to economize on costs and fails to penalize or expose inefficient industries. Since prices do not adjust freely markets are rarely cleared. Not surprisingly, stocks tend to accumulate in certain industries while other commodities are in short supply. The Government responds from time to time to this situation by lowering certain prices and importing essential goods in excess demand, but these procedures are themselves inefficient and costly like all emergency measures. Periodic shortages are followed by temporary glut, consumers resort to stockpiling and urgent import orders often entail high prices.

Thus pricing policies in Egypt are trying to achieve, with deficient methods of price determination, a variety of conflicting objectives. A single policy instrument cannot aim with success at the distribution of income, the allocation of resources, control of aggregate demand, full-capacity performance, and raising revenues.[18] A complete revision of the policy is called for; we understand that the Government is at present concerned with this problem.

Needless to add that the administration of foreign trade with its controls and cumbersome procedures, the licensing system which induces firms to overstate their foreign exchange requirements in their applications to the Treasury, and the delays in issuing licences are all conducive to inefficiencies. Shortage of raw materials and spare parts is a frequent cause of excess capacity. Here again, the problem is complicated because investment plans failed to take proper account of comparative advantages and of the balance of payment problems. The organizational and economic deficiencies of the public sector restrict the possibilities of an export drive which might alleviate the difficulties.

There are two aspects to the issue of nationalization and economic performance: the efficiency of private firms in relation to public concerns and the appropriation of profits. On the first, discussions in Egypt have been marred by unfounded assertions and prejudices. There are no reasons to believe that public managers, as a group, are less able or less competent than their predecessors in the private sector. Political nepotism may influence their recruitment in the new system; family and social nepotism prevailed in the private sector. One may argue that the Government has access perhaps to a wider range of talents than the former private sector as it recruits from a larger social group. We have distinguished three main causes of inefficiencies: the lack of incentives and price and foreign trade controls. With or without nationalizations, the economy would have suffered from the effects of the labour (but not the wage) legislation, certain price controls, and the foreign trade policies pursued by the State. The situation before nationalizations may thus have been preferable from the point of view of efficiency in certain respects: greater price autonomy, greater freedom to innovate, and ability to provide labour with wage incentives. But all that needs qualification: price autonomy may have led to monopolistic pricing, and the freedom to innovate may have been irrelevant if firms lacked the necessary ability or if they lacked the inducement to innovate because of the protection afforded to their markets. All in all, our feeling is that nationalization may have entailed losses to the economy on these counts but that these losses were small. The significant inefficiencies should be attributed to other features of the system and to other policies.

Nationalizations can contribute to economic growth if they result in higher savings. In Egypt, nationalizations have certainly increased Government revenues, but the question is whether the saving propensity of the State is higher than that of capitalists and, if so, whether the gains were not cancelled by the drop in profits after nationalizations. We have been unable as yet to measure the impact of nationalization on savings and will perhaps never be able to answer these questions. Some indirect evidence may however be of interest. A study of the National Bank on the behaviour of companies indicates that, by 1960, they were distributing some two-thirds of their profits to shareholders. This suggests that business saving propensities—not necessarily capitalists' propensities—were relatively small (in countries like the U.K. some two-thirds of profits are retained by the firms). The Government found it easy to justify nationalization precisely on these grounds as it intended to invest all the profits that would accrue to the Treasury. In fact public consumption (see Chapter 8) grew very fast in the 1960s. It is difficult of course to say whether this increase in public consumption would have occurred in any case. We can only pose questions here and leave the reader to reach his own conclusions.

CHAPTER 7

MODERNIZATION:
THE DEVELOPMENT OF INDUSTRY
AND THE SOCIAL INFRASTRUCTURE

'Nous vous demanderons un compte
d'hommes nouveaux—d'hommes entendus
dans la gestion des choses humaines, non
dans la précession des équinoxes'
SAINT-JOHN PERSE

Industrialization

(a) *Introduction.* Industrial developments have a long and
fascinating history in Egypt. The Revolution did not
initiate these developments but, for the first time after
Mohammed Ali and perhaps Ismail, gave the State the
leading role in furthering them. In 1952 Egypt's industrial
sector accounted for some 15 per cent of GDP at factor
costs; it employed slightly more than 8 per cent of the labour
force and contributed only 9·6 per cent of foreign exchange
earnings from merchandise exports. Although still small the
sector had been growing very rapidly in the late 1930s and
after the Second World War. The war played an important
part in preparing the way for subsequent developments.
Although the disruption of international trade hindered
capital formation, it created a naturally protected market in
which demand for domestically produced goods was
heightened by both the curtailment of imports and the
requirements of the large Allied military establishment.
Existing industries had a hard task to meet some of this
demand. They received technical and other forms of
assistance from the Middle East Supply Centre, a very
successful institution established by the British Government
to improve and regulate supplies of basic goods in the area.
But there were dynamic effects, too. Import shortages

mapped the market for entrepreneurs. The inducement of high profits enabled hidden talents to emerge and there is evidence of significant innovational activity. The war gave a boost to small-scale industries and small workshops, where skills were formed and experience gained. More significant, however, for future developments were (a) the accumulation of profits (evidenced by the balance-sheets of industrial and commercial companies) which financed the post-war investment boom, and (b) the employment by the military establishment of some 200,000 workers who provided industry after the war with a large, skilled, and disciplined labour force.

Post-war industrial investment was encouraged by tariff protection. Tariffs were raised above their pre-war levels for a number of commodities, as evidenced in Table 7.1. Although the rise was significant, the degree of nominal protection in 1952 was much lower in Egypt than in Turkey, for example.

TABLE 7.1

Customs duties as percentage of c.i.f. value of selected imports

Commodity	1937	1952
Refined sugar	35	60
Canned fruit and vegetables	20	30
Cotton yarn	25	40
Woollen yarn	20	25
Cotton textiles	20–5	30–40
Woollen textiles	17·5–25	17·5–30
Soap	17·5	30
Paper	15–20	35–45
Cement	20	40

Source: United Nations, *The Development of Manufacturing Industry in Egypt, Israel and Turkey*, New York, 1958, p. 129.

One interesting feature of post-war developments is the changes in the industrial structure. Although consumer goods industries—mainly textiles and food—expanded rapidly, diversification towards intermediate goods and consumer durables began to take place. In 1946 Abboud founded a fertilizer company in Suez; Ford installed a small plant in

Alexandria for car assembly soon after the war; Henri Rabbath started assembling refrigerators and other consumer durables before the 1950s; the first plant for plastic products was created in Alexandria by Shafferman just at the end of the war; and there were notable advances in paper, glass, cement, pharmaceuticals, production of iron from metal scrap, copper, detergents, and a few other chemicals.

The second feature is a high rate of expansion of productive capacity which some Egyptian students of the economy have recently tended to underestimate, either because this growth is not evidenced by the behaviour of available output indices or because the conventional wisdom in Egypt is that industrialization began after 1952. Some evidence of this growth in capacity is provided by capital stock in manufacturing series estimated by Hansen and Marzouk,[1] Mead,[2] and Mabro*[3] and by the more recent and more elaborate work by Radwan.[4] Indirect evidence may also be gathered from an analysis of the financial history of joint-stock industrial companies in Egypt.[5] There is no doubt that an investment boom took place.

Although interesting, the question whether industrialization would have continued at the same rate with or without the Revolution carries all the risks of counterfactual analysis. The investment effort was in fact slackening after 1950, just before the Revolution, but this could have been a normal cyclical phenomenon, a temporary consequence of the fall in cotton prices and hence in incomes in the aftermath of the Korean boom, or the consequence of political uncertainty and unease before the Revolution. Whether the slack was essentially a short-term phenomenon or reflected more fundamental problems of an industry adjusting to a lower rate of growth once having exhausted most of the easy import-substitution opportunities for basic consumer goods, is difficult to answer. Our feeling is that, had the political

---

* Mead, in three alternative estimates, found that the value of the capital stock almost doubled between 1945 and 1950, and doubled once more after 1950, but over 10 years. In Hansen's and our own estimate the contrast is less dramatic but the rate of growth appears to be higher before 1950 than after.

climate been different and cotton prices recovered, entrepreneurs would have continued both to press for higher (or
new) tariffs and to invest. Private capital is not ideologically
averse to investment in this or that type of industry, but
simply averse to private losses. If the aim is to diversify the
industrial structure irrespective of comparative advantages,
tariffs and import controls will probably succeed in achieving
it in the same way as planning and public investment. The
main difference between the two systems relates to the
distribution of income and this difference matters indeed.
One can easily imagine Egypt industrializing at a similar
rate and with a fairly similar structure under another
political system. We doubt, however, whether industry would
have been more efficient, whether its workers would have
been better off and Egyptian society much happier under the
domination of foreign and local capitalists.

The novelty of the Revolution is neither in initiating nor in
furthering industrialization, but, as stressed in the previous
chapter, in introducing from the start new forms of Government intervention.

(b) *Changes in the industrial structure.* The direction of
changes is clear from Table 7.2. Textiles, already dominant
in 1952, increased their share in gross value added at current
prices. This, and other evidence on the growth of textile
output and exports, throws light on an important feature of
Egyptian industrialization in the period surveyed: planners
attempted to take advantage of the country's main agricultural resource, and aimed at transforming an export
economy specialized in a primary commodity into an
industrial economy specialized in the processing of that
commodity. The decline in the share of 'food and beverage'
industries, whose rate of growth seems to have been slower
than that of most others, is also a reflection on the linkages
with agriculture. The growth of agricultural production of
food is lower than the growth of demand and Egypt, a net
exporter of food before the war, is increasingly becoming a
significant net importer. Agriculture, therefore, constrains

TABLE 7.2

Structure of gross value added in manufacturing 1952 and 1966/7
(percentages)

	1952	1966/7
Food and beverages	22·4	11·9
Tobacco	7·4	4·4
Textiles	33·1	38·1
Clothing	1·9	1·2
Wood and products	1·6	1·2
Paper and products	1·3	2·8
Printing and publishing	2·8	2·1
Leather and rubber	0·9	1·3
Chemicals	7·4	12·7
Coal and petroleum	8·6	5·2
Non-metallic products	4·3	4·2
Basic metals	1·6	3·9
Metallic products	1·7	3·3
Machinery	0·7	4·4
Transport equipment	3·1	2·1
Others	1·2	1·2
	100·0	100·0

Source: Department of Statistics and CAPMS, *Census of Industrial Production,*
relevant years.

the expansion of the food industry. The share of basic consumer good industries (textiles, food, beverages, tobacco) has declined from 64·8 per cent to 55·6 per cent between the two years. This corresponds to an important development in chemicals and other intermediate goods such as paper and basic metals. Although the share of machinery in gross value added has considerably increased from a very small initial value, Egypt has not succeeded in developing its capital-good industry in any significant way. 'Machinery' includes mostly consumer durables. It is interesting that the bias against capital-good industries observed in many developing countries under private enterprise should also exist in a planned economy. The bias normally arises because nominal tariff structure affords little or no protection to capital goods in order to encourage investment, and gives higher protection to intermediate goods. The result is that the effective protection of capital-good industries is negative. In Egypt, the absence of significant developments in the capital good sector reveals planners' preferences rather than the results of serious project-appraisal. There is no doubt that Egypt can produce certain types of machinery more efficiently than consumer durables and cars. External economies are probably more significant in this sector than elsewhere because production is intensive in terms of skilled labour. Finally, a capital-good industry may lead to small technological innovations in, say, agricultural machinery. However inconspicuous, technical changes which adapt machinery to local conditions can contribute significantly to productivity.

The pattern of structural change in Egyptian industry is thus typical of most developing countries. The stage reached at present does not appear to be that of advanced industrialization, as the shares of producer-good industries, although significantly higher than in 1952, are still relatively small. Yet advances in intermediate-good industries have been remarkable, involving much diversification. Cotton, whose place in exports has been falling (see Chapter 8), is still the main commodity around which much economic activity revolves. It has become a significant input of industrial production, and indirectly retains its share in exports in the form of yarn and textiles.

(c) *The growth of output.* As official indices of industrial production published by CAPMS are conceptually defective and as the index computed in the 1950s by the competent research unit of the National Bank has been discontinued, we shall assess output movements after 1959/60 by an index of gross value added at constant prices. Data in Table 7.3 imply an average annual compound rate of growth of 5·7 per cent during the period considered. Although the National Bank index may understate the growth of industrial production because of a failure to include new products, the broad picture given by these indices is fairly accurate. An average rate of real growth close to 6 per cent over a relatively long period is an impressive achievement. Much higher annual rates obtained before 1963/4 than in the rest of the period. In fact the annual rate of increase has been declining year after year between 1963/4 when it reached a peak of 12·5 per cent and 1967/8 when the level of output was lower than in the preceding year. This turning-point in the growth

TABLE 7.3

Indices of production and of gross value added at constant 1959/60 prices, 1952–1969/70

Years	Index of production	Years	Index of gross value added at 1959/60 prices
1952	100	1959/60	100
1953	103	1960/1	111
1954	112	1961/2	117
1955	119	1962/3	128
1956	130	1963/4	144
1957	137	1964/5	150
1958	151	1965/6	154
1959	157	1966/7	155
		1967/8	147
		1968/9	161
		1969/70	172

Sources: 1952–9: National Bank of Egypt, *Economic Bulletin*, various issues; 1959–70: Ministry of Planning, *Follow-up Reports*.

performance of industry which affected the whole economy will be discussed in greater detail in the next chapter. It will suffice to say here that the apparent cause is import restrictions following an unprecedented balance-of-payments deficit. The recovery after 1968/9 is probably slightly exaggerated by the statistics. In the early 1970s industrial output may have been growing at around 5–6 per cent, but this is a very tentative estimate.

Data on physical output confirm the pattern of differential growth between industries disclosed by the analysis of structural changes. Physical output in textiles seems to have expanded at about the same rate as the whole sector, while chemicals output grew almost twice as fast.[6] Diversification within branches of industry, indicated by the appearance of new products in the statistics, seem to have been more significant in the 1950s than in the 1960s. In fact most of the new products were introduced either by the PCDNP and by the First Industrial Plan or by private enterprise. The General Plan did not innovate very much in this respect; the main investment effort was directed towards existing lines of production rather than new lines. Hence an emphasis on textiles, fertilizers, cement, petroleum products, and basic chemicals.

(d) *Performance*. There are many other aspects to the issue of performance. The contributions of a sector to increases in employment, national income, savings, and foreign exchange earnings are important criteria. Any economic sector can also contribute indirectly to the activity and growth of other sectors through exchange linkages, external economies, and other spread effects. It can also contribute to its own growth by generating technical progress and hence autonomous increases in total productivity.

The contribution of industry to employment will be discussed together with that of other sectors. In brief, industry—for reasons relating to its small initial size, the capital-intensive nature of modern techniques, and the absence of a significant traditional manufacturing in Egypt—absorbed a small proportion of the increment to the labour force. Indirect contributions are more difficult to measure. Industry could create employment in agriculture, for example, by inducing through its own demand a change in cropping patterns towards labour-intensive crops. This may have taken place to some extent with the substitution of vegetables for field crops, but the role of industrial inter-mediate demand in these changes is small. The main backward linkage between agriculture and industry is cotton; as it is produced and exported with or without industry, no employment effects are likely to occur there. The indirect contributions to employment are more significant with certain services—commerce, finance, and transport—and it is possible to attribute between half to two-thirds of the increment of employment in these sectors to industrial-ization. The same reasoning applies to construction, although

employment creation is most significant during the investment period only; in commerce and transport, employment
is created more permanently as they assist in handling output. In Egypt, the nationalization of industry led the
Government to create an enormous administrative super-
structure. Although this indirect employment effect is
considerable we may legitimately hesitate to treat it entirely
as a benefit.

The contribution of industry to increases in national
income is measured in the next chapter. Not surprisingly this
contribution, though smaller than that of services in the
1960s, remains very significant. To measure the contribution
of industry at world rather than domestic prices would throw
much light on its efficiency. The exercise has been done by
the Ministry of Planning[7] and privately by research students[8]
for the textile industry but the interpretation of the results,
as indeed of the whole method of evaluation at world prices,
should be extremely careful. In essence, measurements at
world prices would be relatively simple and meaningful
(only, however, to assess the efficiency of resource allocation
in static conditions) if foreign markets were less imperfect
and if it were possible to assume full employment and perfect
mobility of resources. Egypt faces a less than perfectly elastic
world demand for its long-staple cotton; the elasticity of this
demand curve and hence the shape of the marginal revenue
curve are difficult to ascertain and they tend to change
continually from year to year.

Another complication is bilateral trade in which Egypt
has been increasingly engaged after 1956, not only with the
Eastern bloc but also, very significantly in recent years, with
developing countries including India, Ceylon, and the Arab
world. Although bilateral trade agreements reflect to some
extent world prices which provide obvious points of reference
for negotiators, and although, contrary to very widespread
views, there is no firm evidence of significant losses arising
from Egypt's trade with the Soviet bloc,[9] the system is
imperfect and makes evaluation complicated. Finally,
resources in Egypt as in all developing countries and to a

lesser extent elsewhere are neither perfectly mobile nor fully employed. In a context of rapid population growth and limited economic opportunities labour tends to become increasingly redundant, not necessarily in agriculture but in the rest of the economy. And there are non-tradeable resources. These qualifications suggest that calculations showing that Egypt loses foreign exchange by processing cotton rather than exporting it raw should not be accepted at face value, and that the quantitative estimates of the losses involved are extremely unreliable. But the exercise is meaningful in one respect. The ranking of different textile activities—whatever actual losses or gains—in terms of foreign exchange profitability is correct. Egypt draws greatest advantage from processing its high-quality cotton into very fine yarn and high-quality textiles. The lower the grading or the quality the less the advantage, and somewhere on the scale—this is the point which is difficult to define and which may vary with time—it may turn out to be more profitable to sell cotton raw. The firm conclusion is that a reallocation of resources from low- to high-grade textile production is to Egypt's economic advantage. A possible but not sufficiently evidenced proposition is that short-staple cotton should be imported for low-quality, mass consumption textiles. Egypt's main industrial problem is that the special nature of its major raw material calls for capital-intensive, advanced, and high-quality processing—a problem which may explain the failure of the textile industry at the turn of the century when protection was refused, and the difficulties encountered by this industry since its beginnings a long forty years ago. Egypt's dilemmas are not simple: the country is poor in natural resources and the major raw material which seems to provide an obvious opportunity for industrialization turns out to call immediately for sophisticated and very efficient methods of production; Egypt has an employment problem and yet its natural endowment calls for very capital-intensive industrialization in precisely the branch where other countries may find opportunities for labour-intensive techniques.

Whether industry generates more savings per unit of income than other sectors is difficult to say. The classical economist's view is that capitalists—or the State in the case of public ownership of the means of production—have higher propensities to save than landlords or peasants. In a closed economy, the savings problem is related to the composition of output between producer and consumer goods. But Egypt is significantly engaged in trade, and barring short-term rigidities which may be very important, the long-run savings problem is related to foreign trade. Taking national accounts at face value it seems clear that in Egypt the modern sector contributes significantly to domestic savings partly because social insurance schemes which provide significant funds are feasible only in this sector.

The issue of export performance is closely related to the previous discussion of the textile industry as the growth of manufactured exports is essentially that of textiles (see Table 8.5). There has been a continuous shift in the composition of textile exports away from yarn (though it still accounts for the larger share) towards cotton fabrics and, within yarn, away from coarse grade towards medium and fine grades. This is an extremely encouraging sign. But it is not clear whether the balance of foreign exchange gains arising from import-substitution (which involves certain losses) and export performance (helped by subsidies) is either significant or positive.

Estimates of the growth of total productivity between 1947 and 1965, using the Cobb–Douglas production function, suggest a very low rate of growth of 0·5 per cent per annum.[10] These results are not surprising as industry in developing countries does not generate much technical progress before it reaches a fairly advanced stage. The growth of labour productivity in industry, a very partial index which reflects the contribution of investment and the effect of structural changes in industry rather than improvements in the quality of labour in *ceteris paribus* conditions, was estimated by Hansen and Marzouk at about 4 per cent per annum in the 1950s.[11] In the 1960s, employment increased by 53 per cent and value added at constant prices by 72 per cent; this suggests a rate of growth of labour productivity of just over 1·2 per cent per annum, allowance being made for the reduction in working hours. This is partly explained by overstaffing of both the shop floor and the offices after 1962 and by the increase in excess capacity, not compensated for by reductions in employment (because of socialist laws), after 1963/4.

To lament certain past mistakes in industrial investment is of no use; bygones are bygones. The urgent task is first to improve the performance of the existing industries, ensuring that their returns correctly measured cover at least variable costs, and this may require far-reaching changes in economic policy; second, to improve both the project appraisal and planning methods for future investment. Egypt has little option but to industrialize: the difficult issue is the choice of a pattern which corresponds as much as possible to present and future comparative advantage.

Social policies

No modern government is entirely uninterested in social welfare, labour and employment conditions, education, and health. In Egypt, pre-Revolutionary governments showed some concern with these issues during and after the Second World War. The Revolution pursued on the whole the same policies, but here again the movement gained momentum, partly because of greater political determination, partly as a result of internal pressures, the conventional wisdom about economic development and rising expectations—rarely because of ideology. To Nasser's credit, however, much was achieved, with exceptions and failures here and there.

(*a*) *Labour*. The first acts of the Revolution in the area of industrial relations reflect the contradictions of a military regime jealous of its authority but concerned at the same time with some forms of welfare. It is sad to recall that the first two victims of an otherwise bloodless and moderate *coup d'état* were two workers, summarily executed at Kafr-al-

Dawar near Alexandria on 14 August 1952 for leading a strike and the occupation of a factory. Whether the event simply reflects the nervousness of a two-week-old regime still unsure of its grip over the country or a more fundamental inability to allow industrial action as well as other forms of protest are important political questions which cannot be fully investigated here. It may suffice to say that the nervousness perhaps explains the violence of the reaction, and the intolerance of the regime towards the autonomous exercise of power by any social or political group accounts for its labour policies.

Strikes became illegal but an Advisory Council for Labour was reconstituted with union representation; trade unions were first encouraged to form, and membership later became compulsory for certain categories of workers.[12] But unions have little freedom of action and are subject to financial, political, and administrative controls as they are organized in the same pyramidal structure as the co-operatives and indeed the whole public sector. Though the old regime was not particularly liberal with workers and forbade certain groups—Government employees and agricultural labourers —from forming unions, important strikes, including a famous police strike, did take place especially in 1946 and 1948. Average real industrial wages, partly as a result of strikes and trade union activities, partly for other reasons, rose between 1946 and 1952 by some 45 per cent. These increases contrast with the relative stagnation of average real wages between 1955 and 1962.[13]

Minimum industrial wages were fixed by previous governments at £E0·100 a day in 1944 and £E0·125 in 1950; but these stipulations were meaningless, as minimum wages actually paid were very close to these levels. The Revolution raised the minimum wage to £E0·250 in 1953 but this law was not seriously enforced until the beginning of the 1960s. Other benefits were, however, granted, such as a new insurance scheme for industrial workers financed by employer's contributions; the scheme, introduced in 1956, was initially restricted to large industrial firms in Cairo and Alexandria,

Sick pay, indemnities for termination of employment (whether voluntary or involuntary), and the length of paid holidays were all increased, and the employer's right to dismiss workers made subject to new restrictions. The Egyptian Government approach to the labour problem is common to many developing countries: having curbed trade union activities, governments attempt to placate the urban industrial labour force through changes in labour laws.

Major changes in labour legislation and policies were introduced in 1961 and 1962. A profit-sharing scheme compelled firms to distribute 25 per cent of their net profits (after various deductions including a 5 per cent compulsory purchase of State bonds) to the benefit of their workers and employees. Two-fifths of the amount was to be paid in cash on a *pro rata* basis subject to an individual ceiling of £E50; two-fifths to a welfare fund jointly managed by employers and workers; one-fifth to a housing fund. Later, these provisions were slightly modified, with two-fifths of the amount now paid to a State insurance scheme and one-fifth to the firm welfare fund; cash payments continued on the same basis and the housing clause was abolished. Cash payments to personnel amounted to £E 3·75 million in 1962 and £E 5 million in 1964/5.[14] Membership of company boards was reorganized; the number of members limited to seven including two elected representatives of the personnel, one weekly paid worker and one salaried employee. Hours of work were reduced to a 42-hour week at the old wage. Workers and employees were, however, forbidden to cumulate two jobs, inter-firm mobility became more difficult, especially in the public sector where the former employer's permission had to be sought before the transfer, and overtime work was, in principle at least, abolished. These various stipulations were clearly designed to create more employment. A place had to be made for new entrants, partly at the expense of existing employees. The minimum wage of £E0·250 was enforced in the public sector. (This regulation, very recently, was extended to private industry.) Average wages of manual workers in modern industry rose sharply between 1962 and 1964. Thus, the average money wage index (1953/4 = 100) for manual workers in industry rose from 128 in January 1962 to 169 in January 1964.[15] Social insurance became compulsory and the employer's contribution was raised from 7 to 17 per cent of salary. Manual workers were guaranteed fourteen days paid holidays plus five national holidays a year. Sickness leave was increased to 180 days a year during which the worker is entitled to 70–80 per cent of his basic salary. Dismissals became almost impossible both in law and in practice especially between 1963 and 1966 when the Arab Socialist Union was at its most active defending workers against their employers in the private as well as the public sector. Workers tended to abuse the sick leave regulations and the absolute security of tenure they enjoyed, and in 1966 the Government made dismissals easier in instances of gross misconduct and tightened medical control over applications for leave. As mentioned earlier, uniform wage schedules applied to the whole public sector: the schedules include eleven grades, and promotion within and often between grades (save at the higher managerial echelon) depends uniquely on length of service. These laws, practically unmodified, form the main body of present labour legislation. Little was added after 1964. They represented at the time of the 'socialist' revolution a significant, but once for all, improvement of labour conditions. The most important material advantage granted —the insurance scheme—is in the form of deferred benefits. Money wages rose considerably during a short period but tended later to stabilize. Thus early gains in real wages are being continually eroded by inflation. An annual relief payment—from £E72 for workers in grade XI to £E144 for workers in grade I—is now granted to all in the public sector, in lieu perhaps of the profit share in cash which some firms, for one reason or another, had ceased to pay in the late 1960s. We have been unable to check with certainty this presumption.

The 1961–2 laws did not liberalize the trade union

regulations. There were no overt signs of labour unrest in Egypt until 1968. On several occasions after the Arab–Israeli war, strikes and demonstrations took place mainly at Helwan and Choubra-al-Kheima, the large industrial suburbs of Cairo. They expressed both political frustration, shared by most Egyptians after the defeat, at the deadlock in which the Middle Eastern conflict found itself, and industrial griev- ances. The Government tended to respond to these strikes by immediate economic concessions followed later by reinforced security measures and occasionally some arrests.

(b) *Education.* Considerable efforts were made after 1952 to expand free public education. State expenditures on education increased from some £E 23 million in 1952/3 (less than 3 per cent of GDP) to about £E 126 million in 1969/70 (almost 5 per cent of GDP). Public investment in education similarly increased from about £E 2·5 million in the first year of the Revolution to a peak of £E 33·3 million in the last year of the First Plan, a remarkable thirteenfold increase. After 1964–5 the level of investment fluctuated around £E 25 million a year representing between 6 to 8 per cent of total annual investment in the economy.[16] The expansion in the number of pupils and students at various educational levels may be surmised from Table 7.4. The fastest growth is in secondary technical education which expanded from a very small base. This category, however, is misleading as it

TABLE 7.4

Number of students and pupils 1952/3 and 1970/1

Year	Primary and Preparatory	Secondary	Secondary (technical)	Teacher training	Universities
			(numbers)		
1952/3	1,540,202	181,789	33,366	20,140	41,496
1970/1	4,589,138	297,887	271,638	25,526	176,023
			(indices)		
1952/3	100	100	100	100	100
1970/1	298	164	814	126	425

Source: CAPMS, *Statistical Indicators.*

comprises all types of non-classical secondary education. Commercial schools tend to dominate in this group. In 1965 vocational training proper accounted for 12 per cent of enrolment in secondary schools. The impression that great attention has been given to intermediary education of future technicians, draughtsmen, foremen, and floor managers for industry should be accordingly corrected.

If all secondary education were lumped together in one category, we would see that the universities expanded at the highest rate. The private returns from higher education are both certain and substantial because of the Government employment policy. All graduates have a right to a job in either the administration or the public sector. The purpose of this policy, officially formulated in 1962 but adopted in practice many years before, is to pre-empt the politically dangerous and perhaps socially undesirable emergence of unemployment among the educated. The policy, however, fuels the demand for higher education; and the Government is both committed to employ the educated and pressured into educating those who seek a relatively well-paid and secure job. The social returns for higher education are low and perhaps negative for certain branches such as the arts, commerce, and law. It is interesting to note that the proportion of arts students in universities declined from 52 per cent in 1950 to 26 per cent in 1965; the share of students in scientific or technical faculties increased from 25 to 40 per cent in the same period.[17] The Government attempted in 1968 to restrict the influx to universities by limiting the number of new entrants to 35,000 a year. It also stipulated that at least 60 per cent should enroll in scientific or engineering faculties and 10 per cent in teacher-training institutes. Despite these measures the supply of graduates is likely to exceed for a long time the requirements of the economy for their skills. It seems that at present engineers, previously in great demand, are in excess supply.

The figures in Table 7.4 suggest that secondary education —technical and traditional taken together—expanded almost as fast as primary/preparatory (164 per cent increase as against 198 per cent between 1952/3 and 1970/1). In fact, secondary education expanded faster (in 1952/3 secondary education covered the last five years of the school cycle; it now includes the last three years). The latest available estimates of school enrolment as a proportion of the population of school age are relatively old as they relate to 1965. They show that the proportion of children in the '5 to less than 14 year' bracket enrolled in schools increased from 26 per cent in 1950 to 46 per cent in 1965 while the proportion of the '14 to less than 19 year old' in schools rose from 7 to 29 per cent.[18] These proportions have no doubt increased after 1965. It seems that primary education is not yet universal but this proposition cannot be firmly substantiated without knowledge of enrolment in the '6 to 12 year' bracket, the relevant age group to that type of education.

In Egypt, secondary education is mainly sought by those who aim at universities, and the curricula are oriented in that direction. It seems that the country stands to benefit from a change in educational policies: more secondary schools of the vocational type and less higher education. Economic and social incentives would no doubt induce many students to seek vocational rather than university training. Until recently the Government recruited graduates from technical schools at a starting salary of £E18 per month while university graduates were employed at £E20 per month.* If the starting salary were the only relevant consideration many would find that four or five years forgone earnings in university are not worth the £E2 differential. But the life earning prospects of the graduate are far superior to those of the technician and his social status higher. The imbalance between manpower supplies and requirements is likely to persist in the Egyptian economy unless the Government repeals its commitment to employ all graduates and improves the salary schedules of middle-range technicians.

In teacher training, the number of students appears to have reached a peak of 49,448 in 1965/6 and then to have declined steadily.[19] This in fact is a purely statistical phen-

* Recently increased to £E25 per month.

omenon. In 1967 training institutions for secondary teachers were attached to universities and the fall in numbers is only apparent; the sources, however, provide no clues for an adjustment. Teacher training—even if we disregard figures after 1965/6—seem to have expanded slower than other types of education. Teachers, however, are an input of educational services, and a failure to train them in sufficient numbers must lead to a deterioration in the quality of Egyptian schools. In fact pupil/teacher ratios have increased between 1952/3 and 1970/1 from 29 to 39 in primary schools and from 10 to 20 in secondary technical. The ratio improved between 1952/3 and 1963/4 in secondary schools, falling from 22 to 14 pupils per teacher, but regained its initial level of 22 in 1970/1 after a steady deterioration. The ratio of pupils to classrooms slightly increased during the same period in primary (from 39 to 42 pupils per classroom) and preparatory (36 to 39); the increases were greater in secondary technical (26 to 34), while the ratio remained almost constant at around 37–8 in secondary schools.[20] In fact, school buildings are used at full capacity, and the very small class-room in the village with forty children must be very overcrowded. In Cairo, certain schools operate two shifts. The most worrying feature is the decline in the number of teachers relative to that of pupils. The quality of the education received in the fairly élitist system prevailing before 1952 was reasonably good without being very high. Increases in student numbers unmatched by a greater increase in basic inputs and facilities has undoubtedly affected in an adverse way the qualities of educational services.

(c) *Health and birth control.* Current public expenditures on health increased at approximately the same rate as expenditures on education (at almost 11 per cent on average per year between 1952/3 and 1969/70), but their level, estimated at £E 38 million in 1969/70, is naturally much lower.[21] They currently represent some 1·5 per cent of GDP. The number of hospital beds almost doubled from slightly less than 36,000 in 1952 to about 71,000 in 1970. Egypt has thus 2·1 hospital beds per thousand inhabitants, a relatively low average ratio which conceals considerable differences between rural and urban areas. In fact, all rural health units—from village dispensaries to the famous Combined Centres—only provided 8,149 beds in 1970. But the number of these units increased very rapidly in the 1960s, reaching 1,786 at the end of the decade; every other village is thus provided with some form of public health facilities.[22] Data on the number of medical doctors are scanty and difficult to interpret. Egypt, like many other large developing countries, is losing large numbers of doctors through the brain drain. The apparent costs to society of this migration are high as medical faculties absorb more resources per student than any other establishment of higher education. Whether these costs are partly compensated for by private remittances is difficult to appraise. It is well known that the distribution of medical doctors in the country is extremely uneven. Here again, economic incentives in the form of rural allowances or tax relief may help in attracting young doctors to provincial towns and villages. Compulsory service for short periods after graduation, the favoured method in Egypt, results in considerable frustration, affects the quality of the services provided, and often leads to abuses.

There is no doubt that considerable progress has been achieved and that the average Egyptian, partly because of higher incomes, partly because of better medical facilities, is today healthier than his elders, twenty years ago. *Per capita* consumption of medicines seems to have increased at an average rate of 1 to 2 per cent per annum, and it is interesting to note in this context that the number of chemist shops— almost all in the private sector—has increased from 680 in 1952 to 1,910 in 1971. Much remains, however, to be done to free Egypt from parasitic diseases and to lower the relatively high level of infant mortality.

Improvements in the state of health enhance the significance of birth-control policies because a fall in mortality rates in the lower age brackets can have important repercussions on the rate of demographic increase. Population policies, necessary as they are in Egypt at present, may become increasingly urgent in the future. The Government's attitude towards family planning and birth control has been rather timid especially in the 1950s when the Revolution expected that economic development would eventually provide an answer to the population problem. The Government did not realize that some action should be taken to initiate or hasten a fall in birth rates until the early 1960s when the economic difficulties facing Egypt began to mount. Nasser announced in 1962 that a population policy had become necessary, and a national family-planning programme was introduced in 1965. In February 1966, free pills were distributed to public health centres throughout the country but users are charged a nominal sum every month. It was estimated in 1971 that 300,000 pill-cycles were being distributed every month and 120,000 loops inserted per year. This recent and rather modest effort does not significantly account for the apparent fall in birth rates started around 1964. The family-planning programme suffers from budgetary constraints, the absence of long-term projects, and the reluctance of international agencies to support financially such a defective programme.

(d) *Housing*. The Revolution showed from the start some concern for the housing problem. The motivations were mixed. Abdel Latif Boghdadi, one of the Free Officers in charge of rural and urban affairs in the early cabinets, had ambitious plans for the modernization of Cairo which involved slum clearance, the opening-up of the famous *corniche* on the Nile embankments, and the creation of new and large squares in the centre of the capital. Another objective was to provide inexpensive dwellings for the poorer sections of the urban population. A public company—later an organization—was created in 1953–4 for that purpose. The scheme resembles the French HLM (*habitation à loyer modéré*) and was actively implemented in the 1950s. Thousands of flats were built in Cairo on the site of the Zenhom slums, and in other poor quarters such as Choubra. The scheme was extended to other areas; the organization also played an important role in the reconstruction of the Arab quarter in Port Said bombed during the Suez war. The *habitations populaires*, welcome as they were, benefited a small proportion of the upper stratum of the low-income urban group—industrial workers, low-grade government clerks, and the like. During the 1960s, public investment in cheap urban housing was at an average annual level of £E 5 to 6 million representing an annual addition of 8,000 to 10,000 rooms.[23] No trend is apparent in the figures, which suggest that the share of national income devoted to these investments is declining. The public sector invests every year a similar amount on 'medium level' housing mainly for officials and public sector employees. Most of the rural housing programmes relate to either newly reclaimed areas or to the Nubian resettlement schemes.

The slackening of Government effort in the 1960s coincided with a considerable fall in private investment in housing between 1960 and 1967. This fall was partly the result of the compulsory rent reductions on old houses, rent-controls on new houses hitherto exempted, and a stringent licensing system, all introduced in the late 1950s and early 1960s. They were also due to the inflation in construction costs and to uncertainties arising from nationalization. Here, again, the Government was trying to achieve several objectives—income distribution, reallocation of private investment from luxury flats and villas to cheap houses and away from housing into other economic sectors—with imperfect instruments. Though private investment in housing expanded after 1967 and regained the level attained in the 1950s, in response to both a high demand and a liberalization of control, the housing problem is still acute. The difficulties of lower- and middle-income groups in the towns have not yet been alleviated; and the rural housing problem is yet untouched.

(*e*) *Conclusion.* Achievements and failures should be

assessed with full consideration for the difficulties faced by a poor country experiencing a population explosion. Egypt does not have the means for establishing a comprehensive welfare state. Much has been done—especially in education. More could have been perhaps achieved but economists should be careful not to underestimate the constraints under which politicians operate. However small, achievements are achievements and recognition should be granted. Much more remains of course to be done. The only contribution that an appraisal of the past is expected to make is to help the formulation of better policies for the future.

CHAPTER 8

ECONOMIC GROWTH AND STRUCTURAL CHANGES

'Et dans l'acclamation des choses en crois-
sance, n'y a-t-il pas pour nous le ton d'une
modulation nouvelle?'

SAINT-JOHN PERSE

Introduction

EARLIER chapters have prepared for an assessment of Egypt's economic development—a slow but complex process under the Revolution. History explains the initial conditions; population growth and natural resources define the challenge—the opportunities as well as the constraints. The policies—from land reform to industrialization—represent attempts to influence both short-term and long-term performance; attempts to hasten the pace of economic development. Questions now arise: how did the economy perform within these constraints and under these influences; how did economic development proceed and what did it achieve? Several criteria are relevant to an appraisal. In this chapter we shall be concerned with the growth of the national income and its components; hence, with the evolving structure of the economy. In the next, the employment problem will be discussed since one aim of economic development is to create productive jobs, widen the scope of employment opportunities available to members of the economy and resorb unemployment. In Chapter 10, changes in the distribution of income will be examined.

Economic growth is a significant but very partial criterion of success. Economic development implies an ability to generate and sustain growth from within. The ways in which increases in income accrue—output growth, windfall gains, artificial expansion of unproductive sectors—matter in this respect. Economic growth is sometimes purchased in the present at the cost of future growth; today's successes which jeopardize tomorrow's performance do not compare with successes which lay the foundation for sustained economic growth. Problems of savings and balance of payments, among many others, are therefore relevant.

Further, economic development involves structural transformations. The converse, however, is not necessarily true. Structural changes may simply reflect changes in the patterns of consumption and employment brought about by an influx of external rents, as in certain oil economies; they may reflect the expansion of the 'informal' service sector in response to population pressures, or the absorption in government employment of an excess supply of educated manpower. These changes are in neither case an unambiguous sign of economic development, and they do not enhance the country's ability for sustained economic growth. They are often symptoms of difficulties rather than progress.

The interpretation of structural changes in Egypt is crucial to an appraisal of the country's performance in recent decades because economic diversification is both an old theme of the national movement and an explicit objective of government policies. The diversification of the economy was supposed to lessen its dependence on the exports of a primary commodity and hence its vulnerability to external events; or, in more positive terms, to enhance the flexibility of the economy, enabling it to respond with benefit to changing conditions in the world market. Can we interpret structural changes in Egypt during the past decades as reflecting a meaningful diversification of the economy?

Economic growth

Official estimates of Gross Domestic Product at factor costs in both current and constant prices are presented in Table 8.1.* A shorter GNP series at constant 1954 prices is

* These estimates suffer from a number of weaknesses which have been discussed at some length for the period 1952–62 by Hansen and Mead[1] and for 1960–5 by Hansen.[2] These authors were mainly concerned with the constant price figures, recognizing that alternative current price estimates are virtually

also included. Detailed discussion of official concepts and data, and comparison with the methodology applied in private studies for alternative estimates, which in any case cover shorter periods, will not alter significantly the broad picture, and hence will not be undertaken in this book. The main points worth emphasizing are that the official constant price estimates may overstate the real rate of economic growth and that the current price figures tend to under-estimate the contribution of certain sectors because of incomplete coverage (construction and perhaps services) or because of defective valuation of certain imputed services (housing), while the contribution of other sectors, such as manufacturing, is probably overstated.* It is difficult to say whether on balance the national income at current prices is overestimated or underestimated.

(a) *The overall rates of growth.* The official figures imply the following average annual compound rates of real economic growth: 1952/3 to 1959/60: 4·4 per cent; 1959/60 to 1969/70: 5·0 per cent. The implied annual rate of growth during the First Five-Year Plan (i.e. between 1959/60 and 1964/5) is about 6·4 per cent; and for the five following years, approximately 3·5 per cent. Hansen and Mead estimated the average annual rate of growth of GNP (at constant prices) at 3·8 per cent for the period 1952/3 to 1959/60.[3] Gross national income, because of terms of trade gains, is estimated to have grown at the slightly faster rate of 4·0 per cent. The discrepancy between their estimate and the official estimate, though not very large, is worth noting as an indication of the range of plausible figures. For the plan period, we are inclined to accept Hansen's estimate of an average rate of growth of GDP of 5·5 per cent per annum.[4] Assuming on the

---

impossible to make. The Mead–Hansen constant price estimates for the 1950s are probably superior to the official data, though we have reservations on both. Hansen's criticisms of official estimates relate mainly to inadequate deflators for industry and electricity and to the inclusion of current price figures (e.g. for construction) in the constant price aggregate.

    * Work done for our research project on industrialization supports these conclusions.

basis of Hansen's results that official sources tend to over-estimate real rates of economic growth by some 15 per cent, we may adjust the implied average rate of growth for the period 1964/5 to 1969/70 to 3·3 per cent.

TABLE 8.1

Gross Domestic Product and Gross National Product,
1952/3–1969/70
(£E millions)

Years	GDP at current prices	GNP at constant prices (1954)	GDP at constant prices (1952/3)	GDP at constant prices (1959/60)
1952/3	806·0	990	806·0	
1953/4	847·0	989	871·0	
1954/5	920·0	1,015	930·0	
1955/6	965·0	1,055	881·0	
1956/7	1,067·0	1,077	897·0	
1957/8	1,126·0	1,141	959·0	
1958/9	1,157·0	1,209	985·0	
1959/60	1,285·2	1,284	1,091·0	1,285·2
1960/1	1,363·5		1,139·0	1,363·5
1961/2	1,411·5		1,190·0	1,411·1
1962/3	1,562·8		1,324·0	1,536·7
1963/4	1,739·6		1,416·4	1,669·7
1964/5	1,975·0		1,480·0	1,762·2
1965/6	2,124·1		1,545·0	1,841·1
1966/7	2,180·4		1,546·0*	1,865·9
1967/8	2,187·8		n.a.	1,847·6
1968/9	2,339·4		n.a.	1,954·4
1969/70	2,552·8		n.a.	2,089·3

Note: * = adjusted. The GDP figures are at factor costs; the GNP series is at market prices.

Sources: Ministry of Planning, *Follow-up Reports*; Central Bank of Egypt, *Economic Review*, 8 (3–4), 1968. D. Mead, *Growth and Structural Change in the Egyptian Economy*, Homewood, Ill., 1967, p. 45 for the 1954 constant price estimates (referred to as the Hansen–Mead estimates in the text).

The performance of the economy during the period under review has been uneven. The official figures give an impression of fairly rapid growth between 1952/3 and 1954/5 which conflicts with the Hansen–Mead picture of stagnation for these years; the latter may be attributed to a sharp fall in cotton prices between 1950 and 1953 and hence to the multiplier effect of a fall in export earnings. Another difference between the official and private estimates relates to the period 1955/6 to 1956/7. Here, Hansen and Mead show a slow recovery, while official data imply a fall in the level of real product. Our feeling is that the features of the Hansen–Mead series are more plausible, with one quali-fication, that they tend to underestimate the growth of industrial and construction output in the early years of the Revolution.

There is general agreement on developments between 1956/7 and 1962/3, the last year of the Hansen–Mead series. High rates of growth obtained immediately after the Suez war for seven or eight years until 1963/4. After that year— and here we rely only on official sources—the annual per-centage increase of GDP fell steadily from 8·7 per cent in 1963/4 to −1 per cent in 1967/8. This was followed by a short recovery in 1968/9 and 1969/70. It is too early to ascertain whether the economy continued to grow in the early 1970s at the 5 or 6 per cent rate which may have obtained at the end of the 1960s; our impression, however, is that performance, at present, is extremely erratic.

An important feature of developments after 1956 should be emphasized: neither the plan, nor the Arab–Israeli war of 1967 marked turning-points in performance. Relatively high rates of growth obtained in the years immediately preceding the plan and in odd years during the plan. The plan, in fact, had a difficult start in the first year; and in the second, a cotton crop failure adversely affected the rate of growth. Similarly, the Arab–Israeli war did not inaugurate a downturn in performance; this had already started, for different reasons, a few years before. The war, of course, was an aggravating factor but not the initial cause of the very poor achievements of the mid-1960s.

(b) *Sectoral contributions to the increase in output.* The con-tribution of various economic activities to the increase in national income and product can be assessed from the sectoral breakdown of national accounts. The sectoral contributions to an increase of £E 294 million in GNP between 1952/3 and 1959/60 were as follows:*

* Based on the Hansen–Mead series.

	Percentage
Agriculture	22·8
Industry and electricity	24·8
Construction	5·8
Transport	11·6
Housing	4·7
Commerce	15·9
Other services	14·4
	100·0

Gross National Income increased during the same period by £E 312 million. Gains from favourable changes in terms of trade contributed therefore 5·5 per cent to the increase in income.

It is interesting to note that the contribution of industry and electricity to the increase in GNP was already higher than that of agriculture. The relatively significant contribution of transport is largely due to the growth of maritime traffic in the Suez Canal which recovered rapidly after the short disruption in 1956–7. The tertiary sector (housing, commerce, and other services) contributed more than one-third of the output increase, while agriculture and industry together account for almost half the total amount.

Considering 1959/60 and 1969/70 in the official estimates of GDP at 1959/60 constant prices, we find that the relative sectoral contributions to the increase in output between these two years are as follows:

	Percentage
Agriculture	15·0
Industry and electricity	27·2
Construction	8·3
Transport	2·7
Housing	6·6
Commerce	7·5
Other services	32·7
	100·0

There is no way of distinguishing between the contribution of output and that of terms of trade gains to the increase in national income as the National Bank import and export price indices have been discontinued and the Ministry of Planning does not provide separate estimates for domestic product and income at constant prices. Partial evidence suggests that the terms of trade—taking 1959/60 as a base—moved slightly against Egypt in the early 1960s but improved in a significant way in the second half of the decade. It is thus possible that the net relative contribution of terms of trade changes to the increase in income was positive in the 1960s and of the same order of magnitude as in the earlier period.

The remarkable feature of the 1960s when compared to the previous decade is the rise in the relative contribution of the tertiary sector to the GDP increment.* Tertiary activities, as previously defined, account for some 47 per cent, and the category labelled 'other services'—which includes the Government—for one-third of that increment. The share of industry (excluding electricity) remained constant at about 23 per cent. The increase in the relative contribution of the secondary sector in the 1960s compared to the 1950s is due to electricity. The fall in the relative contribution of transport to the GDP increment from 11·6 per cent between 1952/3 and 1959/60 to 2·7 per cent between 1959/60 and 1969/70 is due to the closure of the Suez Canal in 1967. If we consider instead the GDP increment between 1959/60 and 1966/7, we will find that the contribution of transport (15 per cent) was significant before the Arab–Israeli war. These figures suggest both the magnitude of the loss incurred by the closure of the canal (partly compensated for by grants from Arab states which appear in the rest of the world account) and the growing importance of the transport sector before 1967. Finally, it is worth noting that the contribution of agriculture

* The series used for the two decades are not strictly comparable as we are using GNP at market prices for the 1950s and GDP at factor costs for the 1960s. No serious distortions arise, however, in this case because the difference between absolute increases in GDP at factor costs and GNP at market prices in the 1950s are believed to be insignificant.

has declined from 22·8 per cent of the GDP increment in the 1952–60 period to 15 per cent in the second period.

That one-third of the increment to real GDP in the 1960s was due to the expansion of services—hence, mainly to the expansion of Government employment—casts some doubts on the significance of recent economic growth. Though 'real' output has been growing in education and health (the contribution of these sectors to GDP increment may have been of the order of 5 per cent), it is extremely doubtful whether the output of other Government services has been growing in any meaningful sense. If adequate national account concepts for Government output were developed and applied, the real rate of growth of Egypt's GDP will perhaps turn out to be 15 to 20 per cent lower than in the conventional accounts. Needless to add that the Government employment policy—which boosts in the short run the apparent rate of growth of the economy—has adverse effects on future economic growth. It reduces the investment potential of the economy and aggravates the trade deficit.

(c) *Sectoral developments.* Gross value added in agriculture (at constant prices) seems to have increased at an average annual compound rate of 2·5–2·7 per cent during the whole period. Gross output, judging from several production indices (such as the FAO, the U.S. Department of Agriculture, and a number of private indices), grew at the faster rate of 3·0 per cent, or slightly more, per annum. The difference between the two indicators is mainly due to the continual rise in the share of material inputs in gross output, a well-known feature of agricultural development.

Broadly speaking, value added in agriculture has increased at the same rate as population and gross output at a slightly higher rate. As agricultural employment has tended to increase, on average, by 1 per cent per annum, we may surmise that the annual rate of increase of labour productivity was 1·5–2·0 per cent during the 1952–70 period. The data do not suggest significant differences in performance between the 1950s and the 1960s. We suspect in this connection that official national accounts tended to understate the growth of agriculture in the 1960s, but the downward bias may be small. There are comforting signs in recent years of an improvement in performance which investment in drainage and land reallocation from low- to high-value crops may help to sustain. An interesting study undertaken by Joy Skegg at the London School of Oriental and African Studies throws interesting light on the sources of growth in Egyptian agriculture and reveals the growing contribution of crop allocation in recent years.[5] According to this study, the contributions of increases in area, increases in yields, and changes in cropping pattern to the increase in value added between 1952/3 and 1963/4 were 29, 67, and 4 per cent respectively. Between 1964 and 1968, the relative contributions of these three factors were 35, 18, and 47 per cent respectively. There is room for progress in Egyptian agriculture despite the land constraint, high yields, and high intensity of land utilization; and changes in crop patterns are but one of many avenues.

The growth of industrial output has been discussed in an earlier chapter. It will suffice to recall here two main features: the relatively high rates which seem to have obtained almost continuously—save for the odd year—between 1946 and 1963/4, and the downturn in 1964/5 when rates of growth of both GDP and gross value added in industry began to decline until they reached negative values in 1967/8. It seems that the short recovery of 1968/9 and 1969/70 was not sustained in the early 1970s.

The behaviour of gross value added in construction is extremely difficult to judge from the official national accounts. The Hansen–Mead estimates suggest an average real rate of growth of 7·7 per cent per annum between 1952/3 and 1959/60. Official data for the 1960s are a mixture of constant and current price figures and could not be relied upon. Hansen attempted to adjust these data for the first half of the 1960s by applying a labour-input index to the 1959/60 value added in construction, and thus estimated the real rate of growth of this sector at 10·4 per cent per annum between 1959/60 and 1964/5.[6] Applying the same method to the second half of the 1960s, we find that the average real rate of growth of gross value added in construction was barely above 2 per cent per annum between 1964/5 and 1969/70. The average rate for the 1960s is thus slightly above 6 per cent a year; but the national accounts taken at face value suggest a rate of 9·2 per cent. We have little confidence in the employment data for construction as they involve a statistical adjustment (of unknown magnitude) between 1959/60 and 1961/2 which gives a false impression of once-for-all expansion. Moreover estimates of real growth based on labour inputs assume no changes in labour productivity.

Transport has been a rapidly growing sector between the Suez and the Arab–Israeli wars largely, as already suggested, because of the growing revenues of the Suez Canal which Egypt was able to appropriate after the nationalization of this waterway. The real rate of growth of this sector between 1956/7 and 1966/7 is of the order of 11·2 per cent per annum. It is fair to add that the expansion of telecommunication services and of goods and passenger transport has also contributed to the growth of this sector; the output of these services may have increased at an average annual rate of 4–5 per cent during the period.

Data on gross value added in housing are as difficult to interpret as data on construction. The share of this sector in GDP has consistently been understated partly because controlled rents are an unsatisfactory basis for valuation, partly because the services of owner-occupied houses are not properly imputed. The Planning Ministry has adjusted value added figures for housing from 1967/8 onward but failed to revise the data for earlier years. Calculations based on investment in housing in the 1950s and 1960s lead us to believe that the average rate of growth of this sector was lower than 2 per cent per year. Expansion was faster in the mid-fifties and the second half of the 1960s than during the plan.

The expansion of commerce and finance tends to be

underestimated in the official accounts. The Hansen–Mead series implies a real rate of growth of 3·5 per cent per year between 1952/3 and 1959/60; their series for commerce and finance is calculated on the basis of a commodity-flow index.[7] Applying the same method for the 1960s will give an average annual rate of growth of 4·7 per cent while the official gross value added figures suggest a rate of only 3·9. The official accounts are not, however, consistently underestimated. Most of the discrepancy arises between 1959/60 and 1964/5 (they show an implausibly low increase of only 18 per cent in these five years). The implied rate of growth between 1964/5 and 1969/70 is much closer to our own figures.

Little can be said on services as the problems of interpreting the concept of real output in this sector are almost intractable. The Hansen–Mead series implies a real rate of growth of about 2·5 per cent per annum between 1952/3

TABLE 8.2

Indices of real gross value added at constant prices by sectors
1952–1970

(a) 1952/3–1959/60

	Agri-culture	Industry	Electricity	Con-struction	Transport	Housing	Commerce	Other services
1952/3	100	100		100	100	100	100	100
1959/60	120	152		168	162	124	127	119

(b) 1959/60–1969/70

	Agri-culture	Industry	Electricity	Con-struction	Transport	Housing	Commerce	Other services
1959/60	100	100	100	100	100	100	100	100
1963/4	112	144	190	204	135	108	115	133
1964/5	118	150	228	197	170	110	118	146
1966/7	117	155	248	188	193	115	133	165
1967/8	120	148	349	163	109	165	134	175
1969/70	129	172	437	242	123	173	147	197

Sources: (a) Computed from D. Mead, op. cit., p. 45; (b) Computed from Ministry of Planning, *Follow-up Reports.*

and 1959/60. For the 1960s, the official rate of growth is 7 per cent per annum. Employment in services has expanded during the same period at a rate of 4 per cent per annum. Given the national accounts conventions we would expect real output to grow at a faster rate than employment as allowances have to be made for structural changes in 'services' employment: the proportion of professionals, modern services workers, high-grade civil servants, and the like tends to increase as development proceeds. These allowances, however, do not explain such a large discrepancy between the rate of real output and employment growth. A rate of growth of 5, or at most 5·5, per cent seems more plausible. The difference between the growth of services in the 1950s and the 1960s remains striking. The cause, as often suggested, is the expansion of Government employment.

Relating these sectoral developments to the growth of the economy between 1952 and 1970 suggests that the period of higher average rate of economic growth (some 7 per cent per year, adjusted) was achieved between 1956/7 and 1963/4. This is precisely the period when both industry and transport, the first thanks to investment and the second to the increase in maritime traffic, were expanding at a fast rate. The growth of services during most of this period was relatively moderate. Decline in the growth of industrial output after 1963/4 and the closure of the Suez Canal three years later seem largely responsible for a steady decline in the rate of growth of GDP, cushioned to some extent by an ambiguous expansion of the services. Agriculture, apart from the occasional crop failure as in 1961/2, has been continuously growing though at a low rate, providing an unconspicuous but solid support to the economy.

The allocation of output

An analysis of the sources and uses of resources available to Egypt for consumption and investment is essential to an appraisal of its economic performance; it may explain the difficulties encountered in certain periods and help form a judgement on the short- and medium-term prospects of the economy. The relevant data are presented in Table 8.3. Although the table is restricted to a few selected years, it reflects fairly accurately the evolution of the main aggregates. Whenever necessary, supplementary data will be provided in the text.[8]

(a) *Investment and imports*. Let us start with investment because of its significance as a determinant of economic growth. The investment ratio was fairly constant in the 1950s, with small fluctuations, around 13·5–14·0 per cent. A rapid rise during the first four years of the plan to nearly 20 per cent in 1963/4, accompanied by a similar rise in the share of imports, proved to be ephemeral. Gross fixed investment as a percentage of GDP at market prices began to fall in 1964/5, the last year of the plan, to the very low level of 11·5 per cent in 1967/8; it stagnated at around 11 or 12 per cent at the end of the decade and fell perhaps to a lower level in the early 1970s. The rise in both the investment and import ratios in the first half of the 1960s was not matched by comparable increases in the share of exports and hence of domestic savings. A relatively small balance of payment deficit equivalent to 1·3 per cent of GDP in 1960/1 was succeeded by very large deficits of the order of 6 and 7 per cent of GDP in the following three years. Actual deficits may have been larger because arms purchases are not recorded and Government expenditures abroad tend to be understated. Although financed by U.S. aid under PL480 and by long-term, cheap Soviet loans, the deficit strained the economy. The withdrawal of U.S. aid in the mid-1960s, the foreign exchange drain arising from the Yemen war and, later, the Arab–Israeli war forced Egypt to check the growth of its imports between 1965/6 and 1968/9; in fact the value of merchandise imports fell from £E 448 million to £E 261 million between these two years.

There is a clear link between the turning-point in performance in 1964/5 and the balance of payment deficits of earlier years. The inability to finance growing imports affected both investments and industrial performance. Given the present structure of Egyptian industry, an expanding volume of imports of raw material and intermediary goods is necessary to sustain the growth of manufacturing output. The repercussions of tighter and presumably haphazard controls on these items have been far-reaching, leading to the emergence of significant excess capacity. Delays in the

TABLE 8.3

Allocation of output in selected years (1952–1970) at current prices
(£E millions)

	1952/3	1957/8	1959/60	1963/4	1964/5	1969/70
Resources						
GDP at factor costs	806·0	1,126·0	1,285·2	1,739·6	1,975·0	2,552·8
Indirect taxes (net)	62·4	98·1	90·4	148·3	238·5	418·5
GDP at market prices	868·4	1,224·1	1,375·6	1,887·9	2,213·5	2,971·3
Exports of goods and services	234·0	247·8	283·0	358·5	411·4	385·3
Imports of goods and services	249·3	267·4	280·9	491·7	467·5	399·4
Net imports	15·3	19·6	−2·1	133·2	56·1	14·1
Total resources available	883·7	1,243·7	1,373·5	2,021·1	2,269·6	2,985·4
Allocation						
Gross fixed investment	118·6	165·4	171·4	372·4	358·4	350·3
Stock changes	x	x	x	x	23·3	x
Public consumption	142·8	200·0	228·1	401·8	437·4	717·0
Private consumption	622·3	878·3	974·0	1,246·9	1,462·9	1,939·7
Statistical discrepancy	−x	−x	−x	−x	−12·4	−21·6
Total expenditures	883·7	1,243·7	1,373·5	2,021·1	2,269·6	2,985·4

(Percentages)

Shares in GDP at market prices						
Gross investment	13·7	13·5	12·5	19·7	17·2	11·8
Public consumption	16·4	16·4	16·6	21·3	19·7	24·1
Private consumption	71·7	71·7	70·8	66·0	66·2	65·3
Net imports	1·8	1·6	−0·1	7·0	2·5	0·4
Domestic savings	11·9	11·9	12·6	12·7	14·7	11·3
Indirect taxes	7·2	8·0	6·6	7·9	10·8	14·1
Imports	28·7	21·8	20·4	26·0	21·1	13·4
Exports	26·9	20·2	20·5	19·0	18·6	13·0

Note: Indirect taxes are derived as a residual for 1952/3 and 1957/8. The share of domestic savings equals the share of investment minus net imports. By definition the sum of the shares of gross investment, consumption minus net imports, equals 100 except when a statistical discrepancy is recorded. Figures of imports and exports for 1969/70 are adjusted.

Source: Computed from Ministry of Planning data. S. Radwan's help is acknowledged.

importation of a spare part or small reductions in the flow of
necessary imports have disproportionate effects on output
because inter-industry linkages transmit excess capacity
from one industry to another.

(*b*) *Exports*. Growing import requirements for capital and
intermediate goods—the inputs of investment and production—can only be sustained in the long run by export
growth of comparable magnitude. Foreign aid has proved
unreliable partly because of changes in the donor's attitudes,
partly because of its political implications. Though great
economic benefits may accrue from aid in the short or
medium run—and Egypt's immediate problems have been
alleviated in the past by U.S. and Soviet aid and more
recently by Arab grants—the long-run objective, surely, is
self-sustained growth. Foreign private investment can of
course make a contribution provided projects are carefully
appraised and its social and political repercussions are taken
into account. But here again, the main economic benefits are
related to growth and exports.

Egypt's export performance, though commendable in
many respects, has not kept pace with growing imports
requirements in the early 1960s. It can be seen from Table
8.4 that the value of merchandise exports increased rather
slowly between 1952/3 and 1959/60; that the performance
during the first three years of the plan was extremely dis-
couraging, partly because of the famous cotton crop failure,
partly because of the disruption in the organization of
external trade following the nationalizations; and that the
main increases in the value of exports took place in two
steps, the first between 1962/3 and 1964/5 and the second,
after the Arab–Israeli war. The former is largely fictitious,
reflecting purely an accounting appreciation of the value of
exports in Egyptian pounds after a devaluation; the latter
reflects partly an improvement in export prices, partly the
impact of new oil finds, and to a lesser extent an export
drive promoted by more liberal policies. The slow performance of merchandise exports is suggested by the fall of

their share in GDP at factor costs, from more than 19 per
cent in 1952/3 to about 15 per cent in 1959/60; this share
continued to decline and was as low as 12·8 per cent in
1969/70. The growth of invisible exports—mainly the Suez
Canal but also tourism—provided, however, some support
until the June war. Their value increased by some 90 per cent
between 1959/60 (some £E 93 million) and 1966/7 (£E 168
million). Specific grants from Arab countries make up for
the Suez Canal revenues as they stood in 1966 but do not
compensate Egypt for the incremental revenues that would
have accrued after 1967 had the war not taken place.

The diversification of Egyptian exports in the past two
decades is an interesting aspect of their performance. In
1952/3 raw cotton accounted for 84 per cent of merchandise
exports; agricultural products for more than 92 per cent.

TABLE 8.4

Value of exports in selected years
(£E millions)

Years	Merchandise exports	Invisibles	Total
1952/3	157·6	76·4	234·0
1959/60	189·9	93·1	283·0
1960/1	189·0	91·4	280·4
1961/2	151·0	88·0	239·0
1962/3	197·8	118·9	316·7
1963/4	238·2	120·3	358·5
1964/5	265·2	146·2	411·4
1967/8	246·5	48·4	294·9
1968/9	304·3	55·3	359·6
1969/70	328·1	57·2	385·3

Source: Ministry of Planning.

These shares fell by 1959/60 to 71 and 78 per cent respectively
and the trend continued throughout the 1960s; in 1969/70,
for example, the share of raw cotton was some 49 per cent of
merchandise exports. An interesting study of export diversification by UNCTAD places Egypt at the bottom of a

sample of fifteen developing countries* in 1953; but Egypt rose to the eighth place in 1968, showing by then greater export diversification than Argentina and, less surprisingly, Ghana or the Dominican Republic.[9] Egypt, though far from being the most diversified exporter in the sample, achieved nevertheless greater progress during the period studied than any of the other countries. Diversification did not mean, however, that many new products absent from the 1953 basket were being exported in 1968, but that the share of

TABLE 8.5

Shares of main products in exports
(percentages)

	1952/3	1959/60	1964/5	1969/70
Raw cotton	84·0	70·8	55·9	49·0
Rice	—	2·5	8·1	11·5
Other agricultural	8·1	4·3	5·6	7·3
Crude petroleum	—	1·7	3·9	1·9
Other mining	0·8	1·7	1·1	—
Textiles	3·3	9·7	14·0	14·3
Petroleum products	1·1	1·5	4·1	0·1
Other manufacturing	1·4	6·9	6·6	15·5
Miscellaneous and re-exports	1·3	0·9	0·7	0·4
	100·0	100·0	100·0	100·0

Note: — means negligible.
Source: Computed from CAPMS, *Statistical Indicators*, various issues.

commodities exported initially in minute quantities increased at the expense of cotton. The composition of the present basket is more balanced with rice, cotton yarn, textiles, and petroleum all accounting for significant shares. Export diversification related both to the agricultural basket where a number of minor products increased their share and to the ratio of agricultural/non-agricultural goods which rose significantly.

Further diversification will depend on oil discoveries,

* Argentina, Brazil, Burma, Ceylon, Dominican Republic, Ghana, India, Jamaica, Kenya, Mexico, Nigeria, Sudan, Tanzania, Trinidad and Tobago, and Egypt.

opportunities for increasing the exports of fruit and vegetables which at present are far from being fully exploited,
and changes in industrial policies. The scope is still immense
and the progress achieved in the past twenty years is more a
reflection of this potential than of enlightened promotional
policies. To sum up, despite interesting features of performance, exports failed the economy at a time when it
decided to embark on long-term investment projects and
when growing population and incomes, unmatched by
corresponding increases in agricultural output, continued to
inflate the food import bill. This failure is largely due to the
slow performance of agriculture, partly to the Government's
inability to check the growth of consumption, and to the
pursuit of inward-looking import substitution policies.
Opportunities existed and continue to exist in the Arab oil
economies, for example, where Egypt has not yet acquired a
significant share of their booming market. This failure is not
due as much to an excusable lack of foresight as to rigidities
in both the economic structure and the policy outlook.

(c) *Savings*. An alternative way of looking at a country's
macro-economic problems is to examine savings behaviour.
Though, in a formal sense, the export/import disequi-
librium is identical with a savings/investment imbalance,
much may be gained by analysing these variables separately.
The most disturbing feature of Egypt's economic performance is a failure to raise the domestic savings ratio of the
economy. Though savings data are notoriously bad in
Egypt as elsewhere—they are often derived as a residual
which catches all the statistical errors and important
omissions in the accounts, especially arms purchases and
special Government expenditures abroad—there is enough
indirect evidence to suggest the absence of a rising trend in
the domestic savings ratio. Whatever their worth, some data
are presented in Table 8.6. The apparent rise between
1964/5 and 1966/7 seems to be largely statistical as changes
in inventories began to be recorded in the accounts, thus
introducing a discontinuity in the series. The fall in the

TABLE 8.6

Savings ratios

Years	Ratio	Years	Ratio
1952/3	11·9	1964/5	14·2
1954/5	11·9	1965/6	14·0
1956/7	13·4	1966/7	14·5
1959/60	12·6	1967/8	8·2
1960/1	14·2	1968/9	9·1
1962/3	11·6	1969/70	10·6

Note: Small differences in the savings ratio between this and other tables arise from the statistical discrepancy shown in Table 8.3.

Source: Computed from Ministry of Planning, *Follow-up Reports*, and other data.

savings ratio after the 1967 war should be assessed in relation to the 1964–7 level since all these years pertain to the same statistical series.

An analysis of aggregate savings behaviour in a country like Egypt is essentially a discussion of Government policy. Broadly speaking, the period can be divided into two parts, the first from 1952 to the early 1960s, and the second thereafter. During the first, both savings and investment ratios remained relatively stable although the investment ratio may have been slightly higher than before the Revolution as a result of a rise in Government capital formation. The Government largely financed its new investments by borrowing from the Central (then the National) Bank. A small discrepancy between savings and investment ratios characterizes this period, implying a balance of payment deficit of equivalent magnitude. This was easily financed by the running down of reserves and sterling balances dating from the Second World War and by foreign aid. No trend appears during this period in the share of either private or public consumption; the former fluctuated slightly around 70 per cent of GDP at market prices, the latter around 16·5 per cent. No particular effort was undertaken to increase the share of taxation in GDP or to promote significantly household or corporate savings through monetary or fiscal incentives.

The features of the second period are different in many respects. The implementation of the plan involved raising the investment ratio mainly through an increase in public investment. The nationalizations were a convenient instrument for the transfer of an important source of private savings—the profits of the modern private sector—to the State, and they offered an opportunity for raising the savings rate on the assumption that Government's savings propensities are higher than the capitalists' propensities. Whether some of this potential was realized or not is impossible to answer. In any case, the task of raising the savings ratio by 6 or 7 percentage points to match the planned increase in the investment ratio would remain formidable whatever the success of the nationalizations. The Government succeeded in steadily pushing up the investment ratio during the first four years of the plan, but there is no apparent decrease during 1960/1 to 1962/3 in the shares of public and private consumption from their 1950s levels, nor an increase in the share of indirect taxes in GDP. By 1963/4 the economy had acquired remarkable features: the highest investment ratio ever attained, the largest balance of payment deficit, and a considerable rise to 21·3 per cent of the share of public consumption. The strains arising from such an increase in these aggregates cannot be sustained for long. The drastic reductions in U.S. aid soon after aggravated further the situation. Something had to give way unless savings could be made to increase in the most abrupt manner.

Bleakly for the prospects of economic development, investment rather than public consumption gave way. The investment rate fell gradually from 19·7 per cent in 1963/4 to 14·5 per cent in 1966/7, the fiscal year just preceding the Arab–Israeli war. The share of public consumption decreased very slightly during these years to the level of 20 per cent. Despite a considerable rise in indirect taxation, whose ratio to GDP grew from 7·9 to 12·1 per cent between 1963/4 and 1966/7, and other increases in direct taxes, the savings ratio probably failed to increase by more than 1 per cent. Increased taxation was largely used to finance an increase in public consumption rather than to reduce the share of aggregate consumption in the economy. Political conditions and the Government employment policy may have drastically restricted the range of choices. The Arab–Israeli war accentuated all these trends, worsening the longer-term prospects even further. The share of public consumption rose steadily to 24·1 per cent in 1969/70, largely because of defence expenditure; the fixed investment ratio fell further to 11–12 per cent, and though the share of indirect taxation continued to increase, reaching 14·1 per cent at the end of the period, the savings ratio fell immediately to well below 10 per cent.

We can discern three main elements behind this evolution. The first is the conflict between ambitious objectives of economic development involving massive investments in slow-maturing projects, such as the High Dam and heavy industry, and a desire to achieve these objectives without sacrificing the growth of private consumption. The regime tried to reconcile long- and short-term time preferences relying largely on aid, but also on political expropriations, to secure large future benefits at no significant costs in the present. But aid appeared to involve political as well as economic costs and proved unreliable; nationalizations added new items to public consumption; in short, the reconciliation was impossible, and sooner or later a choice between the future and the present had to be made. The second element is the emergence of a surplus of educated manpower, the result of both population growth and an expansion of educational services. Here again the regime tried to relieve the immediate pressures by increasing public consumption; the long-term objectives were sacrificed to the present. Moreover, much of the investment in education was robbed of significance for economic development, as education became essentially the passport for a secure and often unproductive government job. The third element is Middle Eastern political conflicts from the Yemen to the Arab–Israeli problem. It is a matter of political judgement to assess how much choice Egypt has in a situation which drains its resources; but this is an area where emotional prejudices unfortunately prevail and it is wiser for an economist to treat the international context as a constraint.

The conclusion, however, that political factors have influenced at all levels the economic decisions of the regime —and hence, to some extent, the behaviour of the main aggregates—is difficult to avoid. The decision to tax or not to tax, to finance development at the expense of one segment of society to the benefit of others, to respond by an employment policy to the pressures of the social group which the regime represents, to accept or reject aid with the ties which unavoidably accompany the grant, and the decision to embark on a developmental strategy which involved spectacular achievement rather than a slower but more regular build-up of the country's productive capacity, are all in a sense political options and have far-reaching political implications.

But it is also possible to discern a typical pattern of behaviour of the regime, already discussed in the chapter on institutional changes. The regime had a limited number of objectives—or in Maxime Rodinson's term a number of 'projects'[10]—which it set about to implement without a coherent view of their implications or an assessment of alternatives. It then responded by *ad hoc*, though sometimes spectacular, measures to mounting pressures, partly generated by its 'projects' themselves, partly by economic and political forces not of its own making. It is significant, for example, that the recourse to increased taxation was related to the growing needs of public consumption and not to the earlier objective of investment and economic development. The absence of a coherent strategy and the delayed response to unanticipated problems after they emerge lead to new contradictions and limit further the small range of options available to a poor economy subject to population pressures and external conflicts. In the end, the initial development objective is itself sacrificed.

Structural changes

Economic development is not simply economic growth, and an analysis of the rates of expansion of various sectors, of their contribution to the increase in national income, and of the constraints on past and future growth may conceal other achievements. Economic development involves structural transformations—the diversification of economic activities and a greater integration, through strong linkages and institutional intermediaries, of these activities. The economic development of Egypt until the inter-war period has been correctly characterized as lop-sided development, as most of the country's economic activities, outside the production of food in agriculture, revolved around the main export good—cotton. Though structural changes predate the Revolution—they began in the late 1920s, and became much more significant during and immediately after the Second World War—the economic policies of the regime were explicitly oriented towards modernization and diversification of the economy.

(a) *The investment pattern.* Changes in the sectoral composition of output were mainly brought about by two factors: the pattern of investment and population pressures. The composition of investment changed significantly between the first years of the Revolution when Government involvement, though gradually increasing, was still very small and the post-Suez period, when Nasser began to implement more vigorously his initial 'projects' (see Table 8.7). The interesting features of this pattern are the sharp decline in the share of housing, the increase in the share of agriculture, the small and diminishing proportion of investment in services, and the rising trend in the share of industry (manufacturing and mining). The diversion of resources away from housing after 1955 enabled the economy to grow at a faster rate in sub-period 2 without a rise in the investment ratio. Part of this rise in the rate of growth is statistical, reflecting an underestimate of real output in housing because of imperfect accounting practice. But the shift is significant from the point of view of economic development as housing provides little employment after the construction of the building and it probably generates less external economies and a smaller

TABLE 8.7

Sectoral allocation of investments 1952–1970
(percentages)

	Agri-culture	Industry	Electricity	Transport and Suez Canal	Housing	Services	Others
1. Average 1952/3–1956/7	11·4	23·8	6·0	14·7	32·5	9·8	1·8
2. Average 1957/8–1959/60	14·9	25·7	4·0	18·8	23·1	12·1	1·4
3. Average 1960/1–1964/5	23·4	26·6	7·4	19·3	10·7	10·0	2·6
4. Average 1965/6–1967/8	21·8	27·4	17·1	13·4	12·5	6·3	1·5
5. 1968/9	19·7	29·5	9·3	20·2	13·6	6·2	1·5
6. 1969/70	17·3	34·8	7·7	20·0	10·2	8·2	1·8

Source: Computed from Ministry of Planning, *Follow-up Reports.*

reinvestible surplus than other sectors. Put differently, houses are in a sense consumer durables and in Egypt the larger proportion of new houses were built for the upper income group. The Government, legitimately, put a higher social valuation on investment in agriculture and industry. The objective seems sound though the Government might have gone too far, especially during the plan, in devoting too small a proportion of investment to housing; and it unfortunately failed to change the composition of this investment in favour of both rural and urban lower income groups.

The rise in the share of agriculture—abstracting from the period 1960–8 when the High Dam was built—is noticeable both in the 1950s and after the completion of the Dam. It reflects the allocation of investment to land reclamation, works necessitated by the conversion of basin to perennial irrigation in Upper Egypt, and in recent years to drainage in Lower Egypt, a project which is long overdue. In the post-Dam era, fixed investment of the traditional type—except for drainage—will cease to be an important factor of agricultural development. As increases in yield and to a lesser extent changes in crop patterns have been, and will continue to be, the main sources of agricultural growth in Egypt, a package of measures which includes extension services, research, marketing facilities, and improved price policies will be much needed for future progress.

The link between the growth in services output and investment is extremely weak, especially in Egypt where considerable expansion (according to conventional measures) has taken place through the employment policy. About one half of the small share of investment in this sector represents the proportion of resources devoted to 'development' services such as education, health, social centres, and public utilities. The other half relates mainly to hotels, public buildings for Government administration, and some private services. The decline in the share of investment in services in the second half of the 1960s is worth noting.

Though the share of industry (mining and manufacturing) has been increasing throughout the period, the rise was not very significant between 1952 and 1965. Industrial investment expanded faster than the aggregate but at a slower rate than investment in either agriculture (even if the High Dam is excluded) or transport. The share of industrial investment during the first three years of the Revolution was relatively high, averaging 22·5 per cent—an indication of the strong element of continuity between industrialization before and after the *coup d'état*. A small rate of growth applied to a relatively high initial base implies, however, large absolute increments; and indeed industrialization under the Revolution was significant in this respect. But it is wrong to assume that it involved a very considerable shift in the pattern of investment under either the First Industrial Plan or the General Plan. A more interesting feature is the increase in the share of industrial investment after 1965. This is partly a consequence of the completion of the High Dam and of a temporary shift away from transport between 1965/6 and 1967/8. It is easy to predict that the proportion of investment resources allocated to mining and manufacturing will continue to increase in the 1970s because of the absence of a new major project like the High Dam and a likely reduction in the share of electricity, once the transmission lines from Aswan and the distribution network are completed. Though petroleum may emerge as an important new sector, manufacturing is likely to absorb a rising proportion of a slow-growing investment fund. The need for careful planning is enhanced as industry is an area where significant mistakes are easily made. The hope is that planners will increasingly perceive the importance of making use of the potential afforded by the High Dam, the opportunities of new types of investment in agriculture and certain services such as tourism, and finally the need to improve both the economic and social infrastructure. As important, perhaps, as changes in the types and pattern of investment are changes in the policy framework necessary to improve the allocation of resources in the economy and to elicit dynamic responses from economic agents in agriculture, trade, and elsewhere.

(b) *Structural transformation and sectoral relationships.* Both the rate and the pattern of investment, together with other factors, enabled structural transformation initiated in the 1930s to continue under the Revolution. The pattern of

TABLE 8.8

Shares in GDP at factor costs
(percentages)

	Agri-culture	Industry and Electricity	Con-struction	Transport	Housing	Commerce	Services
1952/3	35·6	15·3	2·7	5·9	6·4	10·3	23·8
1956/7	33·6	17·2	2·8	5·8	6·6	10·7	23·3
1959/60	31·5	20·7	3·7	7·2	5·7	10·0	21·2
1964/5	27·1	23·1	5·3	8·9	4·5	8·6	22·5
1969/70	25·1	23·2	5·5	5·5	6·0	9·1	25·6

Note: GDP at constant 1954 prices for 1952/3 and 1956/7; at constant 1959/60 prices for 1959/60–1969/70.
Source: Computed from D. Mead, op. cit., p. 288, and Ministry of Planning, *Follow-up Reports.*

change is familiar, with agriculture declining as a proportion of GDP, mostly in favour of industry and construction in periods of high investment activity, and with services retaining a large and fairly constant share. Most economists construe this evolution as a sign of economic growth and development. Changes in the proportions of sectoral outputs in GDP is not, however, a sufficient criterion. The more interesting issues relate to the role of the leading sector of the economy, the integration of different branches of activity in a tighter network of relationships, and qualitative changes in both the economic structure and the institutions which enhance the country's potential for growth and development.

It is a moot question whether industry has played the role of a leading sector in recent developments.[11] Three criteria, perhaps, define a leading sector: (*a*) autonomous growth in response to technical innovations, newly discovered or hitherto idle natural resources, or market opportunities; (*b*) the transmission of an impetus to other sectors creating a new demand for their products and contributing to their development by supplying 'new' inputs; (*c*) a significant contribution to the increase in total income. Egyptian industry has expanded first in response to market opportunities enhanced by an external event such as the Second World War or by protectionist policies. This is perfectly understandable—few countries had a different start. The passage from a first stage when the infant industry is protected to the next, when the manufacturing sector having become more efficient and dynamic begins to compete in both domestic and world markets, was not, however, effected. Whether the time elapsed between the 1930s and the 1950s was too short, whether entrepreneurs lacked the drive or the incentives because of the security of their protected markets, are difficult questions to answer. Probably a mixture of both as well as other reasons. Industrialization, however, continued under the aegis of the State and entered new areas where the learning process is even longer and the possibilities of competing in the world market even more difficult. Despite the growth and diversification of its exports Egyptian industry is inward-looking as regards markets. The first criterion, hence, is not fully satisfied—not because industrialization was planned but because it has not reached the stage when plans take advantage of real opportunities generated by the dynamic performance of industry itself.

The second criterion of a leading sector refers to its

linkages. Egyptian industry has strong backward linkages with both agriculture, the major supplier of domestic inputs especially to textile and food manufacturing, and the world market, on which it relies for the raw materials and semi-finished goods necessary for the production of consumer durables, chemicals, and intermediate goods. It is difficult to ascertain the extent to which industry has created new demands for agriculture; it seems however that the diversion effects (away from direct exports into local processing) were more significant than the creation effects (a stimulus for growth). Industry forward linkages with agriculture are weak although it supplies a share of the growing consumption of fertilizers; it has not yet developed inputs and equipment such as pumps, plastic products, chemicals, adapted to the local conditions of Egyptian agriculture and capable of accelerating productivity growth. Industrialization, of course, stimulates construction and provides linkages with transport and other services.

The third criterion is perhaps more fully satisfied although the contribution of services to GDP increments exceeds that of industry.

There is no doubt that sectoral relationships—measured by the density of successive input–output tables—have become tighter during this period. But the alarming feature, mentioned throughout this chapter, is the independent growth of the services sector, a sector with very weak linkages with the rest of the economy. Its rate of expansion has been roughly identical to that of GDP until 1965, and much faster afterwards. An expansion which to a large extent is neither stimulated by that of other sectors and which, in turn, fails to stimulate them, gives rise to a kind of economic dualism between the Government sector and the productive branches of the economy. The former grows in response to the population and employment problem in a largely parasitical manner diverting resources needed for the development of the latter and hindering, perhaps as a result of its own expansion, their efficient performance.

This is where the qualitative issue arises. There is no

doubt that new institutions have been created by the State in the recent period, playing a definite role in economic development—co-operatives, credit institutions, planning and research institutes. Greater literacy and education have changed ways of life and, no doubt, improved the quality of labour now available to the modern sector. They may also have favourable repercussions on the population problem. But great and perhaps unnecessary rigidities have been brought into the institutional system and there is no way of telling how much they cancel other gains.

CHAPTER 9

THE EMPLOYMENT PROBLEM

Agricultural underemployment

EGYPT's employment problem has often been misconstrued as disguised unemployment in agriculture. Bent Hansen, however, has convincingly argued against this view.[1] Evidence on the behaviour of agricultural wage rates suggests that they are related to the marginal product of labour. The subsistence wage theory, often associated with disguised unemployment, is not borne out by the facts: Hansen found that real wages in agriculture tend to fluctuate from season to season and from year to year. Data on hours worked—from a sample survey undertaken in 1964 by the ILO and the Institute of National Planning—did not reveal substantial unemployment during the months of high activity (e.g. the harvest), which suggests that permanent unemployment is not a significant phenomenon. Seasonal unemployment, however, is a feature of agriculture in Egypt as elsewhere in the world.

The absence of disguised unemployment in the strict sense of zero marginal productivity does not necessarily mean that there is no labour surplus in agriculture. The agrarian system in Egypt has a dualistic structure: it comprises large capitalist farms operated by tenants and wage-labour and small family farms mainly operated by the members of the household. There is also an important pool of landless workers. Landownership is unequally distributed and the man/land ratio varies between family farms. There are markets for the services of both labour and land. Finally, it is legitimate to assume that landlords seek to maximize profits and family farmers total utility. It is not surprising to find that, in such a system, wage rates in the open labour market relate to the marginal productivity of labour. The market for temporary agricultural workers is almost perfect:

many farmers demand labour; a large number of landless workers are willing to supply their services; the employment contracts are typically short and landlords tend to behave as profit-maximizers. In this agrarian system, family farmers with a relatively large endowment of land hire wage-labour and other farmers with small endowments either offer their labour services outside the farm or rent land. Despite these features, factor-price differentials tend to obtain. We have argued elsewhere that imperfections in the land market, minor rigidities in the labour market, and technological constraints prevent factor-price equalization.[2] The well-known observation that in poor agriculture labour intensity and yields per acre rise with the man/land ratio on family farms is consistent with the existence of these differentials. They are a sign of inefficiency in the reallocation of labour on land and hence in the utilization of labour. The factor markets fail to eliminate underemployment of family labour during both the slack and the active seasons. Some would be willing to supply more work if their access to the labour market and more significantly to the tenancy market was free of all restrictions. Because of constraints the equilibrium attained is characterized by lower marginal products of labour and underemployment in some family farms. Landless workers, though not disguisedly unemployed, are likely to suffer from open unemployment.

The available evidence on the size of the 'family labour' surplus in Egypt is controversial. Mohieldin estimated on the basis of the 1961 Agricultural Census that 25 per cent of the male labour force is in excess supply during the seasonal peak (women and children are fully employed during the cotton-picking).[3] The ILO–INP sample survey of 1964 presents a completely different picture: full employment and very long hours of work during the seasonal peak and rather surprisingly little underemployment during the slack.[4] The methodology of both studies is open to serious criticisms. There are good reasons to believe that Mohieldin's estimates grossly exaggerate the magnitude of agricultural under-employment (partly because his concept of labour requirements is largely limited to field-work, partly because of definitional weaknesses in the Agricultural Census which overstate the size of the labour force). The ILO–INP survey, according to Dr. Planck, one of its designers, tended to overstate the amount of work actually performed. The evidence does not support firm conclusions: our assessment, after very careful consideration, is that the family sector in Egyptian agriculture held a small labour surplus during the early 1960s.

These findings have theoretical implications: they suggest that, contrary to a conventional view, agriculture does not always hold a large reserve of redundant workers in labour-surplus economies. The institutions of the agrarian system we have described do not allow for significant absorption of unproductive labour. They tend to produce open unemployment whenever the demand for labour fails to clear the market at the subsistence wage. Capitalist landlords are unlikely to hire more workers than profit maximization requires. The family sector is related to capitalist farms through the labour market and thus displaces part of its own surplus, adding to the pool of landless workers. Here, again, redundancy would manifest itself by open unemployment. It is often argued that tradition commits both landlords and family farmers to supporting unproductive labour in underdeveloped agriculture. We recognize of course that agrarian systems have complex features: elements of social feudalism coexist with economic capitalism, and traditional values retain a certain importance. Population growth, however, creates strains in the system. A social commitment to employ redundant labour, plausible in a static situation, becomes an open-ended commitment which tends to break down where a high rate of population growth adds year after year to the labour pool.

The ability of our dual agriculture to absorb labour when population grows while land remains in fixed supply partly depends on the rate and nature of technical progress. There are reasons to believe that this ability is limited. First, a sustained rate of technical progress equal to that of population increase is difficult to achieve. Second, technical progress need not result in higher wages or greater employment on capitalist farms where its benefits tend to be translated into higher profits. Technical progress could increase absorption on family farms; in most developing countries, however, innovations are more sluggish on small than on large farms. In such an agrarian system, strong forces which lead to a displacement of labour away from agriculture are set in motion.

Two issues require examination at this point: one relates to the release from agriculture of a labour surplus continually generated by population increases; the other to the absorption of this labour in other areas and sectors of the economy.

The release of labour from agriculture

The release of labour takes two forms: migration from rural to urban centres and labour transfers within rural areas from agriculture to non-agricultural activities. Migration is the more important phenomenon because of its scale in most developing countries today and its wide socio-economic implications. The scope for sectoral transfers in the rural world is restricted by a number of factors. The size of non-agricultural sectors tends to be relatively small outside the towns. In Egypt in 1960, rural areas with 62 per cent of the total population accounted for the following shares of sectoral employment: industry, 26·3 per cent; construction, 32·5 per cent; public utilities, 19·9 per cent; commerce, 35·1 per cent; transport and communications, 23·0 per cent; services, 29·1 per cent.[5] Even if the rates of growth of non-agricultural employment were for a time higher in the provinces than in urban areas, the increments to the number of jobs would, for a long period, remain larger in towns. And in most developing countries government policies, the values of ruling élites, the unchecked tendency of industry and new services to concentrate in the major centres all add up to discriminate against the rapid development of rural areas. These factors restrict the absorption of labour in the villages and hasten the rate of migration.

That considerable internal migration has taken place in Egypt during the past three or four decades is apparent from the behaviour of the urban population as disclosed by censuses. We may adopt alternative definitions of urban areas: the first is restricted to the five metropolitan governorates (Cairo, Alexandria, Port Said, Ismailia, and Suez), the second also includes provincial cities (capitals of districts or *markaz* and of rural governorates). The data presented in Table 9.1 show that between 1937 and 1966, the rate of urbanization has been consistently and significantly higher than the rate of natural increase. There has been, however, a marked deceleration in the growth of the five metropolitan governorates while the rate of growth of total urban population increased from an annual average of 3·53 per cent between 1937 and 1942 to 3·74 per cent between 1960 and 1966. It is interesting to note that the rate of growth of the smaller towns, lower than that of the five large cities between 1937 and 1960, rose throughout the period and exceeded the growth of the large cities during 1960–6.

A number of inferences on migration can be drawn from the data, on the assumption that the same rate of natural increase applies to rural and urban areas (not an implausible assumption in the light of our earlier discussion of patterns of fertility in Egypt). In the absence of direct estimates of migration flows, our only recourse is to indirect measures. These show, first, that the ratio of out-migrants to the natural increase of the rural population decreased from an annual average of 44·5 per cent (1937–47) to 22 per cent (1947–60) and rose again to 37 per cent (1960–6).* Although the rate of natural increase was significantly lower in the first than in subsequent periods, rural areas retained between 1937 and 1947 a relatively smaller proportion of the natural increment. The depressed conditions of agriculture during the Second World War (cotton acreage was reduced because of the disruption of trade and agricultural yields declined because

* This ratio is calculated as follows:
$$\frac{\text{rate of natural increase} - \text{rate of growth of rural population}}{\text{rate of natural increase}} \times 100.$$

TABLE 9.1

*Level, shares, and rates of growth of rural and urban
population 1937–1966*

(a) Population (absolute figures)

Years	1937	1947	1960	1966
Total settled population	15,920,694	18,966,767	25,984,101	30,075,858
Rural population	11,429,001	12,603,510	16,120,398	17,691,356
Desert governorates	109,610	160,941	212,606	351,759
Total urban population*	4,382,083	6,202,316	9,651,097	12,032,743
Five metropolitan governorates	2,278,745	3,474,276	5,598,056	6,912,773
Other towns	2,103,338	2,728,040	4,053,041	5,119,970

(b) Shares in total population (percentages)

Total settled population	100·00	100·00	100·00	100·00
Rural population	71·79	66·45	62·04	58·82
Desert governorates	0·69	0·85	0·82	1·17
Total urban population	27·52	32·70	37·14	40·01
Five metropolitan governorates	14·31	18·31	21·54	22·98
Other towns	13·21	14·39	15·60	17·13

(c) Annual average rates of growth

Periods	1937–42	1947–60	1960–6
Total settled population	1·77	2·45	2·47
Rural population	0·98	1·91	1·56
Desert governorates	3·91	2·17	8·76
Total urban population	3·53	3·46	3·74
Five metropolitan governorates	4·31	3·74	3·58
Other towns	2·63	3·09	3·97

Note: * Excludes desert governorates which censuses treat as urban areas.
Source: Computed from *Population Censuses* for 1960, 1966.

of shortages of fertilizers) and the attraction of employment
with the allied military establishment explain this phenomenon. The recovery of agriculture during the 1950s may
have enhanced the ability to absorb labour; but the tendency
of the rate of migration to rise as economic development
proceeds soon reasserted itself.

Another interesting feature is the apparent change in the
pattern of migration during the whole period. The rate of
immigration into the five large towns seems to decrease from

an annual average of 1·76 per cent (1937–47) to 1·27 per cent (1960–6) while the corresponding rate for other cities rose from an annual average rate of 0·86 per cent to 1·5 per cent. Rough estimates of the average annual flow of migration in the three periods show more clearly the magnitude of the reversal that seems to have taken place in 1960–6; the flow towards the five large towns did not vary very much from an annual average of 70,000 between periods, but the flow towards the other cities seems to have increased threefold from 24,000 in the second period to 72,000 in the third. This result is surprising: it suggests prima facie that the larger cities have become saturated. Migrants pushed away from the land or attracted by job and income opportunities in the urban sector moved first to the large metropolis. Later, as employment prospects became tighter, because of the considerable inflows of migrants and a high rate of natural increase, they began to look for opportunities in other cities. This hypothesis, suggested in an earlier paper,[6] should be qualified in the light of new data on the growth of towns between 1960 and 1966 unavailable at the time. They indicate a considerable expansion of two cities—Choubra-al-Kheima and Giza—in the greater Cairo conurbation. Although administratively distinct, Giza and Choubra-al-Kheima are both geographically and economically part of the capital. Adjustment for this factor reduces the quantitative significance of the shift towards provincial cities, but the phenomenon remains noticeable.

It is partly accounted for by the decline of Alexandria, which lost in 1952 its status of second capital and later its active and rich foreign community and some of its importance as a trading and financial centre; also by the decline of Port Said, whose isolated location precluded industrial development. Part of the shift is due to the emergence of Aswan as a new economic pole with the High Dam, iron mines, power stations, and the fertilizer plants (the population of Aswan city more than doubled from 63,000 in 1960 to 128,000 in 1966). Other provincial towns, however, seem to have attracted migrants during this period: the industrial

Mehalla-al-Kobra, Assiut which benefited from its status as regional capital in Upper Egypt, also Zagazig and Fayum.

TABLE 9.2

Population and growth of towns between 1960 and 1966
(population in thousands)

Towns	Population in 1960	Population in 1966	Percentage increase	Presumed direction of net migrations*
Cairo	3,353	4,220	25·85	+
Giza	419	571	36·28	+
Choubra-el-Kheima	101	173	71·29	+
Greater Cairo	3,873	4,964		+
Alexandria	1,516	1,801	18,80	+
Port Said	245	283	15·51	—
Suez	206	264	28·15	+
Ismailia (city)	116	144	24·13	+
Tanta	200	230	15·00	—
Mehalla-al-Kobra	188	225	19·70	+
Mansourah	167	191	14·37	—
Assiut	127	154	21·25	+
Zagazig	125	151	20·80	+
Damanhour	127	146	14·96	—
Fayum	112	134	19·64	+
Aswan	63	128	103·17	+
Minia	100	113	13·00	—

Note: * On the assumption of a uniform natural increase (15·74 per cent during six years).
Source: CAPMS, *Statistical Yearbook, 1952–1971.*

Migration is a complex phenomenon, but despite its social and economic significance there is a dearth of empirical studies on the subject in Egypt. The theoretical literature is dominated at present by the Todaro model[7] which emphasizes the pull exerted by the towns. (The originality of Todaro lies in the relationship seen between migration and urban unemployment.) But in countries like Egypt where land is in short supply, population growth is likely to generate a rural push and Todaro is relevant only in part to the problem. In the agrarian system depicted earlier, population growth unless accompanied by a high rate of technical progress will tend to depress wages on the agricultural market and/or increase the incidence of open unemployment among landless workers. It would reduce incomes and average endowments of land on family farms, thus displacing more workers on to the outside labour market.

We could imagine a situation where wages in the modern industrial sector remain fairly constant in real terms (we have shown elsewhere[8] that this situation apparently obtained in the 1950s in Egypt, and there is similar evidence for India). In a land-scarce economy the rural/urban wage differential could widen through a fall in agricultural wages; not, as often assumed, in the light of recent experience in Africa and Latin America, though increases in the minimum legal wage or average wages in industry. Our contention is that in a country like Egypt, migration would continue to take place albeit at a reduced rate, even if modern sector wages remained fixed and modern employment failed to expand. Migrants would try to enter, or create jobs for themselves, in the 'informal' sector whose role in absorbing labour has not received as yet the attention it deserves. (Theorists tend to lump together employment in this sector and open unemployment.) Absorption by this sector, of course, is not unlimited. An equilibrium may be reached when average incomes of landless workers in agriculture equal those of unskilled labour in the urban informal sector. In a dynamic context, absorption depends on the growth of demand for 'informal' services as income rises in the town.

Let us note, however, that population pressures lead to an increase in expenditures on this item through a variety of ways. One of the most interesting is through the creation of new services; any casual observer in Cairo or elsewhere would have noted the entrepreneurial and innovative abilities of pedlars and other service workers. The sales of flowers by young men at traffic lights is in a sense a new service: the convenience of buying the goods without leaving the car on the way home and without wasting time since the transaction is effected during an idle moment. 'New services', often unwanted, are a device to transfer income, and the scope for these activities seems to be significant in towns. The landless worker squeezed out of agriculture will probably use the informal sector as a port of entry to the modern sector, but may in fact spend the rest of his life there. The access to the modern sector of a rural migrant may be restricted for some time by lack of experience, failure to adapt to the requirements of labour discipline, and unfamiliarity with the technological environment; wages and employment conditions in the modern sector may not be immediately relevant to his decision to migrate to the town.

Our argument is that the determinants of migration should not be uniquely related to the modern urban/rural wage differential and the probability of finding a job. In many instances, push factors in agriculture and the flexibility of the informal sector combine to enable migration to occur.

In one of the rare studies on migration in Egypt, J. Abu-Lughod suggests that there are two types of rural migrants: 'the bright youths who migrate in search of education or wider opportunities' and the 'have-nots of the village'.[9] The latter are numerically dominant. That the larger proportion of rural migrants comes from the poorer groups is borne out by the ILO–INP sample survey. It appeared from an interview of 422 migrants that 26 per cent came from families earning before migration less than £E50 a year; 40 per cent from the £E51–75 bracket; 22 per cent from families with an income of £E76–100 and 8 per cent only with an income higher than £E100.[10] Another survey undertaken in rural areas by the INP in 1965 found that 23 per cent of a sample of 1,360 men would like to migrate, the larger proportion of which were landless labourers (42 per cent). Here again most of those who expressed the desire to migrate (21 per cent) came from families earning less than £E100 per year.[11]

Education is another determinant of migration; while push factors may dominate for landless labourers and members of the poorer landed families, education influences the desire to migrate of other groups. Here again the rural/urban wage differential for unskilled workers is not always relevant. The educated youth aspires for jobs often unavailable in villages. Higher education turns him into an urban dweller from the moment he joins the university or other institutions of learning; agriculture to him, as to any person born in the towns, rarely represents a real option. Lower levels of education do not close in the same way the agricultural option and may create a Todaro-type situation; income differentials between agriculture and the modern sector where education may increase the chances of access, the costs of job search, the deferred rewards (in terms of life-earnings) that may arise from waiting, the probabilities of finding employment within a certain span of time are all relevant to the decision to migrate.

The relationships between migration, economic development, and education are complex. Education spreads and the demand for its services increases with economic development. Education is associated with the prospect of good jobs and high earnings; and if it is extended to rural areas, migration is encouraged because a large proportion of these jobs are in the towns. But when the supply of educated manpower begins, after a time, to exceed demand a new situation tends to develop. Unemployment among the educated will grow and may become significant if allowed to increase unchecked. But the rate of migration may slow down only after a long lag; expectations do not adjust immediately. As this situation develops, employers will probably raise the minimum educational requirements for given jobs. And as these requirements are raised, the demands for more education, longer years of schooling, and higher studies increase. Governments are usually wary of the political discontent of the unemployed and susceptible to pressures for more schools and universities. In Egypt, the Government responded by expanding educational facilities and by committing itself in 1962 to employ all graduates. These policies raise expectations; they remove any uncertainty about the economic benefits of education to the individual able to seek it; they reduce or contain unemployment which might otherwise discourage after a time the educated rural youth from migrating. A spiral is thus set into motion: more education, continual creation of unproductive jobs, and, to the extent that these policies reach rural areas, increased migration.

There is no doubt that these forces have operated in Egypt during our period of study. Their quantitative impact on migration is difficult to assess. Because of the progress of education in rural areas in the past decades, we may assume that its role in relation to migration was not negligible.

Labour absorption

Population growth raises the question of labour absorption in the various sectors of the economy; internal migration, the more specific issue of employment in the towns. We shall use two sources of data: population censuses for the period 1937–60 and Ministry of Planning estimates for 1960–70. The two periods will be analysed separately as the two sets of figures are not perfectly consistent.

The main developments for 1937–60 are shown in Table 9.3. The total labour force increased by more than 1·91 million between 1937 and 1960, but the increase was much larger during the first decade. An interesting feature is that between 1947 and 1960 the labour force increased at a much slower rate than total population (less than 1 per cent against 2·5 per cent per annum). The rate of participation in the labour force—around 37 per cent in 1937 and 1947— decreased to less than 30 per cent in 1960. Changes in the age composition due to increases in the rate of population growth and the extension of compulsory education are responsible for this phenomenon, but it may also reflect an inability of the economic system to provide the necessary incentives that would draw more people from the manpower reserves into the labour force.

Agriculture, despite its large initial share (63 per cent in 1937), did not make a significant contribution to new employment during this period. Indeed, the agricultural labour force failed to expand between 1937 and 1947 and the increase between 1947 and 1960 was relatively moderate. Agriculture employed less than 400,000 of an increment of

1,917,000 over the whole period. More than 1·5 million had to find jobs in other sectors.

Employment in manufacturing more than doubled during the period, but the absolute increment (361,000) was smaller in this sector than in agriculture. Industrial employment grew from a very small base (its share in the total was only

TABLE 9.3

Labour force and employment by sectors 1937–1960
(in thousands)

	1937	1947	1960
Labour force	5,809·2	6,994·6	7,726·6
Agriculture	4,020·4	4,085·7	4,406·4
Mining and quarrying	10·8	13·0	21·1
Manufacturing	352·7	560·6	713·1
Electricity, gas, water	21·0	22·6	36·8
Construction	120·7	113·3	158·8
Transport	138·9	203·3	260·2
Commerce	439·5	590·4	641·4
Other services	701·7	1,051·8	1,369·4
Unspecified	3·5	353·9	119·3

Source: *Population Census 1960*, vol. II, Supplementary Table IV.

6·1 per cent in 1937), and in relation to the rapid growth of industrial output after the Second World War, manufacturing employment expanded at only a very moderate rate (1·9 per cent per annum between 1947 and 1960, to be compared with an average rate of growth of real industrial output of some 7 or 8 per cent). The very nature of modern industrial development—which leads to the adoption of labour-saving technology and involves structural shifts towards capital-intensive industries such as chemicals, petroleum, paper, and metals—explains this performance. The bulk of the increase in the labour force—some 1·1 out of 1·9 million—thus found employment in the tertiary sector (including activities which the census fails to specify). The share of the tertiary sector in total employment increased from 24 per cent in 1937 to 31 per cent in 1960; and for each new job in industry three additional persons were engaged in the services. This ratio is strikingly high considering the stage of economic development in which Egypt was at the time. As construction and transport employed only an extra 169,000 workers, most of the expansion took place in government, commerce, personal services, and in the 'informal' sector to which the category labelled 'unspecified' seems to belong.

A breakdown of employment by urban centres (the five metropolitan governorates) and the provinces for the three census years will enable us to analyse the pattern of absorption in different geographical areas. The data used were adjusted by Mead[12] and cover only adult males (aged 15 and above).

It is not surprising in view of our discussion on migration to find that the percentage increase in employment between 1937 and 1960 was much larger in the main towns (129 per cent) than in the provinces (35 per cent). The more interesting feature is the increase in 'services' employment in the provinces. The tertiary sector, despite its small initial share (18 per cent in 1937), absorbed more workers than agricul-

TABLE 9.4

Labour force and employment in urban governorates and provinces 1937–1960

(thousands)

	1937	1947	1960
Urban governorates			
Total employment	617	943	1,412
1. Agriculture	26	27	65
2. Industry	130	221	346
3. Services	461	694	1,001
Provinces			
Total employment	3,840	4,303	5,182
1. Agriculture	2,950	3,112	3,495
2. Industry	200	293	370
3. Services	690	899	1,317

Source: D. Mead, *Growth and Structural Change in the Egyptian Economy*, Homewood, Ill., 1967, pp. 37 and 39.

ture—209,000 against 162,000 between 1937 and 1947 and 418,000 against 383,000 between 1947 and 1960. As a result, the share of employment in 'services' increased to 25 per cent. Nearly half of all new jobs in the provinces were created in the tertiary sector.

Changes in the sectoral pattern of employment after 1960 —unfortunately assessed with a different set of statistics— follow the same general trend. But there are certain differences. The rate of growth of total employment was much faster than between 1947 and 1960 (2·6 per cent against 1·0 per cent), approximating the rate of population growth. Industrial employment expanded faster than before, not so

TABLE 9.5

Employment by sectors 1960/1–1969/70

(a) Total numbers (thousands)

	1960/1	1964/5	1969/70
Total employment	6,511·9	7,373·9	8,274·7
Agriculture	3,600·0	3,751·0	4,048·3
Industry	625·6	825·0	916·1
Electricity	13·1	18·0	22·8
Construction	166·0	345·2	387·9
Transport	252·7	283·9	347·2
Commerce	663·0	729·7	801·7
Services	1,191·5	1,421·1	1,750·7

(b) Shares of main sectors (percentage)

Total employment	100·0	100·0	100·0
Agriculture	55·3	50·9	48·9
Industry and electricity	9·8	11·4	11·3
Tertiary	34·9	37·7	39·8

(c) Annual average rates of growth (percentage)

	1960/1–1964/5	1964/5–1969/70	1960/1–1969/70
Total employment	3·2	2·3	2·6
Agriculture	1·0	1·5	1·3
Industry and electricity	7·1	2·2	4·4
Tertiary	5·3	3·2	4·2

Note: The data refer to fiscal years. Agricultural employment seems to be restricted to adult males. Industry includes mining and the estimates seem restricted to employment within establishments, thereby excluding jobbing artisans. Services include the Government but not the army.
Source: Computed from Ministry of Planning, *Follow-up Reports*, various issues.

much because of a higher rate of investment but as a result of employment policies; after nationalization in 1961 and 1962 the Government compelled public companies to engage more persons than they actually required. The apparent increase in construction seems overstated: the High Dam, irrigation works for land reclamation, and investments undertaken under the First Five-Year Plan (1960/1–1964/5) only explain part of the increase. Here, again, the tertiary sector absorbed the largest proportion (some 58 per cent) of the increase in the labour force, and as the size of the army—excluded from the data—has expanded significantly during the 1960s, the figures tend to understate the growth of the tertiary sector.

Absorption of labour in the service sector seems to have contained the threat of open unemployment, for there is little evidence of substantial unemployment at least until 1965 or 1966. The 1960 census returned 175,000 unemployed, less than 2·5 per cent of the labour force; sample surveys undertaken in the 1960s estimated urban unemployment at around 3·4 per cent. All this, however, requires many qualifications. The concept of 'open unemployment' does not mean very much in underdeveloped countries, except perhaps for certain categories of workers—the skilled and the educated in the modern sector. It is not easy to draw the line between various types of unemployment in agriculture; nor to interpret unambiguously low rates of participation in the labour force, which could reflect either voluntary or involuntary withdrawals; and it is practically impossible to distinguish at the fringes of the service sector those who are meaningfully occupied from the unemployed.

Conclusion

The developments surveyed in this chapter reveal something above the employment structure of a land-scarce economy and the nature of its response to a population explosion. In Egypt, agriculture—because of resource constraints, institutions, low productivity, and the very labour-intensive technology on family farms which restricts the scope of further factor substitution—made a limited contribution to new employment. Industrialization did not provide an immediate solution; despite high rates of capital formation and output growth the number of jobs created every year was, and will remain for a long time, relatively small. The initial size of the manufacturing sector—a sign and consequence of underdevelopment—is largely responsible for this state of affairs. Egypt departed from the pattern of development described by Clark[13] and Fisher[14] and hence from the historical experience of advanced countries on which their models are based. The country is moving from a stage where agriculture was dominant to the third stage where the share of tertiary activities is becoming very large; the long intermediary phase during which the growth of industry precedes that of services seems to have been by-passed. It also departed from a Lewis pattern, where labour is reallocated from agriculture to industry and rural unemployment gradually resorbed.

The reallocation instead has taken place in favour of services, a mixed sector which comprises many activities whose economic significance is suspect. Absorption in services, which may at first appear as a solution to the difficulties posed by the population explosion, raises in fact a number of problems. The transfer of labour from agriculture, where they would have become increasingly underemployed, to low-paid, low-productivity jobs in certain service activities is not akin to reallocation to industry. Labour does not co-operate with capital in these activities and hence does not generate an economic surplus; the growth of these activities is unlikely to contribute to economic development through external economies or technical progress. The reallocation that takes place in the labour surplus economy is, to a large extent, a transfer of the locus of poverty, underemployment, and low productivity from one economic sector or from one geographical area to another.

In Egypt, the Government created a large proportion of the new jobs which became available between 1947 and 1970; the numbers of its employees (excluding the army) are estimated to have increased from less than 310,000 in

1947 to nearly 770,000 in 1960 and 1,035,000 in 1966/7. It is difficult to believe that this phenomenal expansion was entirely warranted by the needs of public administration or that it led to a corresponding increase in the real output of Government services. Open unemployment was avoided or contained by creating a large mass of underemployed and necessarily frustrated and inefficient public employees and officials. Here, again, the contribution to economic development is likely to be negative, because of the macro-economic repercussions of budget deficits on aggregate demand, prices, and the balance of payments, and the diversion of resources from investment to consumption. Labour reallocation, which some theorists construe as an 'engine of development', probably here involves income transfers as much as income growth. Governments should not be unduly criticized for their policies—their dilemmas are serious and their freedom of choice constrained. The inadequacy of their policies reflects to a large extent the inadequate resources of an underdeveloped country faced with a population problem and subjected to internal and external pressures for rapid development.

CHAPTER 10

CHANGES IN THE
DISTRIBUTION OF INCOME

'. . . Mais c'est de l'homme qu'il s'agit! Et
de l'homme lui-même quand donc sera-t-il
question?'
SAINT-JOHN PERSE

Introduction

AN appraisal of economic development in Egypt during the
past seventy years would be incomplete without an analysis
of changes in the distribution of income. The issue is important in the context of this study and in the more general
field of economic development. The social and economic
policies of the Revolution were often motivated, or at least
justified, by distributional objectives; and many others of
these policies, whatever their explicit aims, had a differential
impact on the incomes of various social groups. At a more
general level, improvements in the standard of living of the
poor, a reduction in the degree of income inequality accompanied by increases in the income of the less-favoured
groups, a better distribution of public goods such as education, health, and social services, and more equal opportunities for the underprivileged are all relevant criteria to an
assessment of economic development. And the study of
changes in patterns of income distribution brought about by
the normal play of economic and demographic forces in
a labour-surplus economy is itself of interest. More fundamentally, our concern, as suggested by the verse at the head
of this chapter, is with real people—peasants, workers,
government clerks among many others—or, by default, with
the groups to which they belong. The questions are: how
various groups of people have fared under the Revolution;
which benefited economically and which incurred losses as a

result of both policies and performance in the past twenty years, and how much accrued to each?

Changes in the average real income of different groups both relative to each other and in absolute terms, and changes in the relative size of the groups are the relevant aspects to consider, as economic development involves both income growth and structural transformations. It is possible to imagine two extreme cases: in one, all the gains accrue in the form of higher average incomes for the various categories distinguished but their share in the total population remains constant; in the second case, average incomes remain constant but the size of a more favoured group increases relative to that of others. The latter case may be termed a generalized Lewis situation since in Lewis's model economic development, under labour-surplus conditions, leads to a rise in the ratio of the industrial to the agricultural labour force without changes in the level of real wages. Benefits in the form of a once-for-all increase in wages accrue to labour transferred from agriculture to industry, not to workers already employed in these two sectors. In the real world, changes in income distribution fall somewhere between these extreme cases which may serve as reference points. It will be interesting to find whether the Egyptian situation approximates to either of these cases.

Factors responsible for changes in the distribution of income are so numerous that it may be vain to attempt listing them. In fact, changes in all the economic and demographic variables, institutions, and policies surveyed in this book bear on the issue. The distribution of income relates first to the distribution of wealth, both human and non-human, in society; and policies which influence wealth, such as education, the land reform, or nationalizations, are relevant to the analysis. Income distribution is the result of market forces whose operations in given institutional contexts are often controlled or influenced by policy. Changes in the determinants of these forces—supply, demand, degree of market inperfections, and hence such variables as productivity and population growth, migration, etc.—in institutions and in, say, income, price, or employment policies are thus of interest. Since the concern is with real disposable income of households, the differential impact of taxation, income transfers, and changes in both the external and internal terms of trade need to be considered. Finally, the consumption of free public goods—an element of real income—is also of relevance.

An elaborate and comprehensive analysis of the distribution of income is precluded by both the availability of data and the scope of this study.[1] We are unable, for example, to fit Lorenz curves or calculate Gini coefficients, an impediment which we only half regret as these measures of relative inequality at different points in time do not reveal which group has become better and which worse off in the process. Though the analysis here will be partial and the conclusions tentative, an attempt to assess the direction—and in some cases, the magnitude—of the main changes in the distribution of income may still yield interesting results.

Consumption benefits of economic growth

One of the main objectives of economic activity is consumption—whether for present or deferred uses. Real *per capita* consumption is therefore an interesting indicator of the immediate benefits derived by the *average* Egyptian from economic growth in the past two decades. Tables 10.1 and 10.2 present some relevant data—*per capita* private consumption deflated by the cost-of-living index and estimates of average consumption of calories, proteins, and textiles. Deflation by the official cost-of-living index may overstate perhaps the growth of real *per capita* consumption, but it is extremely difficult to assess the biases involved. A more serious weakness of the data is that private consumption figures are derived in the national accounts as a residual and are hence extremely unreliable. In interpreting the table, it is also essential to allow for the effects of indirect taxes which could not be netted out from the aggregate at current market prices. It is unlikely that the failure to exclude indirect taxes distorts very much the picture between 1952 and 1962 as they tended to increase during this period at approximately the same rate as both GDP and aggregate private consumption. Between 1962 and 1970, however, they increased at a faster rate than GDP at market prices and at an even higher rate than aggregate private consumption. Real *per capita* private consumption has thus been growing at a much slower rate in the 1960s than shown in Table 10.1.* These considerations put in sharper contrast than the table the difference between the high rates of growth of the 1950s and early 1960s and the very low rates in the rest of the period. The behaviour of *per capita* consumption of calories and proteins provides some support to these conclusions although the data there suggest that the turning-point was a few years later. But this difference may simply represent lagged adjustments in the composition of consumption as

TABLE 10.1

Indices of aggregate and per capita *consumption 1952–1970*

Years	Index of aggregate private consumption (at current prices)	Population index	Cost-of-living index	Index of *per capita* private consumption (at constant prices)	Annual average rate of growth of real *per capita* consumption
1952/3	100	100	100	100	
					⎫ 2·64
1956/7	125	111	101	111	⎬
					⎫ 3·78
1960/1	159	121	103	128	⎬
					⎫ 1·45
1966/7	261	140	133	140	⎬
					⎭ 0·66
1969/70	312	156	140	143	

Sources: Computed from Ministry of Planning, *Follow-up Reports, Population Censuses*, CAPMS, *Statistical Indicators* and National Bank of Egypt, *Economic Bulletin*, various issues.

* We calculated, on the reasonable but unevidenced assumption that three-quarters of total indirect taxes fall on private consumption, that the average annual rate of growth of real *per capita* consumption was zero between 1960/1 and 1969/70 and negative after 1964/5.

TABLE 10.2

Per capita *consumption of food and textiles*

Years	Calories per day	Proteins (grams) per day	Cotton textiles (kg) per year
1951/2	2,324	34·7	2·00
1960/1	2,530	n.a.	2·32
1963/4	2,930	49·0	2·51
1966/7	3,064	46·7	2·85
1968/9	2,891	43·6	2·99

Sources: CAPMS, *The Increase in population in the United Arab Republic*, 1969, and *Statistical Indicators*.

people may curtail other expenditures before food. To sum up, the rate of growth of real *per capita* private consumption which is estimated at 2·13 per cent per annum on the basis of figures in Table 10.1 may have not actually exceeded 1·6 per cent per annum; and all the gains accrued before 1963 or 1964. Calorie and protein *per capita* consumption grew at an average annual rate of 1·27 and 1·37 respectively, and textiles at 2·41 per cent per annum; these rates appear to be consistent with the estimated 1·6 per cent rate for real *per capita* consumption.

The benefits from economic growth take also the form of higher *per capita* consumption of public goods such as education, health, social services, public amenities, and the like. Developments in these areas have been surveyed in an earlier chapter. The growth of this type of consumption, especially for education, has been fast. Real public expenditures *per capita* on education is estimated (by deflating Government aggregate expenditures at current prices by a composite price index including Government wages and wholesale price indices) to have increased at an annual average rate of growth of 4·9 per cent per annum. Consumption of public goods such as defence, internal security, or the administration of justice is a very difficult concept as there may be no relationship between the quality—and in certain cases, the reality—of the service provided and public expenditures. Let us note, finally, the obvious deterioration in the quality of urban life arising from the failure to expand the capacity of the public transport system at the same rate as demand.

Some features of the distribution of income and wealth in 1952

There is no doubt that the distribution of income was heavily lop-sided when the Free Officers took power in 1952. The polarization of Egyptian society between a small group of very rich families—many, including the Royal House, of non-Egyptian origin—and large masses of poor was the result of complex historical and socio-economic factors. The maldistribution of income and wealth, common to many underdeveloped countries, was aggravated in Egypt by specific historical circumstances in the nineteenth century (the formation of large estates through gifts from the Ruler or the State), and later by a *laissez-faire* system which, in a country poorly endowed with human skills and subject to population pressures, permits the appropriation by a small minority of the benefits of economic growth.

The concentration of wealth was most apparent in land where some 2,000 individuals representing an even smaller number of families owned almost 20 per cent of the cultivated area. But it also characterized other sectors of the economy. The Alexandria cotton futures market did not involve much more than two dozen broker firms. Cotton exports which represented more than 80 per cent of the country's export trade were mainly handled by a few large firms dominated by giants like Farghali Pasha, Yehia Pasha, Robert Huri, and a few others. Six banks, out of twenty-four operating in Egypt in 1952, accounted for 78 per cent of all advances and 85 per cent of deposits; Barclays alone accounted for 56 per cent of deposits. In manufacturing monopolies or oligopolies prevailed in many branches including relatively large ones such as food processing and textiles. Two powerful groups—Misr and Abboud—held a significant portion of Egyptian capital invested in the modern sector. Bank Misr created twenty-nine companies at various times after its foundation in 1922. The chairmanship of these companies' boards was usually given to a board member of the Bank. A newspaper revealed in 1960 after the nationalization of the Bank, that fifty persons held 42 per cent of the shares, of whom ten possessed 20 per cent and Abboud on his own 14 per cent.[2] The lists of major shareholders and owners of large companies in the private sector, published after the nationalizations and sequestrations of 1961, include some 600 names some of which seem to recur frequently. Analysing the composition of the boards of the industrial companies in 1947, we found that 960 persons (of whom only 265 had recognizable Egyptian names) filled all the posts, and that a significant number were chairing or sitting on several boards. It was not until 1954 that a reform of the company law limited the number of directorships that an individual was allowed to hold to six and the number of managing directorships to two. Little is known, however, about the distribution of urban real estates which would require, if access were possible, painstaking research in the archives of tax offices. But there is evidence in the censuses of a high degree of concentration in wholesale and export–import trade.

The landed and the industrial bourgeoisies did not form entirely distinct groups. Although there are notable cases of very big landowners who never held a single share in a modern sector company, and of 'modern' capitalists with little or no stake in land, the wealth of the Egyptian and foreign rich bourgeoisie was diversified into land, urban houses, government bonds, and equities. And the high degree of concentration did not imply the absence of small capitalists: Bank Misr had encouraged medium landowners, well-to-do professionals, Government officials, rentiers, and merchants to hold company shares.

Income disparities arising from this distribution of wealth were excessively large. In 1950, a landless family earned some £E26 a year. There were perhaps 1·3 million such families (see below). A big landowner, with 500 feddans— some 600 owned areas in excess of that amount—would have received from renting his land at about £E30 per feddan an

annual gross income of £E15,000 and probably half as much
in addition if he cultivated the land directly. The land tax
made negligible inroads into this income which, in any case,
was generally supplemented by the returns on other sources
of wealth. In 1952 an unskilled worker in construction or
industry earned between £E0·15–0·20 a day or some
£E40–60 a year. Assume a capitalist owning 10 per cent of
the shares of a textile company employing 5,000 persons.
Average wages enable us to calculate the wage bill and the
share of wages in gross value added, the share of gross profit.
Assuming finally that 10 per cent of these gross profits were
distributed in dividends (in 1958, distributed profits
accounted for 40 per cent of gross profits on average but it is
safer to be on the very low side), the capitalist's gross income
from his shares in this company would have been £E20,000
in 1952.

Changes

(a) *Agriculture.* The land reform is the main factor of
changes in the distribution of landownership in agriculture
and hence a dominant influence on changes in the distribution of income. The immediate effect of the successive
laws was to remove the top bracket in the existing distribution
of landownership, thus improving the relative distribution
of income and wealth. In the transitional period, pending the
redistribution of expropriated estates, the land reform
involved a simple transfer of income from the big landowners
to the State. Improvements in the relative distribution of
income were not immediately accompanied by rises in
personal income for the would-be beneficiaries of the
land reform as there is no evidence to suggest that the
Agrarian Reform authorities paid labourers on expropriated
estates more than the market wage. Although rents charged
after the reform in 1952 were lower than before, the fall was
as much due to market conditions as to the legal stipulations
of the Act; it is difficult to form an opinion on how much
better off the tenants on estates administered by the Authorities became after the expropriation.

Land, however, was continually redistributed (though lags meant that the Authority always held a large balance), but here again the first stage of the land reform did not imply higher incomes for the beneficiaries. As explained in Chapter 4, beneficiaries until 1958 were liable for the full compensation price of the land as well as supplementary charges, and the Debt carried 3 per cent interest. Saab calculated that their annual charges per feddan were probably as high, if not higher, than the rents previously paid.[3] The disposable income of the beneficiaries thus remained as low as before, the real benefits being deferred for thirty years. Landlords on the other hand had received from the State virtually worthless bonds. Until 1958, therefore, the State turned out, in one way or another, to be the major recipient of incomes transferred by the Reform. The law, however, was changed on several occasions after 1958 always to the greater advantage of land reform beneficiaries; since 1964, the annual repayment charge amounts to a nominal sum. After these changes, the transfer of landownership implied significant income increases for the beneficiary. The amount by which income may increase would be equivalent to the rent minus 10 or 25 per cent representing the land tax and charges for the former tenant and the same amount plus a profit element for the former wage labourer.

Although the data are very incomplete it is possible to make tentative comparisons between certain features of the distribution of agricultural incomes in 1950 and 1965. We estimated the number of landless families (defined as neither owning nor renting land) in 1950 at 1,270,000 and in 1965 at 960,000.[4] Average daily wages for adult males were £E0·10–0·12 and £E0·20–0·22, and the number of days worked per year 150 and 180 in the respective years. On certain assumptions about the average composition of the working family and a knowledge of wage differentials by sex and age it is possible to estimate the average annual income of a landless family at £E26 in 1950 and £E59 in 1965. As rural cost of living has increased by some 70 per cent between these two years, the increase in real income appears to be of the order of 33 per cent, implying an average rate of growth of 1·9 per cent per annum. It is possible that some of these gains were lost after 1965, but in the absence of recent data on wages no firm suggestions can be made. The interesting feature of this change is the fall in the absolute numbers of landless families (as defined) as well as the rise in real incomes. The share of wages paid out in gross value added—i.e. the share of agricultural income earned by landless workers—seems to have fallen slightly from 9 to 8 per cent.

In 1950 some 787,000 rural families held (either as tenants or owners) parcels of less than five feddans. Here again, it is possible to make crude estimates of their average incomes from data on average gross value added per feddan, rents, and the composition of holdings. The average income is calculated net of land tax but gross of capital charges at £E78 per year; the share of this group in total agricultural income is 17·5 per cent. This average, however, conceals two types of income differential: the first, between owners and tenants, is of the order of 100 per cent per feddan held; the second is between holdings of different sizes. Estimates for 1965 are even more tentative. The number of smallholdings is estimated at 1,600,000, average annual income at about £E125, and the share of this group in total agricultural income at 34 per cent. As changes in average incomes for landed peasants are strongly influenced by changes in the composition of the ownership bracket considered, it is preferable to assess real improvements from the growth of real income per feddan. A comparison of 1965 with 1952 (1950 was a boom year not suitable as a base of comparisons because non-wage income in Egyptian agriculture at the time was strongly influenced by cotton prices world) suggests that gross value added per feddan deflated by rural cost-of-living index increased by some 20–25 per cent, or at an average annual rate of growth of 1·5–1·8 per cent. Gross value added is an imperfect but not too misleading an indicator of income for small owners. Some of them, however, hire labour. If wages are netted out, their real rate of income growth will be lower. For small tenants, rents should also be netted out. Tenants enjoyed probably a higher rate of real income growth between 1952 and 1965 as rents did not rise in the same way as gross value added; but there are no firm data. Let us note, finally, that the 'less than 5 feddan' holding bracket included in 1965 land reform beneficiaries. The increase in the income of these new entrants is much more substantial than that of old owners in the group.

An important change in the distribution of agricultural income between 1952 and 1965 is the disappearance of the 'more than 100 feddan' bracket from the structure of ownership. The '100 feddan and plus' group appropriated in 1950 an estimated 25 per cent of gross agricultural income. The average income from land amounted to £E14,000 per annum, some 540 times as much as the income of a landless family. In 1965, however, 421,000 feddans were held in parcels of 100 feddans, accounting perhaps for a share of 4 per cent of total agricultural income. Average income in this group is estimated at £E700 per annum before tax. Although taxes take a significant cut, some large income disparities between landless workers and the remaining big landowners still persisted in 1965. The new ceiling of 50 feddans on ownership will, however, reduce disparities once again.

A comparison of shares of agricultural incomes accruing to various groups is summarized below:

	1950	1965
Landless families	9·0	8·0
Holders of less than 5 feddans	17·5	34·0
Holders of 100 and plus	25·0	4·0
	51·5	46·0

There seems to have been an increase in the share of the group left out from the analysis (mainly holders of '5 to less than 100 feddans'). This is not surprising as this group includes both former big landlords left with less than 100 feddans who may still appropriate 3 or 4 per cent of total agricultural income and the very stable group of medium landowners whose share of the cultivated area has not much declined.

(b) *Industry*. Nationalizations automatically improved the relative distribution of income and wealth by transferring the ownership of means of production in large areas of the modern sector to the State. The measures were essentially privative rather than redistributive and did not entail, directly at least, increases in income for other groups. They were accompanied, however, by the socialist laws which granted substantial benefits to workers. They displaced managing directors and members of company boards and replaced them by new men whose income most probably increased as a result; enabled the Government to create new jobs; hastened the emigration of foreigners, thus opening up opportunities for Egyptians in a number of activities. The sequestrations also implied higher incomes for civil servants and other officials appointed to the trusteeship of the sequestrated properties. The main change, however, is a considerable reduction in the volume and share of the profit income of households. The direction of distributional changes is clear, but their magnitude practically impossible to assess.

Changes in the income of non-profit-earners—most workers and employees—in industry are easier to ascertain.

TABLE 10.3

Employment and average income in manufacturing 1952 and 1966/7

	Labour force (thousands)		Share of national labour force (percentage)		Average annual income (£Es)	
	1952	1966/7	1952	1966/7	1952	1966/7
Modern sector:						
Employees	32	80	0·45	0·95	312	450 (575)
Workers	250	517	3·50	6·08	88	168 (201)
Small-scale:						
Self-employed	120	170	1·70	2·00	120	280
Workers	80	115	1·10	1·35	32	60
Itinerant and rural	80	90	1·10	1·05	32	60

Note: Figures between brackets include fringe benefits and employer's contribution to social insurances.

Sources: Computed from *Censuses of Industrial Production*, various issues.

Two features of Table 10.3 are of interest. First the shares of all types of manufacturing employment in the country's labour force seem to have significantly increased save perhaps for the category 'itinerant and rural'.* Second, average incomes of weekly-paid workers seem to have increased by a larger percentage than those of employees. Deflating again by the official cost-of-living index, increases in average real income between 1952 and 1966/7 appear to be of the order of 44 per cent for workers and 8 per cent only for employees. Changes in the skill-structure of the labour force in a period of significant industrialization account for part of the increase in the average income of workers. Excess supply of secondary school and university leavers whom the Government employed as clerks in the public sector seems to have dampened the rise of average incomes for employees. The data also suggest that the incomes of workers in the small-scale sector and rural artisans move in line with those of landless families in agriculture, and that owners of small establishments in manufacturing enjoyed the larger gains. Increases in real income in the modern sector are understated by our previous calculations because social benefits and social insurance were not included. Although they do not add to the present disposable income of workers and employees they represent a significant welfare gain. Similarly, the average number of hours worked per week declined from 51 to 49 between 1954 and 1966/7. Increases in real income were accompanied by a reduction in the input of effort and this, again, implies a welfare gain.

In construction, average income of workers increased slightly more than in manufacturing. All construction workers do not benefit, however, from the welfare benefits arising from social insurance and other schemes because a proportion of the labour force in this sector is employed on a day-to-day basis; but the share of the temporary labour force in construction has declined after the nationalizations.

Let us note finally that real income increases in the

* Nothing firm can be said about the behaviour of this group because the data, derived as a residual, are shaky.

modern sector accrued mainly between 1962 and 1964 as a result of the socialist laws. Real incomes did not increase very much between 1954 and 1962 save through fringe benefits, and they may have declined in recent years.

(c) *Government*. Government civilian employment increased from an estimated 325,000 in 1952 to 1,035,000 in 1966/7.[5] The share of this group in the country's labour force rose from 9·6 per cent to 15·4 per cent; its share of the national income, from 8·6 per cent to 13 per cent. Average annual income (at current prices) increased from £E240 to £E323 between the two years. This implies that average money income rose by the same percentage as cost of living, leaving real income unchanged. Changes in the grade-composition of the civil service, however, significantly affect the averages. A disaggregated analysis of changes in Government wage scales indicates that significant increases in income accrued in the lower half of the scale. Thus the maximum improvement is in grade 9 where salary rises in 1964 implied an 85 per cent difference in real income between a 1952 grade 9 employee and a 1966/7 employee of the same grade. However, the real value of nominal salaries at the top of the scale fell by some 10–20 per cent between 1952 and 1966/7.

The nature of the changes in Government salary scales could be interpreted in an alternative way. It is possible to distinguish, for simplicity, two groups: the manual worker and the civil servant. The manual worker's prospects when he takes employment are constrained by a narrow promotional ladder. Salary rises in 1964 raised all wages in this ladder. The expected life-time earnings of a manual worker were higher in 1966/7 than in 1952; all of course at 1952 prices. The university graduate usually enters at grade 6 and he may legitimately expect to climb to the top of the ladder during his life-time. Expected life-earnings on these assumptions did not rise very much between 1952 and 1966/7 as the gains that accrued at the beginning of his career would be largely lost towards the end.

Nominal salaries do not represent the whole income of top

civil servants. Many supplement their earnings with fees for membership of committees, trusteeships of sequestrated properties, travel and other allowances. The socialist laws which forbade cumulation of office have never been seriously applied. And the public sector provides some civil servants with many sources of semi-illicit income. Taking the rise in fringe benefits into account, real income increases between 1952 and 1966/7 may turn out to be substantial.

The army is an important sector of Government employment. In the absence of data, increases in number and in income cannot be quantified. There is no doubt, however, that the army has increased its relative share in the total labour force and that the real income of officers has increased faster than that of any salaried group in the economy after 1952.

To sum up: real incomes of workers in agriculture, industry, and government seem to have increased by similar proportional amounts. In agriculture, however, the gains tended to accrue through the play of market forces, while in the other sectors they are mainly due to legislation. The relative size of the labour force engaged in the lower-paid occupations (abstracting from the informal sector) has declined while that of workers with higher average incomes (industry and government) and small farmers has significantly increased. In general, workers seem to have gained more than employees, although the conclusion may only apply to clerks and low-paid employees.

Rural–urban inequalities in the distribution of public goods

There is little doubt that rural areas have benefited under the Revolution from a rise in the relative share of public expenditures on social services. Achievements after 1952 have been significant. An interesting study by the Ministry of Planning reveals, however, the degree of disparity in the social infrastructure between provinces and urban governorates in 1966/7. This is significant for hospital beds and for the spread of education above the primary level. And the discrepancy between public administration expenditures and

TABLE 10.4

Some indicators of rural–urban distribution of social
facilities 1966/7
(percentages)

	Urban governorates	Provinces
Population	21·8	78·2
Students in primary education	27·6	72·4
Students in preparatory education	35·7	64·3
Students in secondary education	42·4	57·6
Hospital beds	41·4	58·6
Social centres	13·2	86·8
Local administration revenues	29·7	70·3
Local administration expenditures	31·3	68·7

Source: Ministry of Planning, 'Indicators of Regional Development 1964/5–
1966/7', unpublished memorandum, Cairo, 1968, pp. 148–57.

revenues implies a hidden subsidy from provinces to the
urban governorates. That the proportion of students in
primary schools in provinces is close to the proportion of
their population in total is, however, a measure of the
progress accomplished in certain fields.

Economic policies and the distribution of income

The Government price policies have significant implications for the distribution of income which can only be
assessed in a qualitative manner. Rent controls, for example,
transfer income from landlords to tenants. The wheat
subsidy for bread benefits the urban population but is
largely irrelevant to the rural population for whom maize is
the staple. Price policies in agriculture are akin to a tax on
landed farmers, who do not benefit from the full extent of
market price increases for their products. Although pro-
gressive income taxes have put a ceiling on personal incomes
which many, no doubt, succeed in evading, the fiscal system
tends to be regressive because of its heavy and increasing
reliance on indirect taxation. In 1959/60 direct taxes
yielded £E 63 million and indirect taxes (net of subsidies)
some £E 90 million;* in 1967/8 direct taxes yielded £E 117

* Some sources put indirect taxes at £E 112 million in 1959/60.

million and indirect taxes £E 345 million.[6] The former thus increased by 86 per cent and the latter by 284 per cent! An analysis of the relative burden of indirect taxation on different income groups cannot unfortunately be undertaken with the data available at present but may provide an interesting topic for future research. The presumption, however, is that the upper strata of lower-income and middle-income groups are most adversely affected.

The Government employment policy is perhaps, after the land reform and the nationalizations, the major influence on the distribution of income. The difference between the employment policy and the other measures is that it may continue to operate for some time in the future. Broadly speaking, nationalizations meant once-for-all changes, and the land reform redistributions will come to an end unless ownership ceilings are lowered once more—a very unlikely event. The employment policy transfers income from the economy to the educated at the cost of future economic growth.

CONCLUSION

'Tout à reprendre. Tout à redire. Et la faux
du regard sur tout l'avoir menée!'
SAINT-JOHN PERSE

THE problem posed by population growth to a land-scarce
economy anxious to achieve rapid economic development
has been one of the major themes of this study.

Despite very early attempts at industrialization (the
famous Mohammed Ali episode) and despite a phase of
export-led growth when trade opportunities and comparative advantages were exploited, Egypt entered the
contemporary age as an underdeveloped, labour-surplus
economy. The high rates of population growth which
obtained in the early decades of the twentieth century rose
suddenly to a higher level after the Second World War
because of exogenous influences on mortality rates. Egypt's
main asset was agriculture; but unfavourable factor proportions despite high yields from a fertile land implied low
productivity per man. Agriculture, which provided the
largest proportion of the country's income and occupied an
even larger proportion of the population, could not be relied
upon to provide rapid, substantial increments to income,
or to absorb the natural increase in the labour force. Further
agricultural progress called for two complementary measures:
a big water-resource project and a complex package of
institutional reforms and extension services. The expansion
of the cultivated area and the flexibility of crop patterns
depend on the first; the transformation of Egyptian agriculture into a modern, input-intensive garden producing
fruit and vegetables for the booming export markets of
Europe and the Middle East can only be initiated by the
second set of measures. Both policies involve long gestation

periods: the first because of Egypt's peculiar natural endowments; the second because of its underdevelopment. The water-resource project—whether the High Dam or an alternative—required considerable funds; the modernization package called for skills and organizational abilities of a quality and in quantities which a poor country does not possess. Agriculture does not provide in these conditions an easy solution to the problems of a country faced with a population explosion and urged by the ethos of the time to develop rapidly.

It is not surprising that the simple economic programme of the Revolution in 1952 was dominated by Egypt's population problem; nor that it involved economic diversification. In fact its unusual feature, compared to development plans in other countries, is the place of agriculture in the objectives. The land reform was partly to alleviate some of the distributional implications of population pressures in agriculture; the High Dam and land reclamation to provide new fields for peasants displaced from old villages by demographic expansion; and industrialization seemed a possible short-cut to transform the country into a modern and dynamic economy capable of generating significant increments of income and employment. But no birth control or population policies: they were perhaps perceived as negative and devitalizing measures. The 'development optimism' of the late 1940s and the 1950s is reflected in this programme. But who can blame the Free Officers for sharing the faith in a 'big push' for rapid development which prevailed in the post-colonial period?

Economic development is essentially a long-term affair, but population pressures create for governments serious and growing difficulties in the short term. In fact, these difficulties are initially aggravated by the implementation of the development programmes whose ultimate purpose is to remove them. They are aggravated by rising expectations fostered by the promise of improvements; by the expansion of education, a significant component of any long-run development package; and by the consequences of increases in aggregate expenditures unmatched by corresponding increases in aggregate output which a big investment effort often entails. Expectations hasten the rate of internal migration by adding a strong urban pull to the demographic push in agriculture. They place political restrictions on the Government's ability to tax heavily marginal increments to income and often force it to concede to privileged groups larger income and welfare benefits than the country can afford. Tangible benefits expected from the promise of economic development have to accrue immediately to the groups on which the Government relies for political support and for the implementation of its programmes—in other words to the clients and the technocrats. The State may have long time-preferences—implied, in Egypt, by development programmes comprising long-gestation projects such as the High Dam and heavy industry—but private groups in society which the State represents have typically short time-preferences. Education has similar effects especially when the supply of education manpower expands faster than the requirements of the economy. Expectations raise the demand for education, and the understandable fear of the political consequences of educated unemployment may induce governments to adopt employment policies whose effects are to heighten expectations and to lead to further expansion of both education and employment. Governments thus are often committed to allow increases in consumption—or, at best, find that their ability to check the growth of consumption is severely constrained—when their development objectives call for more investment. The macro-economic implications of this state of affairs are familiar.

The problem can also be expressed in terms of an export–import gap. Import requirements for all types of goods increase (capital goods, because of investment; raw materials and intermediate goods, because of the demands of new industries; food, when the combined effects of population and income growth increase consumption faster than agricultural output). Import substitution, paradoxically, encourages imports. But the growth of exports lags behind for a long time because protected infant industries are generally incapable of competing on world markets and because the pace of agricultural development tends to be slow. A balance-of-payment deficit necessarily arises.

In Egypt, the Revolution attempted to raise the investment ratio in order to implement its initial development objectives. High rates of economic growth did obtain as long as the balance-of-payment deficit could be financed. But economic growth ground to a halt because the gestation periods of major projects delayed their expected benefits for too long and because aid, in the form of grants or very cheap long-term loans, ceased to accrue in the required amounts. Stagnation need not be more than a temporary phenomenon. The economy will eventually be able to reap the fruit of its past long-term investments and put to use excess capacity in industry, electricity, and other sectors. The redeeming feature of ambitious investment programmes is that they endow the country with durable assets which may become profitably productive after a time.

We would have been more optimistic about the future if defence commitments and the consequences of population pressures, interacting with education and expectations, had not led to rapid increases in public consumption after 1962 and if foreign indebtedness arising from similar causes—the impact of population growth and early rises in income on the food import bill, the financing of development programmes and arms purchases—did not represent such a heavy burden. Petroleum, of course, may provide a way out either through major discoveries or through very substantial grants from oil-rich Arab countries. This simply suggests that the population constraint on economic development cannot be rapidly lifted in the short run save through the intervention of an outside factor.

Population growth, in Egypt, did not influence development policies and the rate of economic expansion only. In land-scarce economies, population growth tends to affect patterns of income distribution and structural change in specific ways. The absence of idle capacity in land and the limited ability of a small industrial sector to create employment displace labour into the services sector. As internal migration is to a large extent the result of push factors, governments find that the range of feasible policies which could check the migration flow is limited. Regional development and adequate improvements of the rural infrastructure, though necessary and unfortunately neglected, are costly long-term measures. To restrict the expansion of 'modern' employment, because it exerts an urban pull, may be tantamount to advocating a slowing-down of economic development. And as the urban wage for unskilled workers in labour-surplus economies is often held down by population pressures, policies which suggest control of wage increases are largely irrelevant. Compulsory restrictions on migration in conditions of land-scarcity implies diminishing marginal productivities of labour in agriculture and hence reductions in standards of living already low in rural areas. More fundamentally, labour surpluses, whether they emerge in towns or villages, represent a social burden unless governments are prepared to allow the Malthusian mechanism to work, a euphemism for allowing people to starve. The present regime in Egypt has always striven to prevent this outcome.

The burden imposed by the labour surplus is partly transferred to the private sector through the growth of parasitic activities in the 'informal' services sector. Education, however, transforms to some extent what would have been underemployment of the unskilled into underemployment of the educated. If the latter are absorbed by the Government as in Egypt, investment is likely to suffer. For these and other reasons, structural changes, in so far as they reflect an expansion of services employment unrelated to the new demands put on the tertiary sector by the growth of agriculture and industry, or to the development of the infrastructure, are the product of population pressures rather than economic development. A different criterion of structural changes from the Clark–Fisher sequence is required to interpret the economic development of a labour-surplus economy.

Structural changes *within* the tertiary sector are as important as structural changes in the economy. Success begins when underemployment—whether in government or in informal services—starts to shrink in this sector.

Finally, population pressures in a labour-surplus economy influence the distribution of gains arising from income growth. While economic development changes the structure of the labour force, population growth restrains the growth of real wages for unskilled workers, and excess supplies, save for certain categories of professionals and technicians, restrain the rise of average earnings for educated manpower. Egypt is not unique in this case. The gains that accrue to entrants to higher wage groups are more substantial than the gains of those who remain in one group. Hence, the inducement for sectoral mobility and the demand for education. Differentials never disappear because mobility is far from perfect; entry to a better job requires the possession of the relevant qualifications.

In Egypt, the education/employment policy raises the rate of entry to some highly paid but unproductive jobs. There is no doubt that, despite social mobility, the children of the privileged groups have a marked advantage in this area. The diversion of resources away from investment to create these jobs means lower rates of growth of labour productivity in agriculture and industry, a diminished ability to create productive employment, and smaller benefits for the less privileged compared with what the country could otherwise achieve.

This study of the Egyptian economy reveals perhaps a general dilemma. The essence of underdevelopment is the paucity of means. Population growth often adds to the difficulties. Past policies, external factors, and the socio-political fabric may often represent constraints. Economic development is a slow and very long process. Governments, however, are under pressure, from within their countries and without, to achieve rapid economic progress. Attempts to markedly hasten the pace—as in Egypt between 1956 and 1964—may turn out to be short-lived because of gaps in resources, which reflect conflicts of objectives competing for scarce means. Not that all that was done in Egypt at that time is lost—on the contrary; the achievements were in many respects impressive. In assessing this period of Egyptian history or indeed of any developing country's history, it is worth remembering that the time involved is always short and that gestations are long. The poet perhaps best expresses the gist of the message: *Et vous aviez si peu de temps pour naître à cet instant!*

NOTES

CHAPTER I: HISTORICAL BACKGROUND

1. On long-staple cotton and its role in Egypt's economic development in the nineteenth century see E. R. J. Owen, *Cotton and the Egyptian Economy 1820–1914*, Oxford, 1969. The old book by F. Charles Roux, *La Production du coton en Égypte*, Paris, 1908, still retains much value. For an interpretation of economic development during the period covered by this chapter, see C. Issawi, 'Egypt since 1800: a Study in Lop-sided Development', *Journal of Economic History*, 21(1), 1961.

2. S. M. Radwan, 'Capital Formation in Egyptian Industry and Agriculture', unpublished Ph.D. thesis, University of London, 1973, ch. IV.

3. The Law of Five Feddans was introduced by Lord Kitchener in 1912 to protect small landowners against dispossession for bad debt. The Law had an adverse effect on rural credit as the Agricultural Bank practically ceased to extend loans to small peasants.

4. See A. Eid, *La Fortune immobilière de L'Égypte et sa dette hypothécaire*, Paris, 1907, p. 41, where it appears that the value of houses subject to tax in Alexandria increased by some £E 10 million between 1905 and 1907. See also E. R. J. Owen, 'The Cairo Building Industry and the Building Boom of 1897 to 1907', in *Colloque international sur l'histoire du Caire* (Egypt, Ministry of Culture), Cairo, 1972.

5. On the attitudes and economic policies of British officials in Egypt, see E. R. J. Owen, 'Lord Cromer and the Development of Egyptian Industry', *Middle Eastern Studies*, 2(4), 1966, and by the same author 'The Influence of Lord Cromer's Indian Experience on British Policy in Egypt, 1883–1907', *St. Antony's Papers*, 17, Oxford, 1965, and 'The Attitudes of British Officials to the Development of the Egyptian Economy, 1882–1922', in M. Cook (ed.), *Studies in the Economic History of the Middle East*, London, 1970.

6. The classic work on education is J. Heyworth-Dunne, *An Introduction to the History of Education in Modern Egypt*, London, n.d. Reprinted by F. Cass, London.

7. Ministry of Finance, *The Census of Egypt taken in 1907*, Cairo, 1909.

8. B. Hansen and G. Marzouk, *Development and Economic Policy in the UAR (Egypt)*, Amsterdam, 1965, p. 5.

9. Ibid., p. 46.

10. D. Mead, *Growth and Structural Change in the Egyptian Economy*, Homewood (Illinois), 1967, p. 8, n. 11.

11. Data from *Annuaire Statistique*, various issues.

12. E. R. J. Owen, 'Agricultural Production in Historical Perspective, a Case Study of the Period 1890–1939', in P. J. Vatikiotis (ed.), *Egypt since the Revolution*, London, 1968, p. 65.

13. Computed from data in C. Issawi, 'Egypt since 1800: a Study in Lop-sided Development', *Journal of Economic History*, 21(1), 1961.

14. National Planning Committee, Memorandum No. 121, by A. Sharif, 1959 (in Arabic).

15. Ministry of Finance, *Budget Reports* and *Final Accounts*, various issues.

16. A. E. Crouchley, *The Economic Development of Modern Egypt*, London, 1938, pp. 125–6 for a mention of labour shortages between 1856 and 1863 and attempts to establish colonies of Italians, Chinese etc. on the land. Much later, in 1901, the Belgian Consul in Cairo, L. Maskens, complained 'La rareté de la main-d'oeuvre est déjà un inconvénient: il deviendra surtout sensible après la mise des grands barrages en état de fonctionnement'. See Belgium, Recueil Consulaire—Égypte, *Rapport de M. Leon Maskens*, 'Situation économique et commerciale de l'Égypte en 1901', Cairo, 1902, p. 11.

17. See, for example, W. Cleland, *The Population Problem in Egypt*, Lancaster (Pa.), 1936.

18. D. Mead, *Growth and Structural Change in the Egyptian Economy*, Homewood (Illinois), 1967, p. 83.

19. On the Public Debt see A. E. Crouchley, *The Investment of Foreign Capital in Egyptian Companies and Public Debt*, Cairo, 1936; A. M. Hamza, *The Public Debt of Egypt*, Cairo, 1944; S. Cave, 'Report by Mr. Cave on the Financial Condition of Egypt', Great Britain, *Parliamentary Papers*, 1876, vol. lxxxiii; M. H. Heikal, *La Dette publique égyptienne*, Paris, 1912; 'Dette publique égyptienne—note historique', in *Annuaire Statistique*, 1916; J. Ducruet, *Les Capitaux européens au Proche-Orient*, Paris, 1964.

20. C. Issawi, 'Egypt since 1800: a Study in Lop-sided Development', *Journal of Economic History*, 21(1), p. 10.

21. See the very interesting book by D. Landes, *Bankers and Pashas*, London, 1958; A. E. Crouchley, *The Investment of Foreign Capital in Egyptian Companies and Public Debt*, p. 19.

22. See, F. Legrand, *Les Fluctuations de prix et les crises de 1902 et 1908 en Égypte*, Nancy, 1908.

23. See W. Willcocks and J. Craig, *Egyptian Irrigation*, 3rd ed., London, 1913, vol. 2, p. 244. The construction of the barrage itself cost £E 2·44 million. The total in the text includes other expenditures (land compensation etc.).

24. A. E. Crouchley, *The Investment of Foreign Capital in Egyptian Companies and Public Debt*, pp. 93 and 200.

25. H. Myint, 'The Classical Theory of International Trade and the Underdeveloped countries', *Economic Journal*, 68, 1958.

26. W. A. Lewis, 'Economic Development with Unlimited Supplies of Labour', *Manchester School*, 1954.

CHAPTER 2: POPULATION

1. T. Paul Schultz, 'Fertility Patterns and their Determinants in the Arab Middle East', in C. Cooper and S. Alexander (eds.), *Economic Development and Population Growth in the Middle East*, New York, 1972, pp. 447–52.

2. For detailed information on rural/urban differences in the 1947 and 1960 Population Censuses, see B. Hansen and G. Marzouk, *Development and Economic Policy in the UAR (Egypt)*, Amsterdam, 1965, Tables 2.17 to 2.20, pp. 44–5; for the disaggregation by educational attainment of mothers see T. Paul Schultz, 'Fertility Patterns and their Determinants in the Arab Middle East', Table 9.2, p. 415, derived from A. M. Zikry, 'Socio-Cultural Determinants of Human Fertility in Egypt, UAR', unpublished Ph.D. thesis, Syracuse University, 1963.

3. See M. A. El Badry, 'Trends in the Components of Population Growth in the Arab Countries of the Middle East: A Survey of Present Information', *Demography*, 2, 1965, pp. 152–3.

4. H. Rizk, 'Fertility Patterns in Selected Areas in Egypt', unpublished Ph.D. thesis, Princeton University, 1959. On Rizk's results see B. Hansen and G. Marzouk, *Development and Economic Policy in the UAR (Egypt)*, p. 32, and T. Paul Schultz, 'Fertility Patterns and their Determinants in the Arab Middle East', p. 425.

5. See Table 2.3 in the text. Hansen and Marzouk, *Development and Economic Policy in the UAR (Egypt)*, p. 31, draw some comfort from the apparent fall in the fertility of younger women because it points to a future downward trend in the birth rate.

6. T. Paul Schultz, 'Fertility Patterns and their Determinants in the Arab Middle East', p. 451.

7. Ibid., p. 401. This and the following four paragraphs are a critical survey presentation of Schultz's interesting analysis of the determinants of fertility. This section owes much to Schultz's important paper.

8. CAPMS, *The Increase in Population in the United Arab Republic and its Impact on Development*, Cairo, Sept. 1969, p. 175.

9. D. Mead, *Growth and Structural Change in the Egyptian Economy*, Homewood (Illinois), 1967, p. 29.

10. CAPMS, *The Increase in Population in the United Arab Republic*, 1969, p. 259.

11. Ibid.

12. D. Mead, *Growth and Structural Change in the Egyptian Economy*, p. 28.

CHAPTER 3: RESOURCES

1. Data on mining output from Federation of Egyptian Industries, *Yearbook*, several issues and CAPMS, *Statistical Yearbook* and *Statistical Indicators*, various issues.

2. Institut National de la Statistique et des Études Économiques (INSEE), *Memento économique, l'Égypte*, Paris, 1953, pp. 83–4.

3. British Petroleum, *BP Statistical Review of the World Oil Industry 1972*, London, 1973.

4. H. H. Ayrout, *The Egyptian Peasant* (transl. J. A. Williams), Boston, 1968, p. 87.

5. P. Fromont, *L'Agriculture égyptienne et ses problèmes* (Cours de Doctorat, Faculté de Droit, Université de Paris, Domat-Montchrestien), Paris. 1953–4, p. 13.

6. K. Wittfogel, *Oriental Despotism*, New Haven, 1957.

7. B. Hansen and G. Marzouk, *Development and Economic Policy in the UAR (Egypt)*, Amsterdam, 1965, p. 56.

8. See on this subject and for other interesting observations on Egyptian agriculture, R. Dumont, 'Les Problèmes agraires de la R.A.U.', *Politique Étrangère*, 2(3), 1968.

9. The reader should consult on mechanization a dated but interesting study by G. Saab, *Motorisation de l'agriculture et développement agricole au Proche-Orient*, Paris, 1960.

10. All data in this section are from CAPMS, *Statistical Yearbook* and *Statistical Indicators*, various issues.

11. C. Issawi, *Egypt in Revolution, an Economic Analysis*, London, 1963, p. 204.

CHAPTER 4: LAND REFORM

1. The foregoing discussion of the historical evolution of landownership draws on the classic work of G. Baer, *A History of Landownership in Modern Egypt 1800–1950*, London, 1962. See also I. Amer, *al ard wal fallah al mas'ala al zira'iya fi misr (The Land and the Fellah, the Agrarian Problem in Egypt)*, Cairo, 1958.

2. E. Eshag and M. A. Kamal, 'Agrarian Reform in the United Arab Republic (Egypt)', *Bulletin of the Oxford University Institute of Economics and Statistics*, 30(2), 1968, pp. 77–8. The reader should consult this source on which we relied for a number of facts and followed in certain parts of this chapter.

3. On the behaviour of rents, see B. Hansen, 'The Distribution Shares in Egyptian Agriculture 1897–1961', *International Economic Review*, 9, June 1968. On the behaviour of agricultural wages, B. Hansen, 'Marginal Productivity Wage Theory and Subsistence Wage Theory in Egyptian Agriculture', *Journal of Development Studies*, 2, July 1966, and 'Employment and Wages in Rural Egypt', *American Economic Review*, 59, June

1969. Also, International Labour Organization, *Rural Employment Problems in the United Arab Republic*, Geneva, 1969. On supply elasticities and price responsiveness in agriculture, R. M. Stern, 'The Price Responsiveness of Egyptian Cotton Producers', *Kyklos*, 12(3), 1959.

4. A. A. El Dessouki, 'Qibar mulaq al aradi al zira'iya wa duruhum fil mujtama' al misri 1914–52' ('Big landowners and their role in Egyptian society 1914–52'), unpublished Ph.D. thesis, Ain Shams University, Cairo, n.d., p. 117.

5. S. N. S. Cheung, *The Theory of Share Tenancy*, Chicago, 1969.

6. D. Warriner, *Land Reform and Development in the Middle East, A Study of Egypt, Syria and Iraq*, London, 1957, p. 13.

7. G. Saab, *The Egyptian Agrarian Reform 1952–1962*, London, 1967, p. 13, n. 45.

8. G. Baer, *A History of Landownership in Modern Egypt 1800–1950*, p. 221.

9. The legal framework of the land reform, pp. 64–6, is taken from E. Eshag and A. M. Kamal, 'Agrarian Reform in the United Arab Republic (Egypt)', pp. 78–83. For further information relating to the various laws between 1952 and 1963 we also had recourse to the compendium of all agrarian reform decrees and laws appended to S. Marei, *al islah al zira'i wa mushqilat al suqan fil kotr al masri (The Agrarian Reform and the Population Problem in Egypt)*, Cairo, n.d. (*circa* 1964), pp. 309–73. For the 1969 decree, see *Middle East Economic Digest*, 1969. The First and Second Agrarian Reform Laws are discussed in great detail in G. Saab, *The Egyptian Agrarian Reform*, Chs. 2 and 13. This work remains the standard source. Other interesting sources on the subject include D. Warriner, *Land Reform and Development in the Middle East, A Study of Egypt, Syria and Iraq*, London, 1957 (see also the 1962 edition); D. Warriner, 'Employment and Income Aspects of Recent Agrarian Reforms in the Middle East', *International Labour Review*, 101, Jan.–June 1970; W. Thweatt, 'The Egyptian Agrarian Reform', *Middle East Economic Papers*, 1956; P. Pissot, 'La Réforme agraire en Égypte', *Bulletin de la Société Francaise d'Économie Rurale*, Oct. 1958; M. Darling, 'Land Reform in Italy and Egypt', in *Year Book of Agricultural Co-operation*, Oxford, 1956; R. M. Ghonemy, 'Economic and Institutional Organisation of Egyptian Agriculture since 1952', in P. J. Vatikiotis (ed.), *Egypt since the Revolution*, London, 1968, and by the same author, 'Land Reform and Economic Development in the Middle East', *Land Economics*, 44(1), 1968.

10. D. Warriner, *Land Reform in Principle and Practice*, Oxford, 1969, chs. 1 and 4.

11. S. Marei, *The Agrarian Reform and the Population Problem in Egypt*, pp. 57 ff.

12. G. Saab, *The Egyptian Agrarian Reform 1952–1962*, pp. 23–4.

13. National Bank of Egypt, *Economic Bulletin*, 19(4), 1966, pp. 351–61. For the more recent data, see CAPMS, *Statistical Yearbook* and *Statistical Indicators*.

14. G. Saab, *The Egyptian Agrarian Reform 1952–1962*, p. 28.

15. Central Bank of Egypt, *Economic Review*, 8(3–4), 1968, pp. 143–51.

16. E. Eshag and A. M. Kamal, 'Agrarian Reform in the United Arab Republic (Egypt)', p. 86. See pp. 86–9 for some of the facts mentioned here. Also G. Saab, *The Egyptian Reform 1952–1962*, ch. 10.

17. R. Dumont, *Socialisms and Development* (transl. R. Cunningham), London, 1973, pp. 192–4.

18. See E. Eshag and A. M. Kamal, 'A Note on the Reform of the Rural Credit System in U.A.R. (Egypt)', *Bulletin of the Oxford University Institute of Economics and Statistics*, 29(2), 1967, p. 100, and National Bank of Egypt, *Economic Bulletin*, 17(4), 1964, pp. 421–9.

19. Institute of Planning, *Memorandum*, no. 933, Cairo, Dec. 1969 (in Arabic).

20. I. M. D. Little and J. A. Mirrlees, *Manual of Industrial Project Analysis in Developing Countries* (OECD), Paris, 1969, vol. 2.

21. E. Eshag and M. A. Kamal, 'Agrarian Reform in the United Arab Republic (Egypt)', p. 88.

CHAPTER 5: THE HIGH DAM AND LAND RECLAMATION

1. For data on the discharge of the Nile at Aswan, see H. E. Hurst, R. P. Black, and Y. M. Simaika, *The Nile Basin*, Cairo (Ministry of Public Works), 1946, 1959, and 1966, vols. vii, ix, and x.

2. Ibid., vol. x, p. 81.

3. T. Little, *High Dam at Aswan*, London, 1965.

4. A. Daninos, 'L'Utilisation intégrale des eaux du bassin du Nil', *Bulletin de l'Institut d'Égypte*, 30, 1947–8. See T. Little, *High Dam at Aswan*, p. 32.

5. See H. E. Hurst, 'Long-term Storage Capacity of Reservoirs', *Transactions of the American Society of Civil Engineers*, 116, 1951; also by the same author, *The Nile*, London, 1952, pp. 299–300; Abdel Aziz Ahmed, 'Recent Developments in Nile Control', *Proceedings of the Institution of Civil Engineers*, London, 1960 (paper no. 6102); Y. A. Shibl, *The Aswan High Dam*, Beirut, 1971, pp. 133–5.

6. See Y. Shibl, *The Aswan High Dam*, Table 15, p. 79.

7. H. Keller, *Optimum Management of Nile Discharge*, Basle, 1964, p. 15 and Y. Shibl, *The Aswan High Dam*, p. 60.

8. Abdel Aziz Ahmed, 'Recent Developments in Nile Control', and 'An Analytical Study of the Storage Losses in the Nile Basin, with Special Reference to the Aswan Dam', *Proceedings of the Institution of Civil Engineers*, London, 1961 (paper no. 6370).

9. See H. E. Hurst *et al.*, *The Nile Basin*, vol. x, also Y. Shibl, *The Aswan High Dam*, p. 62.

10. Central Bank of Egypt, *Economic Review*, 9(1–2), 1969, pp. 15–23.

11. Food and Agriculture Organization, *High Dam Soil Survey* (United Arab Republic, General Report, FAO/SF: 16/UAR), Rome, n.d. (after 1966).

12. W. F. Owen, 'Land and Water Use in the Egyptian High Dam Era', *Land Economics*, 40(3), 1964, p. 282.

CHAPTER 6: INSTITUTIONAL CHANGES AND SOCIAL POLICIES

1. See P. K. O'Brien, *The Revolution in Egypt's Economic System*, London, 1966, for a well-documented discussion of this transformation. Our interpretation of the event, however, differs from O'Brien's on a number, of points.

2. The report is an interesting document for the history of industrialization in Egypt. See, Egyptian Government, *Rapport de la Commission sur le Commerce et l'Industrie, 1917*, Cairo, 1922.

3. P. K. O'Brien, *The Revolution in Egypt's Economic System*, p. 70.

4. B. Hansen and G. Marzouk, *Development and Economic Policy in the UAR (Egypt)*, Amsterdam, 1965; C. Issawi, *Egypt in Revolution, an Economic Analysis*, London, 1963; D. Mead, *Growth and Structural Change in the Egyptian Economy*, Homewood (Illinois), 1967 and P. K. O'Brien, *The Revolution in Egypt's Economic System*.

5. B. Hansen, *Long and Short Term Planning in Underdeveloped Countries*, Amsterdam, 1967.

6. I. M. D. Little and J. Mirrlees, *Manual of Industrial Project Analysis in Developing Countries* (OECD), Paris, 1969, vol. 2.

7. P. K. O'Brien, *The Revolution in Egypt's Economic System*, ch. 5.

8. B. Hansen and G. Marzouk, *Development and Economic Policy in the UAR (Egypt)*, pp. 304–5.

9. Ibid., p. 305.

10. Presidency of the Republic, *General Frame of the Five Year Plan for Economic and Social Development, July 1960–June 1965*, Cairo, 1960, p. 1.

11. B. Hansen and G. Marzouk, *Development and Economic Policy in the UAR (Egypt)*, p. 295.

12. See Economic Organization, *Yearbook*, Cairo, 1960.

13. National Bank of Egypt, *Economic Bulletin*, 14(3), 1961, pp. 322–33.

14. Data from CAPMS, *Monthly Bulletin of foreign trade*, various issues.

15. Anouar Abdel-Malek, *Égypte, société militaire*, Paris, 1962.

16. See Edith Penrose, 'Planning and the Enterprise', *L'Égypte contemporaine*, 59(333), 1968.

17. Ibid., p. 161.

18. See B. Hansen and G. Marzouk, *Development and Economic Policy in the UAR (Egypt)*, pp. 285–94.

19. National Bank of Egypt, *Economic Bulletin*, 12, 1959: 'Company Finances in the UAR in 1956/7 and 1957/8', pp. 85–104.

CHAPTER 7 MODERNIZATION

1. B. Hansen and G. Marzouk, *Development and Economic Policy in the UAR (Egypt)*, Amsterdam, 1965, p. 129.

2. D. Mead, *Growth and Structural Change in the Egyptian Economy*, Homewood (Illinois), 1967, p. 113.

3. R. Mabro, 'Industrial Growth, Agricultural Underemployment and the Lewis Model. The Egyptian Case, 1937–1965', *Journal of Development Studies*, 3(4), 1967.

4. S. Radwan, 'Capital Formation in Egyptian Industry and Agriculture', unpublished Ph.D. thesis, University of London, 1973.

5. An interesting source is Ministry of Finance, *Statistique des sociétés anonymes travaillant principalement en Égypte*, Cairo, various issues.

6. The best source for data on industrial output is Federation of Egyptian Industries, *Yearbook*, Cairo.

7. Ministry of Planning, *Report on Industry in the First Five Year Plan* (in Arabic), mimeo, Cairo, n.d.

8. I. Bronsveld, 'Exports of Manufactured Products by the UAR', unpublished M.Sc. thesis, London University, School of Oriental and African Studies, 1970.

9. See G. K. Kardouche, 'United Arab Republic: Case Study of Aid through Trade and Repayment of Debt on Goods or Local Currencies', UNCTAD Paper, Geneva, 1968 (Ref. TD/B/C.3/63).

10. E. Shamoon, 'Production Functions and the Residual Factor in Egyptian Manufacturing Industries', unpublished M.Sc. thesis, London University, School of Oriental and African Studies, 1967.

11. B. Hansen and G. Marzouk, *Development and Economic Policy in the UAR (Egypt)*, p. 133.

12. P. K. O'Brien, *The Revolution in Egypt's Economic System*, London, 1966, p. 75.

13. See R. Mabro, 'Industrial Growth, Agricultural Underemployment and the Lewis Model. The Egyptian Case, 1937–1965'.

14. Data from Ministry of Treasury.

15. See CAPMS, *Statistics on Employment, Wages, and Hours of Work* (in Arabic), various issues.

16. Ministry of Planning, *Follow-up Reports*, various issues.

17. Data from CAPMS, *Statistical Indicators* (in Arabic), various issues.

18. Data from Ministry of Education.

19. CAPMS, *Statistical Indicators 1952–1970* (in Arabic), Cairo, 1971.

20. Computed from data in ibid.

21. Ministry of Planning, *Follow-up Reports*, various issues.

22. All data here are from CAPMS, *Statistical Indicators*.

23. Ibid.

CHAPTER 8: ECONOMIC GROWTH AND STRUCTURAL CHANGES

1. B. Hansen and D. Mead, *The National Income of the UAR (Egypt) 1939–1962*, Institute of National Planning, memo no. 355, Cairo, July 1963. See also D. Mead, *Growth and Structural Change in the Egyptian Economy*, Homewood (Illinois), 1967, pp. 43–46.

2. B. Hansen, 'Planning and Economic Growth in the UAR (Egypt), 1960–1965', in P. J. Vatikiotis (ed.), *Egypt since the Revolution*, London, 1968.

3. B. Hansen and D. Mead, *The National Income of the UAR (Egypt) 1939–1962.* See D. Mead, *Growth and Structural Change in the Egyptian Economy*, p. 288.

4. B. Hansen, 'Planning and Economic Growth in the UAR (Egypt), 1960–1965', p. 26.

5. Joy L. Skegg, 'Contribution of changes in Cropping Pattern to Development of Egyptian Agriculture 1952–1968', unpublished M.Sc. thesis, London University, School of Oriental and African Studies, 1971.

6. B. Hansen, 'Planning and Economic Growth in the UAR (Egypt), 1960–1965', p. 31.

7. D. Mead, *Growth and Structural Change in the Egyptian Economy*, p. 288. See Table 8.2 in the text.

8. All data are from Ministry of Planning, *Follow-up Reports*, and other unpublished memoranda.

9. P. O'Brien, P. B. W. Rayment, and M. Schilberg, 'On Commodity Concentration of Exports', unpublished paper, UNCTAD, 1971.

10. M. Rodinson, 'The Political System', in P. J. Vatikiotis (ed.), *Egypt since the Revolution.*

11. See R. Mabro and P. K. O'Brien, 'Structural Changes in the Egyptian Economy', in M. Cook (ed.), *Studies in the Economic History of the Middle East*, London, 1970, for a similar discussion of industry as a leading sector.

CHAPTER 9: THE EMPLOYMENT PROBLEM

1. See references in note 3 to chapter 4.

2. R. Mabro, 'Employment and Wages in Dual Agriculture', *Oxford Economic Papers*, 23(3), 1971.

3. A. Mohieldin, 'Agricultural Investment and Employment in Egypt since 1935', unpublished Ph.D. thesis, University of London, 1966.

4. International Labour Organization, *Rural Employment Problems in the United Arab Republic*, Geneva, 1969.

5. Data from Department of Statistics and Census, *Population Census 1960*, Cairo, 1963, vol. 2, Table 4.

6. R. Mabro, 'Industrial Growth, Agricultural Underemployment and the Lewis Model. The Egyptian Case, 1937–1965', *Journal of Development Studies*, 3(4), 1967.

7. M. P. Todaro, 'A Model of Labor Migration and Urban Unemployment in Less Developed Countries', *American Economic Review*, 59(1), 1969.

8. R. Mabro, 'Industrial Growth, Agricultural Underemployment and the Lewis Model. The Egyptian Case, 1937–1965'.

9. J. Abu-Lughod, 'Migrant Adjustment to City Life: the Egyptian Case', *American Journal of Sociology*, 67(1), 1961, p. 23. See also, by the same author, 'Urban–rural Differences as a Function of the Demographic Transition: Egyptian Data and Analytical Model', *American Journal of Sociology*, 69(5), 1964; and 'Urbanization in Egypt: Present State and Future Prospects', *Economic Development and Cultural Change*, 23, 1965. On the push factor in Egypt, see R. Mabro, 'Migrations internes et sous-emploi urbain, le cas de l'Égypte', *Travaux et Jours* (Beirut), no. 45, Oct.–Dec. 1972.

10. United Arab Republic, Institute of National Planning, and International Labour Organization, *Research Report on Employment Problems in Rural Areas, UAR*, Cairo, 1965–68 (10 vols.); Report B, p. 56.

11. Ibid., Report C, p. 29.

12. D. Mead, *Growth and Structural Change in the Egyptian Economy*, Homewood (Illinois), 1967, pp. 37–9.

13. C. Clark, *Conditions of Economic Progress*, London, 1957.

14. A. G. B. Fisher, 'Capital and the Growth of Knowledge', *Economic Journal*, 43, 1933.

CHAPTER 10: CHANGES IN THE DISTRIBUTION OF INCOME

1. In October 1973, after completion of the manuscript of this book, M. Abdel Fadil has begun work on a research project on income distribution. His contribution will, no doubt, add very much to present knowledge in this field.

2. *Gomhouria* (Arabic), 20 Feb. 1960.

3. G. Saab, *The Egyptian Agrarian Reform 1952–1962*, London, 1967, pp. 42–5.

4. All these and the following calculations are based on data from: Ministry of Agriculture, *Agricultural Census 1950*, and *Agricultural Census 1961* (in Arabic), Cairo, 1966; *Population Censuses*, various issues; Ministry of Agriculture, *Agricultural Economy* (in Arabic), various issues. Income data from Ministry of Planning, *Follow-up Reports*.

5. Government employment from Ministry of Treasury, *Budgets* and *Budget Reports*, various issues.

6. Data from Ministry of Treasury.

READING LIST

This short bibliographical note contains suggestions for further reading on the historical and political background of recent economic development in Egypt and on the main aspects of the Egyptian economy.

HISTORY, POLITICS, SOCIETY

Introductory books on modern Egypt:

LACOUTURE, J. and S., *L'Égypte en mouvement* (Paris, 2nd ed. 1962). English translation, *Egypt in Transition* (London, 1958).
LITTLE, T., *Modern Egypt* (London, 1967).
MANSFIELD, P., *Nasser's Egypt* (Penguin Books, 2nd ed., 1969).
TOMICHE, N., *L'Égypte Moderne* (Que sais-je?, Paris, 1966).

Modern History:

BERQUE, J., *L'Égypte, impérialisme et révolution* (Paris, 1967). English translation, *Egypt, imperialism and revolution* (London, 1972).
VATIKIOTIS, P. J., *The modern history of Egypt* (London, 1969).

Biographies:

LACOUTURE, J., *Nasser* (Paris, 1971). English translation, *Nasser* (London, 1973).
STEPHENS, R., *Nasser, a political biography* (London, 1971).

Politics:

ABDEL-MALEK, A., *Égypte, société militaire* (Paris, 1962). English translation, *Egypt, military society* (New York, 1968).
DEKMEJIAN, R. H., *Egypt under Nasir* (London and Albany, 1971).
HARIK, I., 'Mobilization policy and political change in rural Egypt' in R. Antoun and I. Harik (eds.), *Rural politics and social change in the Middle East* (Bloomington and London, 1972).
KERR, M., *The Arab cold war* (London, 1957).
MITCHELL, R. P., *The society of Muslim brothers* (London, 1969).
RODINSON, M., 'The political system' in P. J. Vatikiotis (ed.), *Egypt since the revolution* (London, 1968).
VATIKIOTIS, P. J., *The Egyptian army in politics* (Bloomington, 1961).

People and society:

ABU LUGHOD, J., *Cairo* (Princeton, 1971).
AMMAR, A., *Growing up in an Egyptian village* (London, 1954).
AYROUT, H. H., *Moeurs et coutumes des fellahs* (Paris, 1938). Several new editions and translations *e.g. The Egyptian Peasant* (Boston, 1963). Reprinted in 1968.

BERGER, M., *Bureaucracy and society in modern Egypt* (Princeton, 1957).

BERQUE, J., *Histoire sociale d'un village égyptien au XX siècle* (Paris and The Hague, 1957).

GILSENAN, M., *Saint and Sufi in modern Egypt* (Oxford, 1973).

LANE, E. W., *The manners and customs of modern Egyptians* (London, 1836). Reprinted in Dent's Everyman's Library.

MAKARIUS, R., *La jeunesse intellectuelle d'Égypte au lendemain de la deuxième guerre mondiale* (Paris and The Hague, 1960).

WAKIN, E., *A lonely minority* (New York, 1963). A study of the Copts.

Culture and history of ideas:

ABDEL-MALEK, A., *La pensée politique arabe contemporaine* (Paris, 1970).

ABDEL-NASSER, G., *The philosophy of the revolution* (Buffalo, 1959).

AHMED, J. M., *The intellectual origins of Egyptian nationalism* (London, 1960). Reprinted in 1968.

AWAD, L., 'Cultural and intellectual developments in Egypt since 1952' in P. J. Vatikiotis (ed.) *Egypt since the Revolution* (London, 1968).

HOURANI, A., *Arabic thought in the liberal age* (London, 1962).

MUSA, S., 'Intellectual currents in Egypt', *Middle Eastern Affairs*, 2, 1951.

SAFRAN, N., *Egypt in search of political community* (Cambridge, Mass., 1961).

THE ECONOMY

Economic history:

ABDEL-MALEK, A., *Idéologie et renaissance nationale, l'Égypte moderne* (Paris, 1969).

ARMINJON, P., *La situation économique et financière de l'Égypte* (Paris, 1911).

CROUCHLEY, A. E., *The economic development of modern Egypt* (London, 1938).

——, *The investment of foreign capital in Egyptian companies and Public Debt* (Cairo, 1936).

DUCRUET, J., *Les capitaux européens au Proche-Orient* (Paris, 1964).

HAMZA, A. M., *The Public Debt of Egypt, 1854–1876* (Cairo, 1944).

ISSAWI, C., 'Egypt since 1800, a study in lopsided development', *Journal of Economic History*, 21, 1961.

LANDES, D., *Bankers and pashas* (London, 1958).

OWEN, E. R. J., *Cotton and the Egyptian economy* (Oxford, 1969).

The economy after 1939:

HANSEN, B., 'Economic development of Egypt' in C. A. Cooper and S. S. Alexander (eds.), *Economic development and population growth in the Middle East* (New York, 1972).

HANSEN, B., and MARZOUK, G., *Development and economic policy in the UAR (Egypt)* (Amsterdam, 1965).

ISSAWI, C., *Egypt in revolution, an economic analysis* (London, 1963).

MABRO, R., and O'BRIEN, P. K., 'Structural changes in the Egyptian economy 1937–1965' in M. A. Cook (ed.), *Studies in the economic history of the Middle East* (London, 1970).

Mead, D., *Growth and structural changes in the Egyptian economy* (Homewood, Ill., 1967).

O'Brien, P. K., *The revolution in Egypt's economic system* (London, 1966).

National accounts:

Anis, M. A., 'A study of the national income of Egypt', *Égypte Contemporaine*, 41, 1950.

Eleish, G. E., 'The applicability and utilization of the input–output model in a developing economy: the case of Egypt examined' in T. Barna (ed.), *Structural interdependence and economic development* (New York, 1963).

Khan, T. M., (ed.), *Middle Eastern Studies in Income and Wealth* (London, 1965).

Population:

Abdel-Aty, S. H., 'Life-table functions for Egypt based on model life-tables and quasi-stable population theory', *Milbank Memorial Fund Quarterly*, 39, 1961.

Abu-Lughod, J., 'Urban–rural differences as a function of the demographic transition', *American Journal of Sociology*, 69, 1964.

——, 'Urbanization in Egypt: present state and future prospects', *Economic Development and Cultural Change*, 23, 1965.

——, 'The emergence of differential fertility in urban Egypt', *Milbank Memorial Fund Quarterly*, 43, 1965.

Cleland, W. W., *The population problem in Egypt* (Lancaster, Pa., 1936).

El Badry, M. A., 'Some demographic measurements for Egypt based on the stability of census age distributions', *Milbank Memorial Fund Quarterly*, 33, 1955.

——, 'Some aspects of fertility in Egypt', *Milbank Memorial Fund Quarterly*, 34, 1956.

——, 'Trends in the components of population growth in the Arab countries of the Middle East: a survey of present information', *Demography*, 2, 1965.

Marzouk, G. A., 'Fertility of the urban and rural population in Egypt', *Égypte Contemporaine*, 48, 1957.

Schultz, T. P., 'Fertility patterns and their determinants in the Arab Middle East' in C. A. Cooper and S. S. Alexander (eds.), *Economic development and population growth in the Middle East* (New York, 1972).

Toppozada, H. K., 'Progress and problems of family planning in the United Arab Republic', *Demography*, 5, 1968.

United Nations, *World Population Conference, 1965, Belgrade* (New York, 1967), vol II.

Weir, J. M., 'An evaluation of health and sanitation in Egyptian villages', *Journal of the Egyptian Public Health Association*, 27, 1952.

Zikry, A. M., 'Urbanization and its effects on the levels of fertility of UAR women', *Égypte Contemporaine*, 55, 1964.

Employment and labour:

ABU-LUGHOD, J., 'Migrant adjustment to city life: the Egyptian case', *American Journal of Sociology*, 67, 1961.

GREENWOOD, M. J., 'The determinants of labor migration in Egypt', *Journal of Regional Science*, 9, 1969.

HANSEN, B., 'Marginal productivity wage theory and subsistence theory in Egyptian agriculture', *Journal of Development Studies*, 2, 1966.

——, 'The distributive shares in Egyptian agriculture 1897–1961', *International Economic Review*, 9, 1968.

——, 'Employment and wages in rural Egypt', *American Economic Review*, 59, 1969.

HARBISON, F., and IBRAHIM, I., *Human resources for Egyptian enterprise* (New York, 1958).

INTERNATIONAL LABOUR ORGANISATION, *Rural employment problems in the UAR* (Geneva, 1969).

MABRO, R., 'Industrial growth, agricultural underemployment and the Lewis model. The Egyptian case, 1937–1965', *Journal of Development Studies*, 4, 1967.

——, 'Employment and wages in dual agriculture', *Oxford Economic Papers*, 23, 1971.

——, 'Migrations internes et sous-emploi urbain', *Travaux et Jours* (45), 1972.

NAGI, M. H., *Labor force and employment in Egypt* (New York, 1971).

SEKLANI, M., 'Population active et structures économiques de l'Egypte', *Population*, 17, 1962.

SHAFEI, A. N., 'The current labour force sample survey in Egypt (UAR)', *International Labour Review*, 82, 1960.

UNITED STATES DEPARTMENT OF LABOR, *Labor law and practice in the UAR (Egypt)* by J. Clarke (Washington, 1965).

Agriculture, irrigation and land reform:

ABDEL-MALEK, A., 'La question agraire en Egypte et la réforme de 1952', *Tiers-Monde*, 3, 1962.

AMIN, G. A., *Food supply and economic development with special reference to Egypt* (London, 1966).

ATKINSON, J. D., *Handbook of Egyptian irrigation* (Cairo, 1934).

BAER, G., *A history of landownership in modern Egypt* (London, 1962).

BESANÇON, J., *L'homme et le Nil* (Paris, 1957).

BROWN, C. H., *Egyptian cotton* (London, 1953).

CLAWSON, M., LANDSBERG, H., and ALEXANDER, L., *The agricultural potential of the Middle East* (New York, 1971).

DARLING, M., 'Land reform in Italy and Egypt' in *Yearbook of Agricultural Co-operation* (Oxford, 1956).

DUMONT, R., 'Les problèmes agraires de la RAU', *Politique Etrangère*, 2, 1968.

ESHAG, E., and KAMAL, A. M., 'A note on the reform of the rural credit system in UAR (Egypt)', *Bulletin of the Oxford Institute of Economics and Statistics*, 29, 1967.

ESHAG, E., and KAMAL, A. M., 'Agrarian reform in the United Arab Republic (Egypt)', *Bulletin of the Oxford Institute of Economics and Statistics*, 30, 1968.

F.A.O., *World Land Reform Conference, 20 June–2 July, 1966* (Rome, 1966).

FROMONT, P., *L'agriculture égyptienne et ses problèmes* (Paris, 1953–4).

GHONEMY, R. M., 'Economic and institutional organization of Egyptian agriculture since 1952' in P. J. Vatikiotis (ed.), *Egypt since the Revolution* (London, 1968).

GHONEMY, R. M., 'Land reform and economic development in the Middle East', *Land Economics*, 44, 1968.

HURST, H. E., BLACK, R. P., and SIMAIKA, Y. M., *The Nile Basin* (Cairo, 1946–1966).

MAREI, S., *Agrarian reform in Egypt* (Cairo, 1957).

——, *UAR agriculture enters a new age* (Cairo, 1960).

OWEN, W. F., 'Land and water use in the Egyptian High Dam era', *Land Economics*, 40, 1964.

SAAB, G., *The Egyptian agrarian reform 1952–1962* (London, 1967).

SHIBL, Y. A., *The Aswan High Dam* (Beirut, 1971).

STERN, R. M., 'The price-responsiveness of Egyptian cotton producers', *Kyklos*, 12, 1959.

WAFA, T. A., 'Les conséquences économiques et sociales de la construction du Haut-Barrage d'Assouan', *Impact Science et Société*, 13, 1963.

WARREN, C., 'The High Aswan Dam and new trends in Egyptian agriculture', *Foreign Agriculture*, 7, 1969.

WARRINER, D., *Land reform and development in the Middle East, a study of Egypt, Syria and Iraq* (London, 1957 and 2nd ed. 1962).

——, 'Employment and income aspects of recent agrarian reforms in the Middle East', *International Labour Review*, 101, 1970.

Planning and Industrialisation:

GERAKIS, A. S., 'United Arab Republic: a survey of developments during the First Five-Year Plan, 1960–61/1964–65', IMF *Staff Papers*, 14, 1967.

HANSEN, B., 'Planning and economic growth in the UAR (Egypt) 1960–5' in P. J. Vatikiotis (ed.), *Egypt since the Revolution* (London, 1968).

METWALLY, M. M., 'The effects of market limitations on industrialisation in Egypt', *Yorkshire Bulletin of Economic and Social Research*, 19, 1967.

PENROSE, E., 'Planning and the enterprise', *Égypte Contemporaine*, 59, 1968.

RADWAN, S., *Capital formation in Egyptian industry and agriculture*, unpublished Ph.D. thesis, University of London, 1973.

SABRI, A., (in Arabic) *The years of socialist transformation: an evaluation of the First Five Year Plan* (Cairo, 1966).

UN, *The development of manufacturing industry in Egypt, Israel and Turkey* (New York, 1958).

Money, taxation, trade and aid:

EL NAGGAR, S., *Foreign aid and the economic development of the UAR* (Princeton, 1964).

KARDOUCHE, G. K., *The UAR in development: a study in expansionary finance* (New York, 1967).

——, 'United Arab Republic: a case study of aid through trade and repayment of debt in goods or local currencies', UNCTAD paper (Geneva, 1968).

LOTZ, J. R., 'Taxation in the United Arab Republic (Egypt)', IMF *Staff Papers*, 13, 1968.

SANCHIZ, J. C., 'Money and banking in the United Arab Republic', IMF *Staff Papers*, 12, 1965.

TANSKY, L., *US and USSR aid to developing countries* (New York, 1967).

US DEPARTMENT OF AGRICULTURE, *Public Law 480 and other economic assistance to United Arab Republic* (Washington, 1964).

Periodicals and serials:

Ahram Iqtisadi (in Arabic)
CENTRAL BANK OF EGYPT, *Economic Review*
Egypte Contemporaine
FEDERATION OF EGYPTIAN INDUSTRIES, *Yearbook*
INSTITUTE OF NATIONAL PLANNING, *Memoranda*
Middle East Economic Digest
Middle East Economic Survey
Middle East Economic Papers
MINISTRY OF PLANNING, *Follow-up Reports* (In Arabic)
NATIONAL BANK OF EGYPT, *Economic Bulletin*

Statistical Sources

Annuaire Statistique, Annual Statement of foreign trade, Census of industrial production, Monthly bulletin of agricultural statistics, Population census, Statistical indicators, Statistical Pocketbook, Statistical yearbook

Note: The statistical appendixes of CBE, *Economic Review* NBE, *Economic Bulletin* and FEI, *Yearbook* are important and very accessible sources.

INDEX